Being Human

Other Books by Dwight N. Hopkins

Black Faith and Public Talk:
Essays in Honor of James H. Cone's
"Black Theology and Black Power," editor

Black Theology in the U.S.A. and South Africa:
Politics, Culture, and Liberation

Changing Conversations:
Religious Reflection and Cultural Analysis, coeditor

Cut Loose Your Stammering Tongue:
Black Theology in the Slave Narratives, coeditor

Down, Up, and Over: Slave Religion and Black Theology

Global Voices for Gender Justice, coeditor

Heart and Head: Black Theology Past, Present, and Future

Introducing Black Theology of Liberation

Liberation Theologies, Post-Modernity, and the Americas, coeditor

Loving the Body: Black Religious Studies and the Erotic, coeditor

Religions/Globalizations: Theories and Cases, coeditor

Shoes That Fit Our Feet:
Sources for a Constructive Black Theology

We Are One Voice:
Essays on Black Theology in South Africa and the USA, coeditor

Being Human
Race, Culture, and Religion

Dwight N. Hopkins

Fortress Press
Minneapolis

BEING HUMAN
Race, Culture, and Religion

Scripture quotations are from the New Revised Standard Version Bible, copyright © 1989 by the Division of Christian Education of the National Council of the Churches of Christ in the USA, and are used by permission.

Cover art: Lawrence, Jacob (1917–2000), *The Library*, 1960. Smithsonian American Art Museum, Washington. © 2005 The Estate of Gwendolyn Knight Lawrence / Artists Rights Society (ARS), New York. Photo © Art Resource, New York. Used with permission.

Cover design: Laurie Ingram
Interior design: Ann Delgehausen

Library of Congress Cataloging-in-Publication Data
Hopkins, Dwight N.
  Being human : race, culture, and religion / Dwight N. Hopkins.
      p. cm.
      ISBN 0-8006-3778-X (hardcover : alk. paper)—ISBN 0-8006-3757-7 (pbk. : alk. paper)
    1. Black theology. 2. Man (Christian theology) I. Title.
      BT82.7.H655 2005
      230'.089'96073—dc22

                                                          2005015202

The paper used in this publication meets the minimum requirements of American National Standard for Information Sciences—Permanence of Paper for Printed Library Materials, ANSI Z329.48-1984.

Manufactured in the U.S.A.
09   08   07   06   05   1   2   3   4   5   6   7   8   9   10

For my older brothers . . .

Robert Jr., Calvin, Leroy, Charles, and James

who together opened up multiple avenues in life
and visions about possibilities without borders

Contents

Preface

Our age is one of vastly expanded human roles and possibilities, introducing new ways and forms of human endeavor. Globalization makes us more aware of diverse and shifting cultural, ethnic, and racial identities. Shifting gender roles have made us more aware of gender diversity. And contemporary science introduces medical and even genetic modifications of basic human features. Yet it is also an age in which our basic humanity is contested, challenged, and jeopardized at every turn by hatreds, strife, and social systems that deal in death as often as life. Confusion reigns in society generally and in medical and legal circles over when human life begins and ends. All these phenomena beg the question of what it means, at root, to be a human. *How can we envision being human in a way that supports and enables human flourishing and provides ultimate orientation in such times?*

In this volume I take a fresh look at what it means to be a human being both in our present context and in our ultimate context. The book explains how religious reflection and discussions about the nature of an individual person—what we call theological anthropology—already assume definite ideas about the self, culture, and race. Too many people do not take the time to really explore what these things mean, and in the past even philosophers and theologians deemed such "accidents" peripheral to an abiding, unchanging human nature. Yet our assumed notions of self, culture, and race largely determine who we are. They are not marginal but germinal. By making these realities and relationships more conscious, people can become more open about their ideals about a good person, a worthwhile life, and human destiny.

In rethinking humanness, then, the collective racial, ethnic, and cultural dimensions of African American historical experience can be seen not as peripheral but as a tremendous untapped resource for theological anthropology. Thus my proposals here are based on my ongoing research in black folk culture, a wellspring of historical reflection on what it means to be human. Core chapters explore notions of race, self, and culture, while the final chapter draws explicitly on folktale portrayals of "the conjurer," "the trickster," "the outlaw," and "the Christian witness. I hope and I expect to draw even more from those sources in my further work on theological anthropology.

*   *   *

I would like to thank the Henry Luce Foundation for a Henry Luce III Fellowship in Constructive Theology, which allowed me a twelve-month research leave to think through the arguments resulting in *Being Human: Race, Culture, and Religion*. At an annual University of Chicago Divinity School faculty retreat, I presented many of the ideas for this book. Gracious thanks to my colleagues Wendy Doniger (my formal respondent), Chris Gamwell, Clark Gilpin, Bruce Lincoln, and Kathy Tanner for their astute critiques and suggestions during the question and answer period. My Divinity School students remain some of the brightest minds who sat through my classes on first-generation black theology, second-generation black theology, black theology and womanist theology in dialogue (co-taught with Dr. Linda E. Thomas), race, contemporary models of theology, Third World theologies, African philosophy, and culture. Their engagements helped me rethink many ideas that would eventually go into this book. Appreciation also for discussions in the University of Chicago Divinity School graduate student Theology Club. My annual ten-week Bible class on black theology at Trinity United Church of Christ in Chicago always brought in a grounded intellect to my thinking and writing projects. Thanks to Dr. Jeremiah A. Wright Jr., Trinity's senior pastor, for allowing me the privilege of working with black church and community folk on the South Side of Chicago. Keith Baltimore has been a steady research assistant, one who not only executes timely research (sometimes on very arcane materials), but also has the ability to offer important editorial remarks on my chapters. James H. Cone, Will Coleman, Jeremiah A. Wright Jr., Edward P. Antonio, Peter J. Paris, Emilie Townes, Kelly Brown Douglas, and Karen Baker-Fletcher have been important discussion partners with their publications and conversations.

Michael West (Fortress Press) and Sarah Lloyd (Ashgate Publishing) showed the needed patience throughout the process.

I have also lectured on various parts of this manuscript to intellectually stimulating audiences. A representative sampling follows: National Conference of the People of African Descent in Metropolitan Community Churches (Houston, Texas); Network on Theological Education (Volmoed, South Africa); Society for Indian Philosophy (Kolkata, India); Graduate Theological Union (Berkeley, California); Loyola Marymount University (Los Angeles, California); University of Cape Town (Cape Town, South Africa); Vanderbilt University Divinity School; Boston University School of Theology; the World Forum on Theology and Liberation (Porto Alegre, Brazil); the Centre for Dalit/Subaltern Studies (Theology) (Delhi, India); Vidyajyoti College of Theology (Delhi, India); Gurukul Lutheran Theological College and Research Institute (Chennai, India); United Theological College (Bangalore, India); and Harvard University Divinity School.

Dr. Linda E. Thomas, my wife, has been there as a critical person who helped me think together many of these ideas from casual ruminations, to serious roadblocks, to exciting changes in direction, to the closing of my laptop when the final word was finished.

Introduction:
Who Are We?

Culture, Self, and Race

What does it mean to be a human being—a person who fulfills individual capabilities and contributes to a community's well-being? And what connects that individual person and community to an ultimate vision, a spirituality, or God? These questions invite investigations into, arguments for, and construction of a theological anthropology. When one thinks intentionally about the being of a human and his or her ties to some concern or force greater than the limited self, then considerations of transcendence and materiality also come into play in complex and dynamic ways. In black theology such a theological anthropology is quite layered:

> *Theology* is critical reflection about the God–human relationship, and *anthropology* is rational inquiry into an understanding of human beings in culture. Black theology then is critical reflection about the relationship between black humanity and God in culture. . . . Black theology inquires into the God–black human relationship wherever black women and men find themselves. The social construction of race has a negative impact on black people globally and therefore is a central category in black theology's analysis of the God–human relationship.[1]

So theology and anthropology merge into conversation about normative claims and cultural location. Because all arguments asserting basic

1

principles surface from the contextual location of the writer or speaker, black theology embraces its African American context as a starting point for dialogue with other starting points. All thoughts about God and being human reveal the limited autobiography of the thinker and, consequently, invite discussion with other particular reflections on theological anthropology.

Being Human: Race, Culture, and Religion results from my pondering such questions. As a second-generation black theologian, I initiated a journey for clarity and answers through intense and critical research on African American folktales. They are a rich repository of African American collective reflection on the experience of being human. My preliminary studies surfaced four types of possible theological anthropologies grounded in black popular sources: the *trickster with reversal,* the *conjurer with nature,* the *outlaw with ambiguity,* and *Christian witness with empowerment.* While construction of a specific Christian religiosity was my primary goal, I sought to draw lessons from a larger corpus of black religion. Christian witness, therefore, would be informed by anthropological insights from the spiritual revelations dwelling in the trickster, conjurer, and outlaw paradigms.

To further engage these popular religious sources from black folktales, I began to compare other bodies of knowledge about being human. Various contemporary models of theological anthropology proved to be helpful for discerning current scholars' understanding of the accepted terms of debate, reigning methodologies, and opinions on what is at stake in our understandings of the God–human interaction. As I thought about both black folktales and contemporary paradigms, I discovered that sources of all persuasions *assumed* that they (the authors) and we (the readers) already understood some key realities decisive to any claims about theological anthropology.

Likewise, as I reviewed my own publications (which consistently drew on African American sources to comprehend disparate dimensions of the sacred and human relation), I found that I, too, took for granted several concepts required for any ongoing construction of a black theological anthropology. Sprinkled throughout my *Black Theology U.S.A and South Africa: Politics, Culture, and Liberation* are various ideas on the God–human reality. Likewise, each chapter of my *Shoes That Fit Our Feet: Sources for a Constructive Black Theology* contains sections on notions of sacred calling to humanity. And my *Down, Up, and Over: Slave Religion and Black Theology* offers an entire chapter on theological anthropology.[2]

After these comparative reviews of black popular culture, theological anthropology paradigms, and my own prior works, I concluded that it was necessary for me first to step back conceptually before continuing my initial writing project of a contemporary black theological anthropology based on the four types found in African American folktales (that is, trickster, conjurer, outlaw, and Christian witness). A move forward mandated a move back, as it were, into an extended conversation with fundamental, widely presumed ideas. Restated, my own published work, current scholarly models, and black folk culture models assumed exact comprehension of the following notions: *culture, self,* and *race.* To talk of a God and human connection without an analytical framework stabilizing the meanings of culture, self, and race would be like erecting a house on a soft and spurious foundation. Thus, this present book serves as a theoretical grounding and launching point for a later work on black folktales and theological anthropology in black theology perspective.

Indeed, to speak of the intertwining of human purpose and human condition with a transcendent something (that is, an ultimate vision, spirit, superlative force, or God) places one directly in the vibrant context in which human–sacred encounters unfold. For me, that encompassing environment means human culture. The human–divine dynamic evolves not above materiality or sealed in abstraction but deeply enmeshed in the messiness of human-made exigencies. We find the human and the sacred meeting in culture. In a word, culture itself must be defined as the first condition of possibility for speaking about the texture of human being as it is implicated with spirit. One needs to understand culture before understanding theological anthropology.

Culture itself emerges from the fluid creative play of a community (the selves) framing the formation of an individual (the self). Human beings and human being are the constituent parts out of which cultures are forged. Without collective selves and the individual self, one could not build a culture. Consequently, we must plunge into murky waters to explore the ebb and flow of the community (the selves) with the individual (the self), a prior conceptual tributary from which the notion of culture flows. Otherwise stated, selves/self are the current below the surface of culture.

Furthermore, looking specifically at the United States of America with its identity, aesthetics, and power relations shot through with race, we find that the idea of race has defined and named all collective selves and indeed each singular self. Race is the first marker that introduces and classifies a person and a group in obsessively racialized America. Here, by necessity, selves/self are rooted in clarity about the notion of race. One cannot entertain an explanation of selves/self without openly recognizing and accounting for race.

In sum, theological anthropology grows out of *culture*; culture arises from particular *selves* and the *self*; and selves/self (at least in the U.S. landscape) automatically involve the *race* of the selves/self who create cultures out of which we construct contemporary theological anthropology. These are the three conditions of possibility for framing our thinking about sacred and human relationships.

Need for New Visioning

We examine theological anthropology from a black theology vantage point not only because conceptual clarity demands such a move. The practical urgency of creating an alternative vision of what humans in the United States and, indeed, the world human community can become also compels us to attempt a liberating theological anthropology. Can we say a word about a healthy God–human encounter, in which each person enjoys self-love and a healthy ego; in which human beings come together to found positive and harmonious communities; in which women and men support and live in balance with plants, animals, and the natural elements; and in which people reflect intentionally about their high calling (which they receive from some greater force or being other than themselves) to anchor their human being with the poor and the working class?

For me, the answer is an overwhelming yes. I believe that not struggling for future envisioning of theological anthropology means maintaining a demonic and toxic status quo. By this I mean that the reigning theological anthropology in the United States cuts against the grain of beneficial living for all breathing, and even nonbreathing, realities. The

U.S.A.'s implicit yet dominant theological anthropology is demonic individualism. The demon reveals itself in a kind of American cultural trinity: (1) historical amnesia, (2) instantaneous fulfillment of desire, and (3) "we're number one" mythology. All three contribute to a rabid individualism that amounts to a rival religion or idolatrous notion of the self, the community, and the divine.

The demon lurks just below the American psychic epidermis. When it perceives a threat, either internal or external, it unleashes a holistic and orchestrated attack via the media, money, military, and missionaries, with the goal of carving up the world in its own image and globalizing its individualist theological anthropology.

Let me elaborate on the three aspects of such an anthropology. First, one subscribes to the accepted U.S. definition of a human being if one partakes of that peculiar arrogance of most Americans who, of all the peoples in the world, can afford to pretend that history (indeed, history of even the prior twelve months) never occurred. This conscious decision to bury one's head in the historical sand contrasts radically with the rest of the world's embracing of past stories. For instance, Native American nations have a profound sense of generations gone before.

Many pertinent historical questions should challenge our heart and head: How did the U.S. body politic form? From what peoples on the West Coast and the Deep South between 1607 and 1865 (from the arrival of the first English-speaking colonialists in Jamestown, Virginia, to the end of slavery and the Civil War) did we derive our national identity? What happened to white workers in the consolidation of monopolized capital at the end of the nineteenth century? How did islands in the Pacific Ocean become a state? When did women become legal adults, free of fathers' and husbands' guardianship? Why did the federal government start utilizing ordinary citizens' tax money as welfare payments to giant corporations? How many U.S. citizens know what were the key national issues last year? Historical amnesia clouds our understanding of ourselves as persons in an ongoing national community.

Second, Americans enjoy a plethora of gadgets to facilitate everything from cooking to sex to entertainment: in-car televisions, foolproof diets, indoor exercise machines, liposuction, mail-order catalogs, instant Internet access, cell phones, and so forth. They desire quick wars of aggression without being made aware of the blood and gore and deaths resulting from all imperialist acts of violence on other countries. A lust for instant gratification is satisfied only in a country that appears to maintain its spirituality by not recycling the memory of its history and not investing the quality time, soul-searching, and persistent patient effort requisite to elevate the status of all its human resources. In other words, microwave desires for instantaneous pleasures become an addiction, leading to an insatiability in all aspects of life.

In contrast, one achieves a more salutary communal and individual way of life by satisfying needs rather than desires. What are the necessities of each member of the population, and how does the nation prudently assess its resources to realize the wealth and health of the majority of the country? In simple proverbial terms, we need a kind of delayed gratification in which the wealthy sacrifice some profits and some private ownership to ensure their nation's well-being and the elevation of the overwhelming majority of the citizenry.

Third, the "we're number one" mythology embodies a demonic spirit. In this instance, national unity is achieved by dehumanizing opponents. It is manifest in a peculiar American ritual of breast-beating exhibited especially during epochs of competition—either in international sports arenas or in international attacks. It is a simple fact that the sales of U.S. flags increase dramatically when the U.S. government has declared war somewhere in the world and begins to count how many "enemy combatants" or "bad guys" the armed services have murdered. Why does the nation feel called to assert its unitary superiority over other people? Why does the country's personality require belief that the United States is the greatest country in the world?

A countervailing option would advance friendship first and a mindset not of either-or but of both-and. How can the United States enter international sports events so that other countries win as well? How can the U.S. government aid other countries so that they can further develop their own culture, history, wealth, religions, and goals? Unfortunately, losing a sports event hurts both the national psyche (that is, if we come in second place, then our self-love, self-confidence, and self-esteem have been damaged) and U.S. capitalists' pocketbooks. Corporations earn more profits when U.S. teams win. A victorious sports franchise can promote more product lines for sale, and when the American populace, because of a first-place showing, experiences a momentary high, in good old American fashion, it goes out and spends more money so the wealthy of Wall Street can grab more income.

Likewise, murdering other populations in their own countries through "legitimate" wars is big business. The military-industrial complex sells to a multibillion-dollar market. Bombs, bullets, guns, armor, tanks, helicopters, planes, ships, submarines, military cars, and so forth are intentionally made to be destroyed by going to war. In the military industry, one stays in business by killing people. If U.S. citizens forced their government to end all of its global wars (open and clandestine) and to cease all shipment of (legal and illegal) military aid abroad, then a multibillion-dollar industry would go out of business. "We're number one" engenders deep psychological boosts for the broader psychic ethos, and it also delivers unparalleled wealth and income into the hands of a small group of American families.

The demon of U.S. individualism accompanied by its trinitarian spirituality (of historical amnesia, instantaneous gratification, and the myth that "we're number one") has kicked into overdrive in the new century. But no human empire lasts forever. Read about the Romans; sit with the British; listen to the Soviets. If the long view of history serves us correctly, then the American empire is on the brink of losing not only its global control but also the depths of its national soul.

And so to achieve theoretical clarity and to correct the country's material and supra-material ailments, a theological anthropology can assist in imagining how self-centered empire transforms into something committed to the welfare of the broken and peripheral communities within and without its borders. Part of the response hinges on how we envision being human, as well as the nature of the God or spirituality one conjures. Another part of the outcome rests on how one perceives the calling or vocation that God or spirituality invites one to believe in, think about, proclaim, and witness to.

As my response, throughout *Being Human* I claim that one becomes a human being by gearing all ultimate issues toward compassion for and empowerment of people in structural poverty, working-class folk, and the marginalized. And, through the spiritual and material healed-being of these exploited strata, all human communities, inclusive of oppressors, perpetrators, and victimizers, become similar to those who were formerly oppressed, perpetrated against, and victimized. Diminishing emotional demons and removing the structures of practical control of one group over another birth true sisterhood and brotherhood in harmony.

Once Again on Black Theology

Actually, this integrative approach—balancing human internal and external challenges, women and men, the micro and macro, the psyche and the body, an individual member and the entire family, Christianity and the other great world religions, the human and all of creation, and the spirit and the flesh—manifests a deep dimension of black theology of liberation's methodology, worldview, and long-term goals.[3] It is no accident that such a conceptual orientation and primordial compassion for the bottom sectors of society pervade *Being Human*. As a second-generation black theologian of liberation, I experience the world from that perspective. Out of particularity grows yearning for universal freedom for all peoples, regardless of who they are.

A black theology of liberation is a specific God-talk and God-walk. But what makes it black? To be black in the United States of America is to realize that one's blackness signifies being created in God's image of high self-love, self-esteem, and self-confidence—all geared to serving the poor and the brokenhearted. A normative strand of solidarity and empowerment threads throughout this book. Though God and the ancestors create and affirm black folk, nevertheless, black people are born into a priori circumstances of a male-centered, wealth-driven, and white-skin-privileged universe. Thus, in the following chapters we will be ever mindful of the presence of multivalent macro-constrictions directly affecting what it means to be human. Further, *blackness* here denotes both a sacred natural creation and complex social constructions.

A black theology of liberation is an intellectual discipline and way of life. The following attributes circumscribe the notion of "black" within the discipline: (1) a point of origin, (2) sources, (3) historical traditions, (4) institutional representations, (5) generational offspring, (6) a reference audience, (7) a body of literature, (8) an international network, and (9) a universal impulse.

Contemporary black theology commenced with a July 31, 1966, publication in the *New York Times* of a favorable theological assessment of the Black Power slogan. (The slogan was issued from Greenwood, Mississippi, to the nation and the world on June 16, 1966.) African American pastors and church administrators published the July reflection document. Black theology, therefore, is one of the few contemporary global theologies that arose from the churches and people's movements in the streets outside of the academy. Since that initial period, black theology has relied on primarily, but not exclusively, African American, African, African diasporic, and Third World sources for constructing theology and approaching the varying components of religious studies. Though contemporary black theology is based in an organized church, community, academic, and international movement, the historical traditions of today's black God-talk hail as far back as the first African communities on the African continent, long before the Christian European and European American slave trade in black bodies (1441 to 1865). Black theology is essentially a proactive dynamism that originates out of the positive encounter of God and the ancestors with African American people. Today's black theology has harnessed that historical narrative to create institutions and disciplines.

The oldest and only organization completely owned by black Americans is the African American church. More recent creations from the 1960s into the twenty-first century include the National Committee of Negro Churchmen (1966); the Society for the Study of Black Religion; the black caucuses in the predominantly white denominations; the progressive wing of the national bodies of the historic African American church denominations; the Black Theology Project of Theology in the Americas; the Black Theology unit of the American Academy of Religion; the (international) Ecumenical Association of Third World Theologians; diverse African American religious programs and black church studies centers at schools of theology, seminaries, and divinity schools throughout the nation; and the various forms of pedagogical classes and conferences in educational institutions and in black church curricula across the United States. Even though the founding elders move toward and into retirement age and some have already crossed over with the ancestors, a second and at least a third generation of black theologians have emerged in both the church and the academy. The theological movement propagated theoretical and faith-filled offspring.

Furthermore, black theology has a focused audience. It makes conscious decisions to reflect critically on the nature of the faith of African American churches, other black religious organizations, and gatherings of individuals. Speaking to this audience, an entire body of literature has been published in journals, magazines, and books. Subject matter crosses all standard disciplines of religious education as well as novel, cutting-edge, outside-the-boundaries intellectual enterprises. The domestic audience and corpus of critical literature stand in solidarity, foster ongoing conversations, and solidify international networks with Africa, the African diaspora, darker-skinned peoples worldwide, and the entire Third World. The specificity of the African American religious communities gave rise to black theology. However, the latter maintains its authenticity as long as it realizes that its calling is in service to universal humankind. Love of the black self, the black church, and the broader black peoples worldwide engenders and compels black theology to be at the service of the entire *Homo sapiens* race.

Ultimately what makes a black theology of liberation "black" is the fact that people of African descent in North America are made in God's image. God chooses to tabernacle with the least in U.S. society, and included in those least are black folk. Thus, wherever divinity empties itself in the human realm, divinity creates new possibilities and embraces the full human identity of the poor among us. The sacred realm salutes the full human identity of African American people, specifically embracing the blackness and culture of a community caught in structural oppression. What wicked powers and peoples demonize as savage and lowly, the divinity seeks out and privileges, resulting in a revolutionary reversal of the status quo's naming powers.

In fact, spiritual power (revealed as political-economic access, coupled with cultural promotion of blackness) defines the gift of liberation from a loving transcendent God and infuses the ultimate vision of freedom for marginalized black folk in the United States. God grants the gifts of blackness and liberation together as sacred indications of divine love for struggling people seemingly ensnared in cultural, psychological, and political quicksand. In the commonsense religious wisdom of African American folk, God can make a way out of no way for the oppressed and the oppressor. Regardless of one's class status, justice remains the perennial option for authentic human being.

This Book's Method

In this introduction I have established the motivating query (that is, being human) and the initial research attempt (that is, theological anthropology emanating from African American folktales). In my research, I initially immersed myself within the depths of black folktales, but, as I reflected on my findings, I found that key conceptual terms needed clarifying. Even a review of my previous publications indicated this requirement to state more clearly the presuppositional ideas of culture, selves/self, and race undergirding any essay on theological anthropology. Contemporary models of theological anthropology also confirm the need for defining these concepts.

Consequently, chapter 1 engages several contemporary paradigms of what it means to be a human being. These current models, black folktales, and my own writings all urged me to spend some reflective time ruminating on the nature of culture (in chapter 2), selves/self (in chapter 3), and race (in chapter 4). The conclusion (in chapter 5) summarizes the key ideas in my argument and introduces some lessons suggested by African American popular culture for a theological anthropology. In this sense, the concluding chapter, drawing on the trickster, conjurer, outlaw, and Christian witness symbols, begins to answer the initial motivating query for this journey. What does it mean to be a person who fulfills individual capabilities and contributes to a community's well-being? And what connects the community and the individual to an ultimate vision, spirituality, or God?

1.

Contemporary Models of Theological Anthropology

In the context of the United States, theological anthropology encompasses the diverse experiences of disparate groups forged into a definition of what makes a North American. For instance, Europeans brought their specific conceptions of divine providence to what they considered to be the "New World"; these ideas came most notably with the 1607 and 1620 arrivals of English citizens in Jamestown, Virginia, and Plymouth, Massachusetts, respectively.[1] Preceding these landings, Native Americans or American Indians (that is, the original people of the land) had already crafted a sense of the spiritual self. Likewise, enslaved Africans and African Americans contributed the witness of a black people saturated in their ethos with a divine–human relationship. And when European Americans took by force roughly half of Mexico in the mid-1840s and Puerto Rico and the Philippines in the late nineteenth century (in addition to the kingdom of Hawaii), brown and yellow peoples added their ways of being human in relation to the sacred to the evolving time and space called America. Chinese, Japanese, Korean, and Filipino immigrants continued to round out the rainbow reality and crucial connection of the human and spiritual.

This chapter examines these contemporary theological anthropologies in North America. What they have in common, among other things, is a critical exploration, both descriptive and prescriptive, of the idea of what is a human being from a healthy spiritual perspective. By *spirituality* I mean a belief in an ultimate power greater than any individual person that is embedded in the textures and contours of

specific human cultures, collective and individual selves, and sociologically and phenotypically determined races. Indeed, these probing theological interpretations of the human question engage at various levels
the themes of culture, self, and race in the North American framework
and explore the unique dynamic between the spiritual and the human.
A theoretical or practical conception of the ties between God and
human presupposes these three religious themes in varied and creative
attempts to develop a U.S. theological anthropology. Put differently, a
condition for the possibility of an American theological anthropology
is discourse on culture, selves/self, and race.

Traditional notions of theological anthropology tend to define the
concept in a general sense; that is, the focus is on the mental represen-
tation of human nature or an intangible question of what it is to be
a person. More narrowly, the concern is that of epistemology: "What
is it about human beings that makes it possible for them in their fini-
tude to know the infinite God?" In addition to these general and epis-
temological dimensions, the theologians who have usually controlled
academic conversations have framed the debate from the perspective
of redemption: "What is it about human beings that makes fallenness
possible in such a radical way as to require the kind of redemption to
which Christianity witnesses?"[2] In broad strokes, these queries focus on
human nature and the human condition.[3]

To flesh out these issues, I will consider critically several contemporary voices on theological anthropology, investigating the contrasts
among European American, feminist, and liberation theologies in their
views on theological anthropology. Before such an engagement, a word is
in order regarding the assorted adjectives modifying the phrase "theological anthropology." Initially one might assume that descriptors qualifying
a theological doctrine would indicate a subjective turn among interlocutors in their talk about notions of the divine. Perhaps the descriptors
"Third World," "feminist," and "liberation" skew a credible theological
discourse. In addition, such an argument might claim, the "traditional"
handling of systematic or constructive theology deploys a rational, scientific, and objective treatment of theological anthropology.

Yet, in the first instance, the proverbial observation still holds: God
might be objective, and universal but particular human communities do
theology. Humans, not God, systematize and construct theories about

divine dimensions of their life. Consequently, the people cataloging, creating, or doing the theology are limited by their own direct and indirect human experiences or by their presuppositional lenses that rationally interpret the divine revelations in human collective and individual experiences and in nature. Here experiences result from data received by our five senses, feelings, intuitions, and supernatural insights and data from nature (the nonhuman world). The constructive theologian's autobiography and the biographies of the thinkers she chooses weigh heavily on the substance of the conclusions she advances. More particularly, in the U.S. context, the autobiography of the humans developing a theological anthropology reeks with preconceptions of culture, self, and race.

In the second instance, traditional elaborations of theology have always been adjectival. Even when theologies refuse to place a qualifier before the noun *theology*, an adjective is implied. One notes death-of-God, orthodox, liberal, neoorthodox, dialectical, neoliberal, proclamation, postliberal, process, social gospel, modern, postmodern, and existential theologies accepted as part of traditional talk about God and humanity.[4] In other words, even when theology has been written by a small but elite group of people from one race and gender, those theologies have not been objective, detached, scientific, and universal. They have been and remain ensconced in specific and local contexts. The difference between these so-called broad interrogations of theology, in contrast to the so-called narrow, adjectival, or hyphenated theologies (such as black, womanist, feminist, mujerista, Latino, Asian American, and Native American), is that the former, as a group, have had the resources to promote their voice, their experiences, and their thinkers as normative or as *the* tradition.

I will explore the contemporary debate over theological anthropology by examining four representative stances:[5] progressive liberal (David Tracy), postliberal (George A. Lindbeck), feminist (Rosemary Radford Ruether), and liberation perspectives in the U.S.A. In examining these theological anthropologies, we should keep in mind certain key factors: First, the name of each viewpoint indicates its point of origin in human "racial" and cultural history as well as in the particularity of a definite self and other selves. Second, each perspective comes out of a tradition defined by the descendants of that point of origin. Third, an author of

theological anthropology tends to refer primarily to the ancestors from
that author's tradition. And fourth, this same writer lives within the
context of socially constructed racial structures, as do all people living
in the United States.

Progressive Liberal

While moving from an earlier affirmation of pro-modernist views to his
present recognition of how the modern European version of democracy
has adversely affected and continues to affect the majority of the world's
peoples found in the Third World,[6] David Tracy continues to seek a
revisioning of the liberal individual from the European Enlightenment.
Key to Tracy's notion of theological anthropology is complex, rational
conversation on the part of the reasoning human subject as that subject engages staple sources from European experiences and recognizes
the existence of others different from the European diaspora. Insofar as
he holds tightly to the critically thinking human subject, Tracy remains
within the modernist liberal camp. Insofar as he embraces non-European realities, he opens up a critique of the universal rational person to
the challenge of various particular human persons, especially those who
have been the object of European democracy.[7]

He asserts, "I do care about the shift to the other and not the self.
The shift is about undoing the arrogance and limits of modernity, especially reason."[8] He demonstrates a dedication to the highest form of
critical intellectual inquiry as well as a commitment to conversation
with the other, the one different from the self. Hence, his is a progressive liberal move. Because the European Enlightenment and modernity
have questioned the literal interpretation of the Bible, the presupposed
authority of the Christian churches, and the defense of the assumed regulatory role of the Christian tradition,[9] Christianity has to be revised.
And even with the onset of postmodernity,[10] Tracy still claims allegiance
to core human values of the European liberal, modern effort: "What
remains constant in the shift from modernity to post-modernity is the
fact that such contemporary critiques of modernity deepen the fundamental commitment to those purely secular standards for knowledge
and action initiated by the Enlightenment. . . . The 'authentic' person is
committed above all else to the full affirmation of the ultimate signifi-

cance of our lives in this world."[11] Tracy perceives the theologian's task as revising the postmodern symbols and the Christian symbols in order to be faithful to the common project of secularity shared by both theologians and nonreligious academics. Tracy affirms that the theologian "believes that the Christian faith is at heart none other than the most adequate articulation of the basic faith of secularity itself."[12] This common faith between the modern/postmodern secularist and the Christian theologian is defined by affirming "the ultimate significance and final worth of our lives, our thoughts, and actions, here and now in nature and in history."[13] In other words, the secularist and the Christian share a faith in the rational powers of the postmodern human being. A rational revision of the Christian symbols, then, provides the best symbolic representations of secular faith.[14]

The key task of the theologian indicates the progressive liberal's notion of theological anthropology. For Tracy, important elements in theological anthropology are conversation, interpretation, and understanding, which together can be the tools to analyze the best ideas of the European liberal traditions.

> In the wider Euro-American society, one need not romanticize the politics of Plato and Aristotle, nor minimize the lack of correlation between the original Greek polis and modern society, in order to realize that the Greek ideal of civilized discussion of issues for the polis remains an exemplary limit-concept even in our present vastly complex society. If we continue to assume the value of reasoned, public discourse in a critical and argued fashion, if we continue to affirm the related values of individual liberties and equality as shared and often conflicting values for a democratic polity, then the discussion of these conflicts cannot be left to either a technological and bureaucratic elite nor to the happenstance of special-interest groups.[15]

For Tracy, the purpose of human beings is to pursue a "common good, a common interest in emancipatory reason and a common commitment to the ideal of authentic conversation within a commonly affirmed pluralism and a commonly experienced conflictual situation."[16] Authentic conversation leads to understanding the true nature and purpose of human being. Conversation becomes authentic when interlocutors let the question and the subject matter take primacy in the dialogue; that is, the talking partners have to surrender their own self-interests and their fixation on self-image. The fluid, back-and-forth movement of communication focused on the subject matter will bring the participants into the event of understanding.[17] Indeed, for Tracy, conversation brings about understanding as interpretation.[18]

Tracy states the principles for authentic conversation: "respect for the sincerity of the other; . . . all conversation partners are, in principle, equals; saying what one means and meaning what one says; a willingness to weigh all relevant evidence, including one's warrants and backings; a willingness to abide by the rules of validity, coherence, and especially possible contradictions between my theories and my actual performance."[19] This process of conversation, interpretation, and understanding is no mere idle effort but in fact has theological import. "For believers," writes Tracy, "to be enlightened religiously is to be empowered to understand: to understand, above all a power that is the ultimate power with which we all must deal." Religious understanding involves the Christian believer's relation to God in such a way that we better understand our human selves—that is, "the pluralistic and ambiguous reality of the self."[20] The notion of ambiguity includes not only ambiguity of the selves in conversation but also the ambiguity of the interaction between power and knowledge in the discourse of European Americans vis-à-vis the texts of oppressed people.[21]

The progressive liberal's ongoing attempts to update the project of theological anthropology include extending an invitation to oppressed people to enter the already existing conversation, interpretation, and understanding dynamic of the European and European American dialogical partners. Yet the essential planks of progressive liberal theological anthropology remain the gifts from the Enlightenment. Drawing boundaries around the European project and against Third World theologians, Tracy asserts without compromise: "we should resist any claim from any Third World theologian that the classic liberal rights of freedom of speech, religion, press, assembly, and so on are no longer important for the dialectic of history and merit no theological defense. Any dialectic that can reject those genuine accomplishments of the bourgeois revolutions should be resisted."[22] Furthermore, he names his social location: "my own white, male, middle-class, and academic reflections on a hermeneutics of dialogue and a praxis of solidarity."[23] With this as his starting point, he clearly and consistently articulates conversation, interpretation, and understanding as the best goal in human discourses to appreciate what he calls difference and the other.[24] He allows for the decentering of the "Eurocentric character of a Christian theology,"[25] mentioning the importance of "the historical struggle of the marginalized and the oppressed in liberation theologies."[26] Ultimately, instead of the U.S.A. being the only center with the rest of the globe as the periphery, he argues for a polycentrism found in the many centers around the world, especially where one discovers the poor and the oppressed. These are the other conversations to which Europeans and European Americans must listen.[27]

Along with the concept of polycentrism, Tracy introduces the idea of fragments, which "show the need to shatter any reigning totality system, such as the 'white' understanding of modernity and culture,"[28] in order to recognize the creative particularities in every culture and affirm "the singularity of each culture."[29] He struggles to break totality systems—offspring of the Enlightenment—by attending "intellectually and spiritually, not to the self but to the other," that is, the victims of the Enlightenment and modernity.[30]

While elaborating a progressive liberal theological anthropology, Tracy adheres to his core values: "the great hope of Western reason, including the hope of adequate interpretation." Though he feels that this is a modest vision, in this postmodern, polycentric, fragmented reality, it nonetheless reflects the goals of conversation, argument, interpretation, and understanding "first created by the Greeks."[31]

In the final analysis, Tracy develops a theological anthropology primarily out of the particularity of European and European American experiences. This necessity arises from the crisis felt by these sectors of society as the United States and the world confront the challenges of a global postmodernism. To identify the people facing this crisis, Tracy asks, "But who is this 'we'? We are those Westerners shaped by the seventeenth-century scientific revolution, the eighteenth-century Enlightenment, and the nineteenth-century industrial revolution and explosion of historical consciousness."[32]

One of the strengths of Tracy's work is his naming his own social location, which could eventually lead to an in-depth engagement with the specific texture of the culture in which his progressive liberal analysis contextualizes its theological anthropology. Exploring the autobiographical self within nuanced culture might reveal insights into how the individual self relates to the collective self and how the racialized self in culture connects to a racialized tradition of collective selves. Tracy seems to hint at this possibility:

> The more general question "What is theology?" first demands, therefore, a response to a prior question: What is the self-understanding of the theologian? To ask that question as a personal and in that sense an irrevocably existential one is entirely appropriate. Yet to do so with the questionable assumption that the theologian is clearly a single self—an individual in the Western sense of Burckhardt, Kierkegaard and Nietzsche—is to betray the real demands of the passionate reflection of true individuality. More exactly, one risks ignoring the actual complexity of different selves related to the distinct social locations and therefore to the distinct plausibility structures present in each theologian. Behind the pluralism of theological conclusions lies a pluralism of public roles and publics as reference groups for theological discourse.[33]

At the same time, one can raise questions regarding a theological anthropology whose constituent parts are conversation, interpretation, and understanding. The key issue is renegotiating the very system that structures the discussion. A progressive liberal theological anthropology does not seem to take full account of the possibility that the Other (of and to whom the progressive liberal has begun to speak) might desire to reconfigure the very scaffolding of the discourse.

Imagine a table created for discussion participants by a group of elites who have already determined the core topics, the language to be used and its key vocabulary terms, and the strict definitions of correct thinking and correct method. Such an approach does not leave room for the Other to participate in the building of an entirely new table, to rearticulate core topics, to use the Other's own language and vocabulary, and to include new and different structures in thinking about the human being. Even if "postmodern intellectuals" seek to turn their listening and analytical ear to "the oppressed" in order to become "human subjects in active solidarity with all those others we [postmodern intellectuals] have too often presumed to speak for," does this revised notion of conversational dynamics offer room for the challenges emanating from the Other?

We might ask, What happens when the oppressed Other speaks differently, uses different criteria for meaning, truth, and so forth? In a word, does the revising and reenvisioning of modernity and postmodernity also allow for a leveling of power in theological anthropology? Or can one revise the bourgeois, modernist project (from the European Enlightenment) or the postmodernist move (symbolized by the fragmented quality of life)[34] without speaking to a redistribution of wealth, privilege, and power among the majority of real people in the U.S.A.? Both surface and subterranean power dynamics will inevitably affect conversation, interpretation, and understanding among the citizenry.

Stressing an other-oriented divine love, Tracy refers to the specificities of the "neighbor" as the object of a hermeneutical theological anthropology,[35] that is, a theological anthropology of interpretation. He demonstrates that such an orientation takes for granted the foundational existence of God's love of *agape* (mutual love). To be a self requires the self and the Other woven together in mutual interaction via *agape*.

> The route to authentic self-hood for the Christian, whatever the particular focus for interpreting that ideal, remains a route of the radical discipleship of an *imitatio Christi*. The demands for real mutuality expressed in the Christian ideal and reexpressed in the *caritas* tradition, the radical self-sacrificial love disclosed in the cross of the Crucified One are themselves expressions of the gospel agapic gift and command to the self to live a radical equal regard for every human being, for the neighbor, not only the friend. . . . The reality of God as love decisively revealed in the event of Jesus Christ is the central clue to the meaning of the self as a human self both loved and loving.[36]

The question persists: what does it say about God as love if the substance of the love lacks justice, if it does not empower those objects of love who are oppressed?[37] Does not "real mutuality" entail a transformation of the self in recognition of other selves? This question has significant relevance for the United States, where one interlocutor is privileged (with access to and control of resources and the structure of the conversation based on the assumed normativity of one type of racialized self), while the Other remains the object of the discourse and without control over its structure or language.

In a word, the forging of the progressive liberal understanding of the human being stumbles on a major obstacle: the unresolved and seemingly inherent tension between the purported basic tenet of "radical equal regard for every human being" and the fundamental right of the individual to create an asymmetrical social, cultural, and economic human community. (If the collective human community's obligation to ensure concrete equality among all citizens was *the* cornerstone of European modernist thinking, then the U.S. Constitution with its theme of individual rights and free enterprise and its uncompromising stance on private accumulation of wealth would not serve as the logical extension of the best of the European Enlightenment experiment in the United States.) While maintaining and privileging the results of the modern bourgeois enterprise, progressive liberal theological anthropology seeks to revise the Enlightenment experiment by including the Other in the very project whose traditions veer away from political, economic, cultural, linguistic, and religious equality for everyone.

Is it possible to fashion a theological anthropology based primarily on the model of bourgeois revolutions? Or does it require a new paradigm grounded primarily in liberation of the poor and the oppressed? On the one hand, Tracy wishes to uphold "the classic middle-class virtues" of the accomplishments of "the modern, bourgeois revolutions." On the other hand, from the Christian gospel point of view, Tracy acknowledges it is among the poor and the oppressed that one discovers Jesus' message to humanity, and, likewise, it is among these sectors of society that one encounters human hope vivified by sacred presence.[38] Indeed, it has been the types of theological anthropology emerging from bourgeois revolutions that have created the poor and the oppressed. Still, Tracy appears to be arguing that these same revolutions possess a sufficient will and internal resources to oppose the structures and material benefits established by the bourgeois class for whom the revolutions were fought.

History has shown, at least in the U.S. context, that the eighteenth- and nineteenth-century bourgeois revolutions resulted in freedom, democracy, individual rights, and natural rights for specific self/selves and races. That is to say, this legacy grants all of these privileges primarily to elite wealthy, white families. As a result of these revolutions, power, privilege, and positions in North America are increasingly concentrated among a few at the top of the socioeconomic ladder, whereas loss of economic wealth, intensified psychological pressures, declining standard of living, and damaged family well-being have become the hallmarks of life for the majority of Americans (most pointedly perceived among communities of color). But the conundrum remains: does distant or recent history indicate that revolutions for the bourgeoisie have the internal resources, convictions, and passions to alleviate poverty, working-class status, and white supremacy—that is to say, to eliminate the very conditions requisite for bourgeois privilege?

Bourgeois revolutions produced a new perception of the human person—the ideal of the bourgeois individual, with his (and later her) individual civic rights and with the individual rights to accumulate wealth privately at the expense of the other selves. Bourgeois revolutions occurred precisely in the narrow interests and for the permanent maintenance of bourgeois rule as an elite minority population dominating the overwhelming majority of society. Only after overthrowing feudalism and establishing a monopoly over private property for wealthy white men were the majority of Americans given limited access to classic (European bourgeois) rights. In order to restructure society so that the bourgeoisie (as the ruling class) can systematically and continually redistribute wealth upward, this revolutionary class articulates bourgeois freedom, democracy, and individual rights so long as the majority of human selves in the United States (and the world) support monopoly capitalism. Bourgeois democracy means that individual rights are allowed if they do not challenge bourgeois rule. Hence, it appears that the minority elite consider their self-understanding of what is a human being as normative for the majority of humanity, who are without private wealth.

Restated, the majority population is given permission to exercise the "classic liberal rights of freedom of speech, religion, press, assembly"[39] as long as these individual rights do not evolve into group rights threatening bourgeois rule.

Postliberal

Like David Tracy, George A. Lindbeck constructs a European and European American theological anthropology from his primary engagement with the sources of that tradition. Lindbeck, however, feels that Tracy concedes too much to the secular demands of modernity and postmodernity, hence removing the foundation from the very purpose of the Christian believer as authentic human being, which is to immerse oneself into the uniqueness of Christian discourses and confront and change the non-Christian world. Lindbeck believes that Tracy incorrectly deduces a common human experience in secular and Christian cultures and concludes that secular culture and Christian culture merely express the same universal experience. After stating his own stance, Lindbeck dismisses Tracy's position as an "experiential-expressive one":

> [Religions] are . . . patterns of ritual, myth, belief, and conduct which constitute, rather than being constituted by, that which modern people often think of as most profound in human beings, viz., their existential self-understanding. This model of the human being . . . is the inverse of the experiential-expressive one. The humanly real . . . is not constructed from below upward or from the inner to the outer, but from the outer to the inner, and from above downward. The acquisition of a language [is] necessarily from the outside. . . . The Christian theological application of this view is that just as an individual becomes human by learning a language, so he or she begins to become a new creature through hearing and interiorizing the language that speaks of Christ.[40]

For Lindbeck, an existential self-understanding results from being taught and exposed to a religious dynamic introduced from outside of the individual, in contrast to a notion of the nonreligious and the religious adhering to some mutual reality inherent in what it means to be humanly real. Lindbeck claims a radical differentiation between one's prereligious state and one's learned religious way of life. To become authentically "a new creature" (in Christ) one undergoes a profound and qualitatively distinct move into the realm of being religious. Therefore, Lindbeck's model of the human being is an effort to move beyond Tracy's modern/postmodern liberal perspective. Lindbeck concentrates on building a postliberal theological anthropology. For him, Tracy's progressive liberal assumptions make philosophy (that is, nonreligious questions derived especially from the liberal, modern, and postmodern experiments) the starting point for answering what God has called human beings to be and do. For Lindbeck, Christianity provides its own criteria. Speaking specifically about dogmatic questions, but maintaining this posture throughout his debate with the progressive liberal position, Lindbeck argues:

> If religious issues are to be settled on religious grounds, then no non-theological theology of propositions can be used to decide the question of whether dogmatic infallibility is either meaningful or possible. . . . Religious discourse has its own integrity, and no matter what is the best way to analyze propositions in other realms and for other purposes . . . this does not determine the appropriate way to talk about the central affirmations of the Christian faith.[41]

Instead of trying to change the gospel message in accordance with the demands of modernity or postmodernity (that is, external issues and concerns determine the internal Christian culture and language), postliberal theological anthropology calls on believers to learn their own unique native tongue, that is, to entrench themselves thoroughly in the grammar of Christian speech rather than secular speech. Constructing self-identity requires grasping the importance of language within specific cultural contexts. Lindbeck underscores the specificity of linguistic frameworks and meaning:

> We are now much more keenly aware than in the past of the situational or contextual character of all meaning. The linguistic analysts, especially Wittgenstein, speak sometimes of meaning as a function of "forms of life." Unless we know the ways language operates in the detailed behavior of individuals and communities, we do not know its signification. Words and concepts have meanings insofar as they have uses, and to know their meaning is, at least on one level, to know their use. This is why knowledge of the situation or context is of vital importance, for it is the context which both occasions and explains the When, the Why and the How—that is, the meaning—of what we say.[42]

Consequently, the believer needs to relearn the language of the Bible and see secular culture and philosophy through that language, worldview, and culture. How language operates in the Bible and the contexts for the deployment of languages in various biblical situations determine the content for what it means to be a Christian human being in the midst of a non-Christian culture. And, in Lindbeck's viewpoint, though the outcome is ultimately left to God, this appropriation of biblical language as it operates in definite contexts will lead to Christianizing secular culture.

Lindbeck perceives Christianizing culture as a biblical imperative. Christianizing culture becomes a by-product of the believers' immersing themselves deeply in the Christian language. In the past, God used the church to Christianize cultures. But the Christian cannot provide a blueprint. Lindbeck writes: "only when the songs of Zion are sung for their own sake will they be sung well enough to gain currency in society at large. The cultural mission cannot be programmed but is, from the human perspective, an accident or by-product of the Christian community's faithfulness in attending to its own language and life which, of course, includes service to others."[43] This process of relearning Christian syntax and biblical language on their own terms and then offering Christian culture to secular culture is sorely needed to combat the secular cultural vacuum existing today in what Lindbeck calls traditionally Christian countries like the United States. By offering a Christian culture to replace secular culture, Christians provide a specific religious language, idioms, and metaphors through which the national goals of the United States can be expressed. With all citizens articulating Christian language and experiencing Christian culture, "questions of meaning, purpose, and destiny" become much clearer.[44] We are called to interpret the world through the usage of biblical literacy, not with the secular and philosophical concepts advocated by progressive liberal theology.

To better understand the postliberal's theological anthropology, we must grasp Lindbeck's exact deployment of the notions of language and culture in the Christian religion. First we should clarify what religion is not: for postliberals, religion is not constituted or defined by secular philosophy, society, or culture. Common human experiences between secular life and Christian life do not provide the presuppositional ground for common expressions of a supernatural or transcendent universal experience. In other words, Christianity is not an expression of a foundational common human experience shared with the secularist or even with members of other non-Christian religions. Christianity uniquely constitutes human experience and constructs reality. Lindbeck opposes any theological positions directly or indirectly suggesting a transcendental reality comprised of a common human thread.

Like languages and cultures, religions do not spring from a common font of "universal experiential essence"[45] out of which particular religions, languages, and cultures flow. Postliberal theological anthropology perceives linguistic and cultural forms shaping and defining human experience, and not the other way around. If a generalized, common human experience (with secularity and Christianity both manifesting the same essential human experience) were the threshold to faith, then humans would be called to have conversation among all parties, and, through conversation and interpretation, a common understanding would arise about what should be the way of civilized and rational cohabitation in postmodernity. But for Lindbeck, this would leave open the possibility of subsuming the Christian language and culture underneath secularity or non-Christian religions. Instead of Christianity absorbing the latter, the reverse would unfold. Different religions signify different experiences and not universal human experience. The Buddhist, the secularist, and the Christian actually live through three different experiences. They participate in separate processes.

For Lindbeck, religions denote exact meanings; they are akin to languages. Lindbeck's "emphasis is placed on those respects in which religions resemble languages together with their correlative forms of life and are thus similar to cultures (insofar as these are understood semiotically as reality and value system—that is, as idioms for the construing of reality and the living of life)."[46] One becomes religious similar to the way one acquires a language and culture. One accepts, digests, and makes one's own that which is learned from and created by others. Religion must be accepted on its own terms and not translated into foreign tongues. "The grammar of religion, like that of language, cannot be explicated or learned by analysis of experience, but only by experience. . . . In short, religions, like languages, can be understood only in their own terms, not by transposing them into an alien speech."[47] Through repetition of telling the story and practicing rituals and grammar, one internalizes a group of skills of a specific religion. One learns how to be religious as one is taught a culture.

Lindbeck calls us to be authentic by accepting what he sees as a specific Christian vocation: because the religion of the Bible defines beauty, goodness, being, and truth, non-Christian realities need to be transformed into "figures . . . of the scriptural ones." For it is the Bible that absorbs the world rather than the world the Bible.[48]

Summing up the antagonistic difference between his postliberal approach and that of the progressive liberal, Lindbeck concludes: "The crucial difference between [progressive] liberals and postliberals is in the way they correlate their visions of the future and of present situations. [Progressive] liberals start with experience, with an account of the present, and then adjust their vision of the kingdom of God accordingly, while postliberals are in principle committed to doing the reverse."[49] To be a human for the postliberal is to immerse oneself in biblical literacy and the Bible's worldview,[50] to pull together like-minded Christians into enclaves of mutual support, and to advance a Christian perspective and practice into civic society and secular culture.[51] Lindbeck claims that "the viability of a unified world of the future may well depend on counteracting the acids of modernity. It may depend on communal enclaves that socialize their members into highly particular outlooks supportive of concern for others rather than for individual rights and entitlements, and a sense of responsibility for the wider society rather than for personal fulfillment."[52] In other words, if one lives in the biblical universe in religious enclaves, the result may be the Christianization of culture.

Several red flags arise in Lindbeck's discussion of theological anthropology. First, he apparently sees one Christian culture that permeates the communities of all Christian believers. However, though many profess to follow the one Christ, a multitude of different cultures have absorbed Christianity into their own indigenous, pre-Christian cultures. Hence, unique racialized and indigenous cultures of people have transformed the nature of an originally generic Christian culture. Especially for many communities of color or Third World peoples in the U.S.A., the form of the proclamation, the style of the ritual, the vibrancy of bodily participation in religious worship, and how logic is enfleshed in culture are sometimes considered just as important as the content of universal Christian dogma.

Second, though Lindbeck believes that Christians and the followers of other world religions experience different theological anthropological realities, he fails to acknowledge that Christians in the U.S.A. experience different material realities too. The heterogeneous realities of various cultures in the U.S.A. explode the notion of one common language and culture for American Christians. For African Americans dwelling in structural poverty, the political economy of their community directly affects how they receive the gospel message as well as what questions they pose in response to the gospel. Moreover, among Christians in North America, the various types of spoken English influence how these people of faith live their lives as Christians and express their beliefs as a community.[53]

Finally, while Lindbeck bases his theological anthropology on the Bible, as Itumeleng Mosala has shown, there is more than one word of God in the sacred scriptures.[54] Lindbeck fails to acknowledge this reality when he instructs us to learn the language of the Bible as sacred witness and, thereby, let the biblical world determine the secular world. In addition to Mosala's notion of contrasting words of God and, in fact, contrasting Gods in the Bible, we can also cite how the Bible is practiced differently based on the social location of the communities that appropriate the Word. For example, white Christian slavemasters and enslaved Africans and black Americans exegeted, or interpreted, the Bible (in some cases the very same passages) with completely opposite analyses. Christian masters portrayed biblical passages in a metaphorical and spiritual way, except citations of such verses as "slaves, obey your masters." In contrast, the Reverend Nat Turner (an enslaved African American Baptist) heard God's voice in the biblical text and organized an armed rebellion against the material system of enslavement.[55] Hence, Lindbeck's postliberal view fails to acknowledge diverse Christian interpretations of scripture and the presence of a variety of cultures and languages that influence the Christian world.

Feminist

Feminist scholars would critique both Tracy and Lindbeck for intimating that their arguments represent classical and universal ideas of theological anthropology. In fact, from a feminist perspective, these two thinkers develop concepts of what it means to be a human being from the specificity of men's experience. Thus, instead of describing theological anthropology in a general sense, progressive liberal and postliberal claims could more accurately be described as elite men's theological anthropology. As Rosemary Radford Ruether, an important contemporary feminist scholar, argues,

> The uniqueness of feminist theology lies not in its use of the criterion of experience but rather in its use of *women's* experience, which has been almost entirely shut out of theological reflection in the past. The use of women's experience in feminist theology, therefore, explodes as a critical force, exposing classical theology . . . as based on *male* experience rather than on universal human experience.[56]

Ruether's observation implies a methodological turn. Theological anthropology is particular and contextually bound; one does not speak of theological anthropology in general. Who are the humans in the God–human connection? What is their status in society? What do they look like? These questions pertain to both the person developing the theological anthropology and the people or community about whom the theologian writes. Part of Ruether's approach is to make the sociology of theological anthropology transparent, thus preventing it from remaining hidden in the dominant discourse. When men write about theology, in the overwhelming majority of cases, they fail to indicate publicly that their theological anthropologies signify the finite and limited realities of men, a minority population within the United States and the world. Hence, progressive liberal and postliberal positions are not objective and universal authorities.

In direct contrast, feminist scholars make explicit their theological stances. The norm or critical principle for feminist theology is the development and promotion of the full humanity of women. "Theologically speaking, whatever diminishes or denies the full humanity of women must be presumed not to reflect the divine or an authentic relation to the divine."[57] The starting point in the conversation over what it means to be a human commences, for feminists, with women's realities and what is beneficial to those realities. Furthermore, this means that women become agents in history and assume a posture of defining their own authentic and full humanity.[58] Women speak for themselves by naming both the negative ramifications of a patriarchal culture and their own understanding of what it means to be a human being in relation to God. The development of a feminist perspective is a major turn in theological anthropology. Prior to the challenge from feminist scholars, theological anthropology assumed elite male experience as normative.

Learning from what they identify as the exclusive dimensions of male definitions of theological anthropology, feminist scholars construe an understanding of the human person that intentionally features the particularity of woman's experiences while embracing the authenticity of man's reality. Ruether claims that "women cannot affirm themselves as *imago dei* [in the image of God] and subjects of full human potential in a way that diminishes male humanity." She advances an expansive, inclusive method: "Women, as the denigrated half of the human species, must reach for a continually expanding definition of inclusive humanity—inclusive of both genders, inclusive of all social groups and races. Any principle of religion or society that marginalizes one group of persons as less than fully human diminishes us all."[59] Thus the achievement of woman's full humanity entails the full humanity of men and all of creation.

Ruether's position on theological anthropology does not cater to an abstract and general notion of woman. Hers is a double-edged sword. She opposes, on the one hand, the elite European and European American male experiences of progressive liberal and postliberal theological anthropologies, and she criticizes male liberation theologians, on the other, for not recognizing the hierarchies that exist even among the poor. Consequently, Ruether introduces ideas of poverty and class in her discussion of women. The leading factor is not a general "woman" but a specific sector of oppressed women. In her words, feminism "goes beyond the letter of the prophetic message to apply the prophetic-liberating principle *to women*. Feminist theology makes explicit what was overlooked in male advocacy of the poor and the oppressed: that liberation must start with the oppressed of the oppressed, namely, *women* of the oppressed."[60]

In addition to the mistaken analysis of male liberation theologians, feminist theological anthropology must take seriously a similar critique internal to its own understanding of who is the female human person. "Sociologically, women are a caste within every class and race. . . . In a real sense, any women's movement which is *only* concerned about sexism and no other form of oppression, must remain a women's movement of the white upper class, for it is *only* this group of women whose *only* problem is the problem of being women, since, in every other way, they belong to the ruling class."[61] Hence, Ruether's analysis leads to at least two further conclusions. First, a narrow focus exclusively on women leads to the inevitable co-optation of the definition of women's full humanity (in diversity) by the "white upper class." Second, a generic emphasis on woman forces women whose human identity entails class and race to be invisible. Therefore white upper-class women tend to describe the nature of woman through their restricted lens.

To construct a theological anthropology from any specific sector of society that represents and forces its minority self-understanding and its provincial self-interests apes the material structures and harmful culture instituted by patriarchy. Therefore Ruether goes on to depict two damaging obstacles created by patriarchy to prevent the full humanity of women. Both are manifestations of hierarchy and dualism. One is the psychic dualism claiming that men are biologically prone to reason, calmness, and deliberation while women have a natural proclivity for intuition, emotionalism, and spontaneity. As Ruether writes, "to put it bluntly, there is no biological connection between male gonads and the capacity to reason. Likewise, there is no biological connection between female sexual organs and the capacity to be intuitive, caring, or nurturing. Thus the labeling of these capacities as masculine and feminine simply perpetuates gender role stereotypes."[62] If the mental or psychic difference were to reside in a biological distinction, then gender and sexual hierarchy within the human condition would be mandated by the normal course of a static human nature.

The second obstacle of hierarchy is sociological. In a patriarchal society, woman's place is in the home, the domestic arena, and the man's role is public, in the workplace, and in decision-making roles in politics and economics. To redeem the status of both men and women, all must reconnect to the state of the human as being in the image of God (*imago dei*), which leads to full recovery of psychic potential and a transformation of the social differentiation between the genders.[63]

Furthermore, the classical doctrines of male theological anthropologies presume the symbolic use of *men* or *male* to represent all genders. Such discursive moves affect not simply the words or talk about the God–human encounter. If that were true, altering the words from male to female or just expanding the language to include women would suffice. As Ruether explains,

> sexual symbolism is foundational to the perception of order and relationship that has been built up in cultures. The psychic organization of consciousness, the dualistic view of the self and the world, the hierarchical concept of society, the relation of humanity and nature, and of God and creation—all these relationships have been modeled on sexual dualism. Therefore the liberation of women attacks the basic stereotypes of authority, identity, and the structural relations of "reality."[64]

Sexual symbolism, with its implied superiority of the male person, is linked directly to a patriarchal structure in human culture. Words do not have power in and of themselves; their potency manifests in how they forge internal psychic and external systemic configurations that make a difference in human female and male interactions. For Ruether, the core of disequilibrium within the identity of human community arises out of the cultural inequalities represented by skewed sexual symbolism. One's definition of gender and sex roles thus directly determines how one operates in the realm of the psychic, the civic order, and the cultural sphere and influences one's notions of the self and selves. Hence, a return to the *imago dei* (that is, where the image of God in the human person creates a healthy human and divine engagement and reveals itself as the dynamic of redemption) will undo old conceptions of theological anthropology and refashion what it means to become a new robust human community.

The question of redemption in feminist theological anthropology raises concerns about what Ruether terms "feminist metanoia and soul-making," a conversion journey in which the individual attains self-realization. This soul-making or redemption into the new human and holistic individual unites our minds with our bodies, reason, and passions; joins impulse with our thoughts, slow clarity, and maturing perceptions; encourages growth of both self alone and self in relationships;

and affirms self and other. Redemption, or transformative *metanoia*, consists of re-alignment with wholesome relationships, a journey of changed connections with oneself, community, society, and culture, and with all of creation.[65] Ultimately, for Ruether, the realization of the new woman will indicate the liberation and full humanity of all and lead to the institution of nonhierarchical structures. Such a transformation "demands not just a new integrated self but a new integrated social order."[66]

A new integrated social order brings to life a new humanity. According to Ruether, in fact, Jesus and the theme of Christology shed light on the future creativity that is to come on earth. From the perspective of feminist theology, Jesus is the liberator proclaiming judgment on status quo relationships maintaining privilege, domination, and deprivation. While calling for renunciation of such evils, it is not Jesus' male gender that determines his liberation mission to transform the human being. Rather, Jesus embodies "the new humanity of service and mutual empowerment" beginning with the bottom of hierarchical webs of oppression, especially low-caste women and, through them, touching all of humanity.[67] Following the path of Jesus launches one into a dynamic of radical transformation of the self, resulting in a calling to service that does not end with the most marginalized cultures of humanity but, with a special sensitivity to the marginalized, pursues empowerment for all.

Consequently, feminist theology, in contrast to progressive liberal and postliberal theologies, would argue for an inclusive construction of theological anthropology affirming what is fundamentally desirable and nurturing in human culture and in all of nature (plants, animals, and the earth). Specifically, theological anthropology, drawing on one being created in God's image and heeding the call from Jesus, means a kind of democratic participation, promoting everyone's equal value and equal access to all the best created by human culture, fostering the ownership by working people of the wealth they created, men's and women's mutual sharing in the domestic and public spheres, and harmonious interweaving of ecological and human systems.[68] The linchpin for the redemption and forging of an authentic self in the context of culture and nature is the experiences of oppressed women. Succinctly elaborating her theological anthropological vision by further drawing on her Christology, Ruether writes that "Jesus' vision of the kingdom is one of radical social iconoclasm. . . . This is not simply a reversal of domination, but the overcoming of the whole structure that sets people in oppressive relationships to one another. Jesus addresses this message particularly to the poor, not in order to exclude the rich, but in order to make clear to them the conditions under which they will enter the kingdom."[69] The theological notion of *imago dei* becomes the practical imitation of Jesus. And therefore with the new woman come a new society and a new earth.

Liberation

The final examples of contemporary theological anthropologies come from the diverse movements of liberation theologies among people of color in the United States.

Black Perspectives

For black theology, we engage the thought of James H. Cone.[70] Whereas Ruether and feminist theologians commence with women's experience, Cone starts with race and the black American human person. To Cone, feminists are strong on developing a new woman, but they need to work harder to perceive the core importance of race in forging the new human being. When it comes to the past, current, and future status of African Americans, in Cone's view, most white feminists have a proclivity and alacrity to side with white men regarding what people are created and called to be and do. If we are to forge a new humanity in the United States, then the black human experience has to be fundamental.

In his theological anthropology Cone persistently emphasizes, among other realities, the decisive roles of liberation and freedom. In this regard, he interweaves the themes of God, Christology, and humanity. Human liberation becomes God's salvific work through Jesus Christ; therefore, Jesus Christ's humanity and divinity act as the initiation point for an analytical investigation of liberation. Oppressed humanity, especially oppressed black humanity, perceives its historical fight against exploitation grounded in Jesus Christ who is the gift of freedom for the oppressed. "Liberation is not an object but the *project* of freedom wherein the oppressed realize that their fight for freedom is a divine right of creation."[71] In the initial act of creating human beings, God offered the right to struggle for freedom as a paramount gift, especially for those heavily laden with burdens of violence and injustice.

As Cone says, "God in Jesus meets us in the situation of our oppressed condition and tells us not only who *God* is and what *God* is doing about our liberation, but also who *we* are and what *we* must do about white racism. If blacks can take christology seriously, then it follows that the meaning of our anthropology is also found in and through our oppressed condition, as we do what we have to about the presence of white racism."[72] For Cone, Jesus is not for everybody in an abstract universal theological anthropology. Jesus is for the oppressed, whose true human identities arise in their struggle for liberation. Again pursuing a christological lens, Cone describes theological anthropology as the human person being endowed with freedom because the core content of Jesus' gospel is liberation. To realize that content is to be fully liberated, to attain freedom. Human beings cannot be who Jesus wants them to be if they are slaves to someone else. Consequently, the black oppressed are called to rebel against systems of oppression. And the privileged and nonblack oppressed only become fully human when they join oppressed blacks in the struggle to follow Jesus' mandate to be free. Liberation, then, means the practical application of human freedom.

Cone emphasizes the importance of the practical application of human freedom because the movement to realize anthropological freedom grounds itself in God's freedom, which is freedom to be in relation with human beings "in the social context of their striving for the fulfillment of humanity."[73] Here the gift of God through Jesus Christ translates divine salvation into earthly liberation. At the same time, the human recipients of God's salvation-liberation axis are required first to acknowledge their vertical relationship in theological anthropology—that is, the "anthropology" flows from the "theological." Only by recognizing God's gift of freedom to the oppressed, whereby marginalized communities respond to the good news of Jesus the liberator, can oppressed humanity ascertain that its ultimate allegiance is not to principalities and powers of this earth but to God. God's own freedom to be with the bottom of society through the vivifying activity of Jesus Christ empowers the poor in such a fashion that they obey only the divinely created gift and contemporary vocational imperative to fight against those who thwart the divine plan to set the captives free on earth now. In a word, the vertical fellowship with God results in political commitments to change the human world.[74]

In Cone's logic, to be created and called by divine freedom leads to an undeniable conclusion: individual liberation actualizes in collective cultures. "Authentic liberation of self is attainable only in the context of an oppressed community in the struggle for freedom. . . . There can be no freedom for God in isolation from the humiliated and abused."[75] As one becomes what God has called her or him to be, the individual's response to divine initiated freedom is specific to that person. In this sense, Cone claims, freedom is what happens internally in each individual; "it is what happens to a man's being."[76] Though there may be visible manifestations of this interior development (for instance, Cone cites picketing, rioting, marching, and voting), when a human being perceives the self as the self is and not as a creation of others, he or she is free as created in God's image and in response to divine vocation. In this instance, one is capable of determining the parameters of one's own existence.

Moreover, for Cone, human freedom has more exact meaning when related to the contemporary United States. Blackness defines the symbolic reference point for oppression and, simultaneously, signification of a certain and definite liberation. Therefore, in the U.S. context, freedom affirms blackness. Cone argues that "to be free is to be black—that is, identified with the victims of humiliation in human society and a participant in the liberation of oppressed humanity. The free person in America is the one who does not tolerate whiteness but fights against it, knowing that it is the source of human misery."[77] Consequently, blackness (as the human condition of suffering and the way of Jesus' vocation for us to be free and liberated) specifies both the oppressed race of blacks and those who enter the condition of blackness.

Still, while affirming blackness in its particularity (regarding race) and in its universality (regarding social option), Cone underlines a clear path for the black race primarily in the context of self-love vis-à-vis divine love of oppressed black human beings. "In a world which has taught blacks to hate themselves, the new black man does not transcend blackness, but accepts it, loves it as a gift of the Creator. For until he knows that, until he accepts himself as a being of God in all of its physical blackness, he can love neither God nor neighbor."[78] What Cone here attempts to extrapolate from the theological physiognomy of black and white phenotypes in the United States is what he considers the theological blind spot of white theologians. In the preciseness of the North American parameters, an unstated assumption underlying race relations between white and black cultures is the white theologians' and broader white society's belief and practice that God has created the white phenotype to be superior to black physical features. The logic of Cone's arguments is that white theologians privilege their European and European American ancestors as primary, if not exclusive, sources for theological anthropology not only because these scholars believe such thinkers are more intellectually credible, but also because the thinkers are physically white. They rank the highest in scholarly interpretations because, among other things, they possess a more acceptable, recognizable, and agreeable physical appearance. As an unquestioned and assumed given, white thoughts and bodies constitute universal reality. That is why, when it comes to developing theological anthropology, the majority of white intellectuals fail to specify that they are fashioning a *white* theological anthropology. They have the privilege of discursive power to assert "theology" or "religious studies" as universal objective endeavors when, in fact, they are simply mining the creative sources from localized European and European American cultures. Hence, whiteness is revealed as the unstated operative norm.

Cone charts an unambiguous conceptual framework in his theological anthropology, which he calls "liberation," or freedom to be in relation to God. To reach this divinely intended human reality of fellowship with God, the black community emphasizes conversion, prayer, and community worship. This vertical dimension of freedom connects horizontally at the same time with freedom in relation to self and the oppressed community. And liberation as freedom does not conclude or end with a static point in human history. The crafting of the authentic human person is an ongoing project of freedom in human history, and not a once-and-for-all disembodied spiritual act. Yet human history does not limit liberation; liberation is beyond human history and not confined to this world. Liberation beyond human history stands for the divine future breaking into the present. Consequently, liberation stands as the project of freedom in hope.[79] And whoever seeks to attain liberation and freedom as a human being is obligated to privilege the poor because Jesus voluntarily sought a preferential option for the poor. "Therefore, whoever fights for the poor," argues Cone, "fights for God; whoever risks his life for the helpless and unwanted, risks his life for God."[80]

Some internal tensions surface in Cone's theological anthropology. If the poor act as normative in the definitional description of the human community created and called by God, and members of this human community are differentiated by culture and race, then how does the plumb line of the poor interweave among whites themselves? Restated, are poor whites—members of white culture and the white race—to be privileged in Cone's theoretical scaffolding? Are not whites dwelling in structural poverty also made in the image of God, and therefore do they not fall within the purview of Jesus, whose sole purpose was to actualize the anointing of divine spirit to set the captives free and to liberate the oppressed? Or has the entire white culture and race succumbed irreparably to the evil tentacles of systemic white supremacy? Do none from that social and phenotypical context experience or reveal the in-breaking of the divine that black theology longs for?

Womanist Perspectives

Womanist theology, another indigenous form of liberation theology within U.S. culture, has developed to distance black women's positive faith, thoughts, and realities from the racism of white Christian feminists and from the sexism of black male theologians.[81] Womanists ask, How does one claim or live into God's gift of full humanity as a woman of African descent living in North America? What does it mean to embrace the created and called obligations to be a black woman in spite of and through the anti-God scholarship, theologies, and practices of sexual oppression, racial discrimination, and class exploitation?

Jacquelyn Grant takes on this theological anthropological dilemma by interrogating critically religious notions of servanthood. She has investigated nineteenth-century white feminists and discovered their concern with being "servants of men." Yet black women today (as in the past) endure a social status below white women; hence black women, for Grant, are the "servants of the servants."[82] Further pursuing a deconstruction of the doctrine of Christian servanthood, Grant asks, "What is the meaning of such conciliatory notions as 'we are all called to be servants'?"[83] Such a liberal theological platitude as servanthood obfuscates the distinction between service and servitude, a distinction that, unfortunately for black women, has too often collapsed into one and the same theological definition and practical obligation.

Because servanthood language blocks black women from being what God has created and called them to be—accountable to God and exercisers of their full divine gifts as they see fit, free of gender, race, and economic impediments—Grant depicts the issue as a theological challenge to black women's humanity. Defining what she sees as the theological quandary, Grant asks, Whose female experiences undergird the development of theology—the female descendants of slaveholders or the female descendants of slaves? How can one advocate the divine vocation of black women to be instantiated in a theological doctrine of service when black women have been imprisoned by the horrors of service? The exploitative nature of that service, in effect, has meant that African American women have lacked concrete, structural political, economic, and social mechanisms for their empowerment. Consequently, a theological anthropology pertaining to the divine command to serve manifests as overspiritualization: continual pain under the guise of authentic Christian witness and perpetual suffering under the mantel of a higher spiritual calling.

As an alternative to a deconstructed servanthood dogma, Grant proffers a reconstructed category termed "inclusive discipleship," in which interdependence and justice act as operative norms.[84] Discipleship remains a theological imperative for the human community (hence, a theological anthropological enterprise) with several interrelated denotations. In Grant's estimation, "the recognition of the humanity of people must be a basic part of our search for the reigndom of God."[85] Constituent categories of this humanity and God's new community dynamic are: "(1) an affirmation of human dignity; (2) the practice of justice in human relationships; (3) the establishment of equality among human beings—men and women, differing racial and ethnic groups, etc.; (4) self-affirmation as a necessary category of human reality; (5) self-reliance, self-definition, and self-control as components of humanity; and (6) economic empowerment for historically oppressed peoples."[86] Thus, within Grant's womanist analytical framework, a healthy theological anthropology entails both spiritual and tangible planes of the humanity of people. The transcendent dimension highlights lofty ideals of human dignity, justice, and equality among diverse human communities. Simultaneously, spiritual attributes of the human person are incarnated in the materiality of economic empowerment; the ideals of dignity, justice, and equality, therefore, require a sacrifice—the redistribution of wealth. Similarly, because humans were created in the image of God and have the vocational duty to search for the in-breaking of the divine, individuals, especially members of oppressed groups, need to develop the ability to affirm themselves based on God's criteria and not those of oppressors. Foundationally, the new reconstructed marks of humanity suggest the realized power to control, define, and rely on the self as a gift of God to the oppressed.

Emilie M. Townes claims a womanist theological anthropology through her argument for a womanist spirituality of wholeness (with relationality as content) and social witness (with justice as substance). "Womanist spirituality," Townes articulates, "is the working out of what it means for each of us to seek compassion, justice, worship, and devotion in our witness. This understanding of spirituality seeks to grow into wholeness of spirit and body, mind and heart—into holiness in God."[87] The God–human connection revealed in wholeness centers on "is-ness," the inextricable webs of the spiritual and the physical ties displayed in the black context. The holistic and relational is-ness of the African American person verifies itself not in transempirical worlds, but in the palpable, discernible concrete existence that welds a unified "relationship between body, soul, and creation. In this sense, it is consonant with African cosmology that understands all of life as sacred."[88] Contrary to Western thought's dichotomized self–other opposition, according to Townes, womanist theological anthropology "advocates a self–other *relationship*, for it is in the relational matrix that wholeness can be found for African Americans."[89]

Moreover, wholeness and relationality stand not-in-and-of-themselves. These value-laden notions demand fulfillment of ethical imperatives of moral responsibility and accountability to the way of being and culture of all those of African descent who survived the forced diasporic dispersion. Here one intimates a one-for-all and all-for-one communal process glued together by defense and development of black bodies and black souls, for such a unity has maintained the African American human person's sanity and determination. Without recognizing and intentionally following such a corporate compass, future generations of black folk will inevitably endure a historical amnesia and fundamentally a loss of a distinctive African American identity granted by the divine spirit.

Finally, womanist spirituality expressed as social witness comes from African American women's lives, particularly their moral, justice-oriented wisdom. Such a wisdom surfaces in black women's "autobiographies, speeches, novels, poems, sermons, testimonies, songs, and oral histories."[90] From this experienced wisdom, Townes initiates a process of defining a vigorous and flourishing human person, one who takes seriously the dimensions of survival and being as well as the nature of creation, gender roles, the color caste system within the black community, and identity issues. For Townes, womanist spirituality intended for a thriving humanity interconnects body and soul and personal and communal, all grounded on and infused with the Spirit.

Karen Baker-Fletcher introduces into theological anthropology the call for womanist gifts of power. Her theology does not allow belief in the solitary subjectivity of an acting divinity who, by its all powerfulness, appears to obviate human-initiated practice. Rather than portraying God as dominating or unilateral in God's creation of and call to the human person, Baker-Fletcher argues for defining God's being as one of co-creating with human beings. On the one hand, she attempts to avoid any patriarchal norms of God as the sovereign lord bolting from the heavens to solve human predicaments, thereby fostering a type of quietism on the part of creation. On the other, she seeks to skirt a deistic stance calling for God to be absent from the created realm, resulting in a form of humanocentric way of life in which people go it alone without the Spirit's intervention.

Baker-Fletcher perceives black women birthing something new while engaged in struggle and transformation along with God in God's creative activity, a participatory covenant and co-creativity she deems African American women's gifts of power. She describes womanist womanhood or way of being human as seven attributes defining these gifts of power:

faith, which has to do with the power of belief in a God of infinite possibilities for fulfillment in creation; voice, which has to do with the
power of prophetic speech and naming; survival, which includes gifts
of healing, resistance against evil, "making do," and "making a way out
of no way"; vision, which has to do with prophetic sight; community
building, a form of social salvation and healing; regeneration, which
requires memory and the passing on of wisdom, knowledge for survival, healing, and liberation; and liberation, acts of struggle for freedom and social reform.[91]

In their theological anthropologies womanist scholars have brought
forward the web-like qualities of black women's lives and experiences.
Linda E. Thomas writes how the black woman's life and body embody
many oppressed communities. While taking on macro-structural and
micro-structural systems and drawing on African forebears, black women
theologians' thought and practice include gender, race, class, sexuality,
and ecology.[92] Kelly Brown Douglas terms this integrated approach to
the human condition as concern for the human person's sociopolitical
and religio-cultural wholeness and all aspects of a culture.[93]

The hallmark of womanist theological anthropology—the inclusion
of people's constituent experiences—is called into question by Renee L.
Hill, a self-identified lesbian womanist scholar. She affirms womanists'
underscoring the complexity and ambiguity of human oppression and
its results, the multilayered and across-the-board forms of human liberation. But she exhorts womanist thinkers to be all-embracing in their
explorations and judgments of what they signify as the humanity of
black women. In a word, their theological model, to be taken seriously
in its universal applicability, must pass the sober challenge of internal
consistency. Hill identifies a significant issue missing in most womanist
scholarship: God's gift of sexual orientation. She presents a trenchant
critique:

> However, Christian womanists have failed to recognize heterosexism
> and homophobia as points of oppression that need to be resisted if *all*
> Black women (straight, lesbian, and bisexual) are to have liberation and
> a sense of their own power. Some womanists have avoided the issues

of sexuality and sexual orientation by being selective in appropriating parts of [Alice] Walker's definition of womanism. This tendency to be selective implies that it is possible to be selective about who deserves liberation and visibility.[94]

Hill asks how womanists can argue adamantly against the contradictory exclusivity lodged in black and feminist talk about the God–human encounter while they inconsistently, if at all, recognize the theological humanity of divergent sexual orientations from the dominating, female heterosexual norm. She challenges womanist culture to allow a non-heterosexual self to serve as an archetype and a prototype of God's creation of and call to humanity.

Hispanic/Latino Perspectives

Hispanic/Latino theological anthropology also uncovers a complex picture of what it means to be genuine and whole human beings. Miguel H. Diaz, in his work *On Being Human*, emphasizes human agency and human practice, cultural humanization, person in community, practice and aesthetics, and God's preferential option for the marginalized.[95] David Maldonado Jr., in his assessment of Latino/Hispanic theological anthropology, raises similar yet more expansive dimensions. He claims that

> the discussion of theological anthropology from a Hispanic perspective has led us to a broader definition of the task. It is not limited to traditional debates about the nature of humanity at the individual level, but requires examining human existence in its broader and contextual realities. It calls for consideration of historical, cultural, and communal sources, as well as economic, political, and social forces that shape and define human existence. This is not to suggest social determinism and to deny the significance of the person and self, but rather to call attention to the significance of the social context in which life is known and experienced. The individual is not understood in isolation, disconnected from the human and social environment, but rather as a social being in dynamic interrelationship with the human reality.[96]

In detailing his argument, Maldonado contends that the Hispanic perspective takes seriously human embodiment in human culture and the
social environment. In this sense, a constructive statement on the God–
human interaction combines notions of cultural roots, ethnic identity,
historical visioning, social location and oppression, and community.[97]
In contrast to dominant or traditional stances' fixation on the nature
and existence of one person, Maldonado postulates that a Hispanic
project interrogates and draws on the discipline of history, sociological analysis, and racial, gender, economic, and ethnic studies relative to
community realities.

For Maldonado, ethnicity serves as the main entry into what it means
to be a Hispanic or Latino American. And this ethnic self/selves evolve
historically out of the hybrid blending of Spanish, Amerindian, and
African peoples and out of the inhumane colonization of Latin America
and Africa by Spain, Portugal, France, and, of course, the U.S.A. His-
panic/Latino people's sense of identity is rooted in their shared culture,
including a "common language, religious antecedents, family values,
and other cultural aspects of community." Furthermore, social-scien-
tific data unveil an undeniable fact: Hispanics/Latinos occupy disproportionately the lower socioeconomic segment of U.S. society, having
"low income, low educational attainment levels, poor housing, poor
health, underemployment . . . issues of racism and cultural nativism."
Perhaps the sine qua non of Maldonado's God–human ties in Hispanic/
Latino life is the concept of community: for him, to be a Latino/His-
panic human, by definition, is to be delimited, found, and affirmed in
community.[98] An accent on the group does not deny the unique importance of the individual self; nonetheless, an anthropological hermeneu-
tic brings to bear an intentionality concerning the communal and the
collective selves.

Virgil Elizondo, considered the father of Hispanic/Latino theology, paved the way and thereby presented the crucial scaffolding for
Latino/Hispanic theological anthropology. Situated within the specificity of Mexican American culture and community, Elizondo delineated Latino identity as uniquely created by both the Spanish Catholic
and the Anglo-American Protestant conquests, which resulted in colonization and exploitation. Yet the negativity of Christian European

contact in the Americas yielded a *mestizaje* ethnicity—a new mixed or mestizo population. Constituted by Mexican and American fusion, Mexican Americans are not mere additive conclusions or juxtaposed compounds of two larger cultural and social forces. On the contrary, they are an entirely new cultural group gifted with its own independence and originality from the two conquering parent bodies. Hence, Elizondo isolates analytical notions of hybridity and autonomy in theological anthropology.

Perhaps his most controversial contribution rests on his bold assertion that Latino comprehension of the new divine-intended human interaction lies already in embryo form within the actual Latino *mestizaje* community today. "*Mestizaje*," Elizondo asserts prognostically and hopefully, "is the beginning of a new Christian universalism . . . [in which] the fullness of the kingdom has already begun, the new universalism that bypasses human segregative barriers." The new culture, self, and selves of the divine eschaton have broken into human history and revealed themselves in celebrative hybrid garb not woven out of a single culture but integrated fully by many cultures into one human community.[99] The *mestizaje*, already present, marks that novel beginning of the future.

Summing up a theological anthropology, Diaz proffers seven models or attributes. Latino/Hispanic developments of the divine–human reality or what human beings have been created and called to do by an ultimate spirit manifest in: "1) the Galilean identity of Jesus; 2) accompaniment; 3) cultural humanization; 4) human praxis and struggles; 5) engendered relationships; 6) creaturehood; and 7) trinitarian relationships."[100]

Mujerista Perspectives

Drawing on and coming out of Latino/Hispanic discourses, Ada María Isasi-Díaz advances a mujerista theological anthropology—"developing a method to do theology that uses religion of grassroots Latinas as its source."[101] From the standpoint of Latinas (that is, Hispanic women), theological anthropology entails at least three key concepts. *La lucha* (the struggle) touches on the daily and ordinary struggle of Hispanic women to survive and live life fully, the act of communal celebrations in the midst of everyday life. *Permítanme hablar* (allow me to speak) insists on the Latina as one who makes known her past and participates in making present and future history. It defines the Hispanic woman as protagonist. The third concept is *la comunidad/la familia* (the community/the family). Part of being a Latina is discarding the negative realities while maintaining the family, which is defined as relationships extended all the way out to the broader community. In *la comunidad/la familia*, Isasi-Díaz argues, Hispanic women experience a sense of unity, cohesiveness, self-identity, and self-worth.[102]

Asian American Perspectives

Asian Americans endure a unique debilitating context in their construction of a positive theological anthropology. From the dominant society comes the suspicious gaze that Asian Americans are not quite *American* human beings. On multiple levels, they endure a betwixt-and-between civic status. In fact, they are perceived as foreigners no matter how many generations have been born and lived in the United States. In addition, within their own communities, they struggle over intergenerational pressures with parents and other elders, who urge children to maintain Asian and Asian American cultures and languages, that is, to maintain the specificity of an Asian American human beingness. And various stresses also arise in figuring out one's specific Asian background and how that relates to the general Asian American community. Similarly, the question of what is an Asian American human person is greatly affected by the high percentage of Asian Americans who marry non-Asian people, primarily European Americans. This in turn poses an additional layer of human identity queries for mixed racial-ethnic children. Therefore, to construct a healthy theological anthropology of identity, Asian Americans face the twin obstacles of forced liminality and perceived deviance from Americanness.

In response to this dilemma, Fumitaka Matsuoka argues for the necessity of accepting liminality as "holy insecurity"—in other words, to appreciate Asian American identities, to fight against racism and sexism, and to see Jesus as standing with the oppressed. Matsuoka writes, "The ordering of life for Asian Americans, seen from the Christian faith perspective, is likely to focus on the needs of the disinherited and disfranchised in society. . . . Trust for the disfranchised, empathy for the disinherited, and dignity for the hopelessly uncredentialed are far more significant than certainty of a belief, consistence in logic, or even the hope for a progressively better future."[103] Voicing Asian American self-definition and cultural assertion, Matsuoka argues that Asian Americans must claim their own agency.

> The first function of our ethnic assertiveness is the defense of our ethnicity against the pressures of cultural naturalization. . . . A notable sign of this newly emerging ethnic visibility and assertiveness among Korean and other Asian American Christians is that of collective identity in place of individual selfhood. Most often, when individual Asian Americans insist on "being ourselves," we are in fact defending a self we share with others. . . . If the first function of Asian American ethnic assertiveness is the defense of ethnicity against cultural naturalization, the second function is the celebration of our collective identity. . . . The third function of ethnic assertiveness is to build and sustain the reborn community—to create institutions, gain control of resources, and provide educational and welfare services.[104]

Asian American women experience both racial and gender oppression in facing dual expectations: they are to be both submissive mothers in the domestic sphere and exotic trophies for non–Asian American men.[105] Drawing on her ethnographic fieldwork among Christian Korean American women, Jung Ha Kim reassigns subversive interpretation to and creative implications for dominant portrayals of Asian American women. Such a reconfiguring results from the "handed-down wisdom" of the women. Women appropriate initial derogatory terms such as *feminine*, *deceptive*, and *behind the scenes* and deploy them in the interests of women. Consequently, the historical barriers relegating women to the domestic sphere and out of the public domain of power and control have unsuspectingly and inadvertently spurred on Korean American women to develop an informal culture of collective resistance. Jung Ha pens this analysis:

> "Churched" Korean American women also utilize extensive forms of nonverbal daily communication skills in the context of their church: frequent giggles, knowing glances, holding of hands, bitter smiles, light

hitting on arms, and constant eye contact. All these nonverbal forms of communication and articulated wisdom for survival can be seen as instrumental for fostering resistance and self-empowerment among "churched" Korean American women.[106]

Thus a creative self-constitution of and a ritualized agency for women's humanity enable them to make history and create the present, thereby debunking prevalent stereotypes, such as the "model" passive Asian American woman. The ideal status is to realize active social agency by seizing and incorporating whatever resources are at hand into intergenerational commonsense wisdom. In this regard, even silence becomes a weapon of struggle to attain full humanity and "a sense of freedom, resistance, and liberation."[107]

Native American Perspectives

For Native Americans or American Indians, theological anthropology begins with the inextricable living and balanced cohabitation between humans and all of creation. The authors of *A Native American Theology*, Clara Sue Kidwell, Homer Noley, and George E. Tinker, postulate:

> For Native Americans, their intimate relationship with the natural environment blurs the distinctions between human and non-human. Human beings are not the only people in the world. The world is populated with a large number of persons, human and non-human, whose interactions constitute the Native world. We must move beyond the Christian tradition of humans as unique creations of God to the idea that the world of persons is all embracing. Native people believe that they share the world with spiritual beings with whom they must establish relationships.[108]

In fact, the intertwining of spirituality into the totality of human and nonhuman life permeates American Indian cultures to such a degree that elders responsible for ceremonial rituals deny that religion is an indigenous institution. They argue instead for the pervasiveness of spirituality infused throughout the complete cultural way of life and social makeup of what it means to be defined as a Native person. Particular sacred ceremonies (such as the Green Corn Ceremony, the Sun Dance, and sweat lodge rituals) embody spiritual power and sacred presence in the ongoing collective effort to renew the world. One does not have to create a religion. One lives the everyday spirituality of all of creation.

The communitarian/communistic nature of Native cultures means that to be a human being situates one essentially within kinship account-ability and opportunities that subordinate accenting the individual. "Who one's family is defines one's sense of self." "Kin relationships structure the rights, obligations, and responsibilities of individuals to groups." However, at the same time, this cultural relegation of an individual to the collective is cognizant of the unique entity and personal identity of each human being, delineated by one's particular relation to the spirit world.[109] Since this sacred world inheres in all of creation, perhaps American Indian voices deploy the most complex worldview of all contemporary models of theological anthropology. Native people's theoretical conceptions broaden the notion of theological anthropology with its traditional fixation on human predicaments and social problematics. While attending to these foci, American Indians' reflections on their selves yield central attention to all realms of the spirit world, of which human beings are merely one aspect. Hence, the "goal of life is maintaining a proper relationship with the spiritual world."[110] And key to universal balance, as it pertains to Native understanding of the human person, is the status of and community's relationship to the land. "This sense of spiritual association with land, the marking of boundaries and renewal of the earth through ceremonies, and the concept of Earth as mother and nurturer, give land a special place in Indian senses of identity."[111]

In discussing Native American women's involvement in crafting a theological anthropology, Andrea Smith focuses on the overall thrust of Native people's journey toward and concentration on a spiritual equilibrium tied to land, in the interest of collective identity. "Native women," she writes, "concur with Malcolm X that the real fight is a land-based, national one."[112] As Third World peoples living in a First World super-power, the Americas' original people stake out unique claims for national sovereignty as part of their spiritual connection to land, communalism, and peoplehood.

Culture, Self, and Race

These contemporary models of theological anthropology in the North American arena signify the emergence of various experiences of what it means to be a human being, particularly from a Christian perspective. Though each voice mines creatively and formulates innovatively its own contribution in the conversation, I would argue that the disparate voices advocating their own particular lenses and unique contexts share at least one common theme: the use of *culture, self, and race* as subject matter in the spiritual connection to humanity, the elaborate explication of what people have been created to be and called to do. While these three notions are frequently used by theologians, one rarely finds a sustained, consistent grasp of them as normative principles. They remain, however, core concepts in each theological anthropology examined in this chapter. Indeed, culture, self, and race are the bones upon which the flesh of progressive liberal, postliberal, feminist, and liberation theological anthropologies cling.

Toward the end of explicit clarity, chapters 2, 3, and 4 of this book take on the ideas of culture, self, and race, respectively, as the conditions for the possibility for devising a constructive statement on theological anthropology today. An unstable content for these three conceptualizations tends to undermine the full force of the anthropological arguments advanced by contemporary theologians. Everyone utilizing the same words does not necessarily mean the same things. Consequently, to mark the nuance in definitions among the interlocutors presented here in chapter 1 around culture, self, and race and as a way of plowing the ground for my own presentation of theological anthropology, the following three chapters unfold out of logical necessity. The taken-for-grantedness of the notions of culture, self, and race, by all schools of religious scholarship, indicates how vital these terms are for varying theses and how central their presumptions are to coherency of diverging systematic reasonings about theological anthropology.

Finally, the exploration of theological anthropology, like all intellectual claims and theoretical discussions, does not take place in an abstract, noncontextualized reality. The content of one's argument and choice of sources reflect class, gender, racial, colonial/neocolonial, and sexual-orientation privileging and preferences, especially when authors do not openly assert the context of their talk about God. Ideas do not fall from the sky, as if sitting in front of one's computer isolated in the attic removes one and the discussion of ideas from the particularities of social interests situated among diverse strata, most importantly in the U.S. ethos where the dominating scholarship objectively in effect or subjectively in intent chooses a preferential option for the North American ruling class.

Therefore, as an admission, my entire project seeks a connection to the interests of the materially poor (of all races, ethnicities, genders, sexual orientations, colonies, and neocolonies) and voices locked out of the prevailing U.S. political-economic paradigm. And through that entry point of the conversation, one embraces the well-being of all peoples and their extended family members (that is, fish, birds, animals, water, air, and plant life). All of creation derives from some force or power greater than the constituent parts of creation. I choose to examine this origination from the perspective of a supreme spirit who, among other revelations, manifests, for me, decisively, but not exclusively, in Jesus the Anointed One. And chapter 5 will reweave my argument via a more direct theological anthropological statement from black folktales.

2.
Culture:
Labor, Aesthetic, and Spirit

For several reasons, the notion of culture arises immediately after a comparative assessment of contemporary debates on theological anthropology.

First, contemporary debates regarding theological anthropology presuppose attempts at constructive statements about the God–human encounter taking place within culture. Put differently, current agreements and disagreements over human nature and the human condition are contextualized and constituted by the substance of human culture. For example, progressive liberal scholars draw creatively on the best human reasoning from the culture of the European Enlightenment tradition as it is tempered by the faces and agenda of the oppressed—the non-European, colonial victims of modernity. In order to yield a more profound interpretation and understanding, reasonable partners devise a theological anthropology by participating equally in critical conversation. Furthermore, this sacred–human interplay hinges on recognizing the distinct culture of the individual interlocutors and the new fused horizon resulting in, among other things, the potential for a novel culture in which all share the fruits of conversation together.

Postliberals acknowledge the centrality of culture in the very substance of theological anthropology. For them, a perceivable and unique secular human culture prevails largely because of the pervasive presence of a liberal and philosophical ethos. Similarly, a specific Christian culture with identifiable language exists. Postliberals believe that this Christian culture is urgently required to replace the threat and reality of secular culture, particularly in a "Christian" nation like the U.S.A. Akin to other intellectuals of religion, feminist theologians adhere to the importance of culture in exploring the question of the human person's created and called purpose. Their theoretical quarrel with progressive liberal and postliberal discourses to a great extent revolves around fundamental divides over the role of disparate cultures in the definition of theological anthropology. In a word, feminist scholars present trenchant critiques unveiling male elaborations of the human person as merely that: a male intellectual deploying male experiences and casting these opinions into the totality of scholarship under the false guise of universal human culture. The central challenge of feminists, then, is the advancement of women's experiences and female culture into the conversation.

And liberation theologians of various stripes within North America concur on the nature of poor people's culture—whether that be common narratives, the experiences of forced migration, women of color's unique gifts, loss of land, discrimination against non-English languages, or any undertaking signifying what it means to live a minority status based on any combinations of race, class, gender, and sexual orientation. By virtue of the positioning of talks about culture within contemporary disputes, a statement on a constructive theological anthropology necessitates an unraveling of the contours of culture.

Second, since black folktales serve as the primary sources for my own theological anthropology and are perceived in common conversation and scientific scholarship as cultural forms, the tales themselves require an explanation of what is culture. (Of course, other disciplines and interpretive lenses apply to black folktales, including politics, economics, sociology, and psychology.) With their aesthetic function and encompassing nature, black folktales are chosen as explicit sites of anthropological studies because they represent how a people organizes itself through rituals, symbols, language, functions, structures, and primordial beliefs.

Not only do the tales themselves exemplify statements created by and concerned with the totality of the human being, they also point to themes of human nature and the human condition. The tales are built on the raw materials of stories about spiritual presence among ordinary people. And so to build reflective and self-reflective judgments regarding the workings of a divine reality and to comprehend the sacred–human being relation, folktales suggest a seemingly endless array of possibilities. Constructing a contemporary theological anthropology from folk narratives is, at least, a cultural performance.

Third, the constructive and contemporary theological anthropology I will advance later aims toward an explicit Christian statement, and Christianity logically presupposes the divine descending vertically into the horizontal cultural plane. Even without biblical "evidence" or textual verification, one can deduce that if an ultimate power greater than oneself exists, the human person only has knowledge of or encounters such an entity in culture. One becomes aware of this ultimate spirit, hope, vision, faith, or presence by this revelation revealing itself. If one could discern the ultimate without the ultimate coming into the penultimate, then the penultimate would have the potentiality and actuality of initiating (and, thereby in a way, controlling) the divine–human encounter. With that all-determining power, why would the human person need an ultimate? Obviously, the range of Christian responses to the question of the nature of the ultimate is vast, from a humanist position that God created humans with free will and then removed Godself from human affairs in order to allow humans to arbitrate the will in human culture, to a more fundamentalist stance of an absolutist, all-controlling deity.

Finally, biblical instructions call for a clarification of the notion of culture in theological anthropology. Philippians 2:5-8 reads: "Let the same mind be in you that was in Christ Jesus, who, though he was in the form of God, did not regard equality with God as something to be exploited, but emptied himself, taking the form of a slave, being born in human likeness. And being found in human form, he humbled himself and became obedient to the point of death—even death on a cross." Here the ultimate reality or being decides to relate to the penultimate by emptying itself into the cultural clothing of the human realm. God pours out Godself into human culture.

Similarly, the birth narratives indicate the conscious decision of divinity to reveal itself in human culture, this time underscoring marginalized culture. An unwed pregnant woman engaged to be married gives birth to an illegitimate son in a barn with livestock, straw, dirt, and cow feces because there were no accommodations in an inn; one could speculate that the family did not have any wealth to use to bribe an innkeeper for lodging. And the political and military authorities (that is, the apparatus of the state and those who control the state) search for this child in order to murder it.

In Jesus' inaugural remarks about his purpose on earth, as announced in Luke 4:18-19, he emphasizes the fact that God consciously chose to enter human affairs on behalf of those in systems of exploitation— such as the materially poor, those in prison, the brokenhearted, and the oppressed in society. A central thread in the biblical narratives is the incarnation of a divinity among people in dire predicament, far from the centers of power and wealth. In a word, Christian revelation is a cultural dynamic colored by the social conditions and collective experiences of peripheral communities in the biblical witness.

Theological anthropology is thus a cultural process, in which an ultimate intermingles with the penultimate (that is, the God–human connection is profoundly situated in culture). To comprehend more fully this intermingling or connection, we will now examine the notion of culture.

The Notion of Culture

Culture, as defined by Randwedzi Nengwekhulu, has three intertwined aspects. It is (1) "the totality of the results of human labour, i.e. the results of material and spiritual wealth created by human labour, culture is 'the development of human productive forces.'" Human labor is complemented by what Nengwekhulu calls (2) "spiritual culture. This includes philosophy, science, ideology, art, literature, religion, education, etc. . . . expressed in and through concepts of spirit and spirituality." And these two (human labor and the spiritual) are closely tied to (3) "'artistic culture' which is in reality the figurative objectification of artistic creativity."[1]

Culture, defined in its three manifestations of human labor, the spiritual, and the artistic, is influenced by the interplay between the material and the spiritual. Nengwekhulu underscores the relative autonomy of the spiritual aspect from the material. That is, the spiritual aspect of culture is not a passive reflection of the material economic. Spirituality is relatively autonomous. It too can take the lead in the human labor-spiritual-artistic relations. Nonetheless, though relatively autonomous, the spiritual is rooted in the material elements of social life. Hence, changes in the economics of production are accompanied by changes in the other features of culture.

At this stage of the discussion, a tripartite definition of culture helps to underscore the interconnections between material and spiritual realities in such a way that all of humanity's activities include the realm of culture. In addition, even though, in terms of real human activity, the material and the spiritual exist simultaneously, there is a clear distinction between them.

Culture: Holistic, Interdisciplinary Dynamic

Before unpacking the three-part typology of culture, we will examine culture as a holistic, interdisciplinary dynamic, beginning with identifying some implications of human labor. In contrast to popular intuitions and more academic formulations that focus almost exclusively on the aesthetic and spiritual appreciation of culture, we proffer a preliminary appraisal of human labor—our novel analytic introduction into the cultural field.

The human labor dimension of culture raises issues of political economy. But it does not pertain to a crude Marxist concept where the economic base gives rise to a superstructure which is merely a passive reflection of the material base. Here, the spirit of the artistic (that is, the superstructure) has no impact on labor or wealth (that is, the economic base). Stuart Hall, drawing on Raymond Williams's *The Long Revolution*,[2] argues "against the literal operations of the base-superstructure metaphor, which in classical Marxism ascribed the domain of ideas and of meanings to the 'superstructure,' themselves conceived as merely reflective of and determined in some simple fashion by 'the base,' without a social effectivity of their own." Thus, to understand the human labor aspect of culture within the context of political economy should not mean giving in to a unilateral economic determinism,[3] since this would obscure the full liberating creativity and potential of spiritual and artistic parts of culture. It is a two-way process where base and superstructure affect each other.

In addition, Hall discerns this comprehension of culture in contrast to highbrow cultural conclusions, in which a notion of "real culture" emanates from the realm of high-class ideas. In this skewed lens, culture becomes one of perfection or "the sum of the 'best that has been thought and said,' regarded as the summits of an achieved civilization." This "civilized" elite or bourgeois culture excludes vibrant possibilities from the remainder of society (indeed, the majority of the citizenry) and therefore, for Hall, requires a democratization and socialization. To combat this deviation, he suggests that culture really consists of disparate forms of a social process—"the giving and taking of meanings, and the slow development of 'common' meanings—a common culture." Hence, he takes on the "idealist" and "civilized" notions of culture by reformulating culture as "ordinary."[4]

Again drawing on Williams's work, Hall further clarifies culture as referring to and being disclosed in social practices. By social practices, he underscores the interrelatedness of "elements or social practices normally separated out," so that culture as a whole way of life evinces not simply practices (in some sociological works) or ethnographic accounts (in some anthropological renderings), but an organized intertwining of human efforts. Culture is "threaded through all social practices, and is the sum of their interrelationship." Culture underlies all social practices as patterns of organization or forms of human energy. The theoretician's task is to unravel the layered attributes of these relationships as they are organized throughout society. Hall terms this reconfigured appraisal of culture (that is, reconfigured over against the idealist, civilized, and vulgar Marxist approaches) as "radical interactionism," a nonprivileging of any one practice as the sole cause of the others.[5]

Similarly, W. Emmanuel Abraham (Ghana) adheres to a more comprehensive notion of culture. Though not employing the suggestive phrase "whole way of life," Abraham's standpoint on culture verifies this expression. For him, culture encompasses not only the spiritual and material but also the emotional, intellectual, and ethical aspects that "characterize the heritage of a society or social group."[6] With further nuance, he expands the qualities of culture to include those of politics, economics, education, art, literature, and religion. In a certain interpretation, Abraham mirrors Stuart Hall's thinking and Hall's appropriation of Williams's work. Abraham exhibits a sensibility for the complexity and challenge of deciphering an investigation of culture that yields no simple description. Thus he opposes a static locking of culture into a metaphysical idealism or a false civilized elitism. And, in symmetry with Williams, he shuns the model promoted by crude Marxist thought that limits culture to a function of economy.

Abraham's take on culture is notable for including such phenomena as the emotions, the intellect, and religion without obscuring concepts of politics, economics, and so forth. In this fashion, he broadens the notion of culture beyond a commonsensical intuitive posture that would constrain culture within the boundaries of art and a narrow assessment of the aesthetic. And he launches the conversation beyond the arguments sometimes captured in reaction to the base–superstructure program already established by crude Marxism. Indeed, he unlocks the broader and more creative potential of perceiving culture pervading the vectors of human energy or practices (as identified by Hall and Williams), which too often go unrecognized. That is to say, the very texture of human being (that is, to feel, to think, to believe) exists as a cultural moment. Abraham establishes a threshold for viewing the sacred seeping into the more obvious traits of the human person.[7]

Drawing on his own heritage, Abraham also cites the African as a complex cultural being—"an accumulation of a variety of cultural fragments. He [or she] is endowed with a base of . . . traditional culture, which is by now irreversibly impregnated at various levels by elements of other cultures, some of which were imposed and others sought and acquired."[8] In this regard, culture denotes a syncretism, a core intermixed with various and sundry strands combined to yield the culture of a people. Because he utilizes African heritage (more pointedly, his Ghanaian lineage) to substantiate his claim, I find it highly instructive for forging clarity on the notion of culture. Here I note that African American folktales (the offspring of the African matrix), as the primary source for my own constructive theological anthropology, result from a hybridity or syncretism as well.

To appreciate this syncretism one does not have to submerge oneself in the vibrant and intricate controversy over whether all African culture disappeared in the European slave trade or not, which arose out of conflicts between the work of anthropologist Melville J. Herskovits and that of sociologist E. Franklin Frazier. A similar discussion has been carried out between William A. Bascom and Richard M. Dorson, both anthropologists.[9] And neither does one have to belong to an Afrocentrist

audience to accept some continual impact of African culture on those
enslaved in the so-called New World and on their descendants today.[10]
Likewise, at various historical junctures, some creative and vital interface
occurred between Native Americans and black Americans.[11] And Frazier
and Dorson both claim a heavy dosage of European and European American substance in black culture.[12]

Concluding his theoretical remarks, Abraham suggests a three-part
typology for culture in general: "The culture of a people has many
dimensions. They include a pedagogical one, teaching the common
wisdom to succeeding generations and yielding the symbols and means
for communicating that wisdom; an ethical one, declaring principles
of sensibility and action, and sketching out the basis and limits of tol-
erance and cooperation; a prophetic one, bearing on the norms and
future history of its people."[13] The importance of culture, for him,
does not lie in an abstract descriptive quality. Nor is it just an interesting cerebral exercise. Culture matters for the well-being, survival,
freedom, and future of a people: it teaches intergenerationally, provides boundaries for right and wrong action in community, and establishes norms that serve as internal self-critical mechanisms in order for
a people to keep renewing, renourishing, and, thereby, growing. Since
theological anthropology wrestles with what human beings have been
created and called to be, believe, say, and do regarding matters of ultimate concern, it therefore must participate in these instructive indicators of culture. Consequently, culture and theological anthropology
take stands within the human predicament on perceived rights for definite communities.

Human Labor

Within the human labor category of culture offered by Nengwekhulu
(with "spiritual culture" and "artistic culture" constituting the additional factors in a holistic cultural dynamic), Amilcar Cabral's insights
build on Abraham's position linking culture with pedagogy, ethics, and
the prophetic; that is to say, culture is rooted in and directly affected by
social location. Cabral, from Guinea-Bissau in West Africa, takes up the
debate about the human labor or political-economic trajectory in the
notion of culture advanced by Nengwekhulu.

Let us ground this discussion of theological-anthropological implications of culture in terms of human labor in the context of poor black people living in the United States. This sector of the African American community and the American population finds itself located in a specific political economy. The vast majority of the racial group identified as black fall within the working class or live in structural poverty. By working class, I mean black folk who do not monopolize and own wealth in the way that the top 10 percent of the U.S. population monopolizes and privately owns and influences the overwhelming majority of private wealth and retains exclusive purchase on public policy. Hence, the revisiting of economics vis-à-vis culture is warranted at this point.

Cabral identifies broad material features of culture. He notes

> strong, dependent and reciprocal relationships existing between the *cultural situation* and the *economic* (and political) *situation* in the behavior of human societies. In fact, culture is always in the life of a society (open or closed), the more or less conscious result of the economic and political activities of that society, the more or less dynamic expression of the kinds of relationships which prevail in that society, on the one hand between [the human person] (considered individually or collectively) and nature and, on the other hand, among individuals, groups of individuals or classes.[14]

Culture emerges out of the human energy, creativity, and struggle exerted by the human person (individual self or communal selves) in relation to nature (technologically refined and raw natural) and in relation to various human beings occupying definite societal positions. Culture, then, does not operate as a concept isolated from the material formations of how people organize both their micro-everyday living and their macro-systemic arrangements. Human beings may be conscious or unconscious of their cultural choices and intended creations. Culture, furthermore, has definite links to prevailing political and economic activities and ties to specific traditions again influenced by culture's relation to the historical development of humanly created economic and political setups. Cabral's accent on the dependent and reciprocal connections of the cultural and the political-economic allows for more interplay among these human factors: not a unidirectional rigidity but a reciprocal movement obtains here.

Cabral also adds a view of history and the mode of production as they play a part in cultural development. Whatever culture's traits, it acts as an essential part of a people's history, and, for Cabral, history and culture both have the mode of production for their concrete basis. His definition of the mode of production fosters an understanding of the overlap among culture, history, and mode of production.

> Now, in any given society, the level of development of the productive forces and the system for social utilization of these forces (the ownership system) determine the *mode of production*. In our opinion, the mode of production whose contradictions are manifested with more or less intensity through the class struggle, is the principal factor in the history of any human group, the level of the productive forces being the true and permanent driving power of history.[15]

Culture is greatly determined by the economic interactions and positioning among people. More specifically, one's ownership of, power over distribution of, and relation to material wealth (nature, technology, machinery, and people) can have a direct impact on one's cultural creativity and perception of culture. Likewise, class relations (that is, who owns wealth rather than only income and who owns, controls, and distributes the materials used for economic production in a society) express the movement and traditions of human interactions. Human connections to the level of material wealth and creative technology (of the factors that define economic class) enable human beings to advance societies and make history. We can only progress or regress (that is, influence the flow of history) relative to what is materially real and the vistas of human visioning.

A difference exists between this notion of culture and that of crude Marxism. A crude Marxism does not allow the artistic and the spirit (that is, the superstructure) to ever impact labor and wealth (that is, the material base). In contrast, Cabral allows a reciprocal connection between base and superstructure. What Cabral emphasizes, within this connection, are the class relations or material base as the "principal factor in the history of any human group."

Because class connections are dynamic, are expressions of the mode of production, and are the principal factor in history, and because culture both has the materialist base of the mode of production and is an element of human history, when one speaks of culture, one simultaneously speaks about history and the mode of production. Therefore, however one defines culture, if culture is somehow wrapped up in the mode of production (that is, issues of ownership of wealth), then culture touches on classes and their social, economic, and political differentiations.

Cabral, no crass economic determinist, states that culture is constituted by oral and written traditions, works of art, dance, cosmological ideas, music, religious beliefs, social structures, politics, and economics. Still, his underscoring the culture-history-political economy specification facilitates a perspective of culture as a category of historical and fluid resistance. Because culture has a materialist relationship, the advancement of progressive culture (against the monopolization of power over others) can, in its reciprocal relationship to its materialist connection, both reflect the level of wealth ownership and distribution and spur on opposition to nondemocratic social relations in the areas of material life. Culture can assume an agential role in the resistance to and possible transformation of how people operate in the structures of a society's economics and politics. Indeed, cultural resistance, Cabral submits, generally precedes comparable resistance in the domains of economics and politics.

Again exemplifying the reciprocal nature of culture, Cabral claims that those who intentionally participate in liberation movements signify "the organized political expression of the culture of the people who are undertaking" the effort for the democratization of ownership of wealth, environment, and social activities. Not only can culture influence certain parts of the mode of production, politics can affect certain dimensions of culture; thus politics, by way of culture, can act upon the mode of production as well.[16]

Like Abraham, Cabral identifies the marks of culture as, among other things, pedagogical, ethical, and prophetic, and he contributes additional categories. He clearly opts for a popular culture, that which emanates more or less from social sectors lacking ownership and control over wealth. While embracing the creativity from all civic strata, including the privileged, Cabral emphasizes "people's culture." He offers these final cultural goals: the development, first, of popular culture or people's culture based on positive values indigenous to this grouping; development of a national culture based on the history of struggle for justice; promotion of political and moral awareness along with patriotism (a patriotism circumscribed by the democratization of the mode of production and all that relates to it—that is, history and culture); development of scientific culture to foster material progress; the advancement of a universal culture inclusive of art, science, literature, and so forth; and the assertion of humanistic practices such as solidarity with, devotion to, and respect for other people.[17]

Cabral's method of focusing on the initial dynamic of people's culture would indicate a significant role for black folktales—a unique tradition of those African Americans occupying structures of poverty and extreme locations away from ownership of wealth and distribution of wealth (that is, peripheralized citizens within the mode of production). I concur with his emphasis on moving from this particularity out into the universal implications of people's culture as they contribute to the general human storehouse of experiences, while, concomitantly, learning from and appreciating what overall human creativity and energies offer all specific cultures.

If theological anthropology unfolds within culture, if political economy pertains to a part of cultural content, and if class differentiations express the mode of production within political economy, then Lucius T. Outlaw's further nuance regarding the economic-political-ideological living phenomenon in culture aids our discussion at this point. Outlaw argues that economic classes result from their connection to the mode of production, but he wants to delve into the mixture of political and ideological causality (linked to class). That is to say, how is it possible to foreground the influence of class relations while also accounting for the agential and proactive role of politics and ideology as parts of culture? For Outlaw, "classes . . . are effects of 'an ensemble of the structures of a mode of production and social formation . . . and of their relations, first at the economic level, second, at the political level, and third, at the ideological level.'"[18] Classes, therefore, come about not exclusively from economic factors or motivations. Classes arise from the determinations by the mode of production as well as social-political and ideological relations.

Outlaw then clarifies more specifically how classes are constituted by both *structures* and *relationships*. Structure signifies one's position in the ownership and distribution of the economic production process, while relationships underscore one's political and ideological realities, linked but not wholly limited to the economic. The structural location, moreover, simply denotes that objectively everyone has class location vis-à-vis the mode of production. In fact, some people own wealth, and others merely work to receive income. Appeal to a unifying and positive cultural goal of *e pluribus unum* does not obscure this objective fact. Social agents, therefore, occupy a given social location independent of their will. Outlaw terms this the "structural determination" of classes.

Next, he moves to the distinction between "objective" or "structural" and one's class position in the social relations of production— that is, how one relates to reality through the media of the political and the ideological. At these junctures, social agency can decide to act to maintain the economic status quo or seek transformation. The rise of the economic productive forces (wealth, technology, and use of nature) includes a rise of political and ideological relations among citizens. In general terms, those who disproportionately own, have access to, and exert decision-making power over a country's productive forces develop certain political modalities and ideological justifications to maintain their objective ties to the mode of production. Because the political and ideological aspects provide more autonomous activity than one's link to the economic, there exists a fluidity in the choices that different classes make and the choices even acted on intra-class.

This inter- and intra-class maneuverability of relationships in the political and ideological domains, for Outlaw, is further brought to light in his notion of "subgroupings." Classes are constituted by subgroupings. (The idea of subgroupings, moreover, helps to clarify some parts of the characteristics of race; see chapter 4.) These conceptual additions provide the conditions for the possibility of the human will to act. He states, "However, classes can be further distinguished by subgroupings. There can be 'fractions' and 'strata' that have their bases in differentiations within the relations of production and in differing political and ideological commitments/relations of various groupings of people. And there are 'social categories,' i.e., groupings of agents defined principally

by their place in political and ideological relations such as intellectuals or a state bureaucracy."[19] Though they might have objective structural economic positioning in society, disparate subgroupings can in
fact act contrary to their class/structural location. Consequently, working-class people, in concert with the bourgeois class, can act politically
and ideologically against their own position in favor of the owners of
wealth (an instance of inter-class agency). So, too, members of the owning class, in opposition to their class colleagues, can act politically and
ideologically against their own economic status and in favor of working
people (an indication of intra-class agency). Thus ideological and political intricacies sometimes supersede and condition one's perception of
the economic. Culture, as a total way of life inclusive of class structures, relationships, and subgrouping realities, means the possibility of
ever-changing micro-everyday activities and macro-structural configurations. In other words, class and subgroupings can transform cultures
because cultures are, in large part, the creations of proactive human self
and selves.

The Artistic

Culture, drawing on Randwedzi Nengwekhulu's previously cited explanation, consists of the totality of human labor, spiritual culture, and
artistic culture. Our extended conversation regarding the political economy of culture attempted to broaden out Nengwekhulu's dimension of
human labor. Now we view what he terms "artistic culture," but what I
prefer to engage conceptually as culture's aesthetic trajectories. For this
part of the discussion, we draw on Barry Hallen's interesting conclusions from his work on Nigerian culture since the 1970s.

Hallen's scholarly work (that of a formally trained philosopher)
approaches indigenous worldviews of the aesthetic by conversing with
the elders of a local community. In his case, he argues that the systematic comprehension of the aesthetic aspects of culture is disclosed in the
intellect of the *onisegun*, the masters of medicine, herbalists, or alternative medical doctors, who are the repositories of the collective wisdom,
experience, and traditions of the Yoruba.[20] After decades of interviewing
and being, in turn, interrogated by the *onisegun*, Hallen discovered that
cultural aesthetics pertained not so much to arts or crafts, though these

were part of his analysis, but to the relevance of beauty as a manifestation of the aesthetic. Here, too, beauty was applied not primarily to arts and crafts but to people or human beings.

The aesthetic or beauty of a person referenced the body and the type of clothing worn by an individual. For instance, one is admired for one's beauty because of the color and fitting of one's clothing; thus beauty of the physical is enhanced by the type of outerwear or exterior trappings displayed in bodily appearance. Yet even this perspective of beauty is consistently coupled with ethical traits of the individual's personality. Hallen comments, "In virtually every account of the term, . . . beauty as a physical attribute was rated superficial and unimportant by comparison with good moral character as a . . . form of 'inner' beauty."[21] One recognizes beauty manifested in the corporeal highlighted by clothing or other outer adornments, but still, deeper beauty must be detected by righteous ethics in conduct. The absence of a good moral character defiles perceived beauty, making the latter rather superficial. In contrast, individuals can lack in good looks, rhetorical eloquence, and social adeptness but embody a good person's personality.

Therefore, beauty and character accompany one another. The *onisegun* claimed consistently: "If the person . . . is good looking . . . , but his or her innermost self . . . is bad, they will still call him or her an immoral person. . . . Whenever anybody does bad things, it means his or her inside self may be bad." The inside of an individual controlled the community's determination of the individual's beauty. When a physically attractive individual actually turns out to possess bad moral character, this signifies that the innermost self of the individual is bad or immoral.[22] The verbal and nonverbal behaviors become decisive in adjudicating the presence of beauty in character. The aesthetic or beauty in culture coexists with and accompanies moral attributes, and thus the community (the collective selves) offers a norm to ferret out beautiful and nonbeautiful character in the human being (the individual self).

The aesthetic of the person is accompanied by the aesthetic of the natural. "By natural," Hallen purports, "is meant the 'world of' nature, of all those things that are neither human nor man-made. In this instance, 'human' being also is a part of nature, of course, but what sets it apart from all other things in the world is the kind of self."[23] The human self is distinguished from nature by the human's intelligence, ability to speak, and possession of moral character. With this differentiation in genus, the aesthetic of the natural consists of the human self admiring or valuing an object of nature simply for its external, physical beauty. For instance, the coloration of the natural or the fullness of its bodily traits can point to beauty in and of itself. Such an aesthetic passes the consensual judgment understood or enunciated by a communal perspective. Still, in the same cultural context the aesthetic of the natural can result from its utility, somewhat like that criterion elaborated about the aesthetic of the person (physical qualities are ultimately subordinated to moral character in assessing beauty). In this context, one labels the character of the natural based on situating the natural object within human groups and assessing beauty relative to the natural object's utilitarian functions for that community.[24]

Finally, Hallen offers the aesthetic of the human-made, the consequence of human creation and energy to manufacture that which is neither strictly the natural nor inherently already given in the description of the person. Common characteristics of such beauty include color, newness, the finishing process, or the shininess of human-manufactured objects. Hallen concedes that these aesthetic traits are found in descriptions of art, but what he hopes to add to this commonly accepted portrayal is the aesthetic aspects of and usually disregarded beauty of "plebeian objects," such as a person's farm, thereby aiding in righting "the aesthetic imbalance" resulting "from collectors' and art historians' disproportionate concerns with figurative carvings and sculpture." Again, like the aesthetics of the person and of the natural, the aesthetic of the human-made draws its character (that is, a community's hierarchy of values regarding better and lesser quality) from the usefulness and durability of the human-manufactured object.[25]

J. P. Odoch Pido, from his extensive knowledge of the Acoli community (in northern Uganda), cites a similar interweaving of behavioral and physical qualities relative to the idea of aesthetics. Within this framework, aesthetics, for him defined as good appearance, is constituted by avoidance of too many extremes in the material makeup or natural attributes of the object of beauty. For example, one can be tall but not too tall, and neither too fat nor too thin. Furthermore, "in addition to [this] inherited proportion and complexion," one appreciates beauty due to the nature of the "characteristic makeup, hair, and cloth-ing . . . styles."[26] Pido goes on to deploy the concept of "classic beauty" when the beauty of an individual self merits the approval of the norms of community. Though such beauty initially appears to suggest appro-bation, it also intimates a negative response for two reasons. First, classic beauty has a tendency to attract an "evil eye," one who has no righteous intention. And second, in a more theological vein, such a beauty could rival absolute beauty only inherent to God. Consequently, in his fur-ther refinement of the beautiful trajectory in the aesthetic, Pido presents "good" (in contrast to classic) beauty, which possesses or evokes unam-biguous approval on the part of one's community. He argues the follow-ing:

> The socially approved appearance is human, not overly extreme, and is what I refer to as "good," as opposed to classic, appearance. Good appearance is attractive, likeable, and beautiful; it influences in a pos-itive fashion the relationships among the individual who bears this appearance and the people around him [or her]; consequently, it makes the person comfortable and secure, especially around people he [or she] is well acquainted with.[27]

At first glance, one perceives a potential contradiction in this depic-tion of beauty. Beauty is welcomed and affirmed in community; still, beauty has to not be automatically accepted but interrogated for its potential underlying negativities. Pido resolves the apparent dilemma by drawing in the idea of fame and its attendant problematic. Fame, exemplary of the complexities of beauty, carries with it a certain degree of discomfort and insecurity for individuals who have the attribute—"often a source of focused public gaze, obsession, and even envy and hate toward those who have it." Concomitantly, it suggests for the com-munity that shortcomings accompany beauty; for instance, lack of industriousness or other imperfections. Hence, the human self does not participate in any abstract portrayal of pure beauty, for that would defy normative communal claims and, perhaps even more important, chal-lenge the status of God's unblemished aesthetic.

Pido broadens the definition of beauty or an aesthetic of the body to include good behavior as an integral component of desired beauty within communal context. Good behavior, akin to good beauty (in contrast to classic beauty), avoids extremes. And sought-after behavior does not evince a natural state. On the contrary, how one acts in an acceptable manner derives from a combination of training and experience. In general, "a person is said to behave well when he or she is humble, tolerant, kind, considerate, and morally right." Accordingly, the truly beautiful, for Pido, embodies the marriage of good appearance and good behavior.[28] Beauty, in this regard, is a history or process of acquiring attributes through socialization as part of social interaction, sometimes by instructions and at other times by trial and error. One attains beauty when one's physical properties are amplified by the repeated grooming of doing in accord with those who surround the physically beautiful individual. In this more precise way, the group fosters and forges an aesthetic of the body and an aesthetic of behavior into the truly beautiful.

Innocent C. Onyewuenyi of Nigeria uses three frames to define the idea of the aesthetic (or artistic culture) as the second subset of the larger notion of culture. Art, for him, is constituted by the functional, depersonalization, and a community orientation. The arts (visual, kinetic, poetic, and musical) participate in functionality when they "are designed to serve practical, meaningful purposes, and that beauty of appearance is secondary. All the same, functional beauty can also be regarded as beauty."[29] A mask or other form of art exhibits the presence of or lack of beauty not because it might seem ugly or beautiful in appearance, but because of its role in the ritual of dance or the practice of religions or its otherwise serving the vivification of a local context. In a word, it facilitates life-giving or community-building energy. Not allowing for the idea of art for art's sake, functional beauty is measured through societal norms and traditions.

Onyewuenyi asserts that artistic individuality and social functionality combine within the attribute of depersonalization. Drawing on variegated exemplars of African art, he declares:

> When we say that African art is depersonalized we mean that the artist's concern is not to express his/her own individual ideas and feelings. The African artist works from a background diametrically opposed to the Nietzschean expressionist influence. . . . He/she performs rather in such a way as to fulfill the ritual and social purposes of a community for

whom the arts are meant to regulate the spiritual, political, and social forces within the community.[30]

In one way, beauty, aesthetics, or artistic sensibilities of individual creativity harmonize with the other people around the particular artist. Such an aesthetic venture suggests great art as that which forges and engenders positive community interaction. It adumbrates the possibility of gifted artists embodying and being embedded with the well-being of one's social location. Furthermore, art links to the spiritual, political, and social forces in which a community is engaged. In this manner, art and the artist perform a function amid the power plays deployed by different selves or groups of individuals. The product and the producer of aesthetics do not transcend politics; both operate within social specificity.

Concluding his three facets of the aesthetic or artistic, Onyewuenyi adds the element of community orientation. The practices of functionality and depersonalization orient themselves toward serving the health, needs, and desires of community. Clearly the aesthetic discloses itself as an interrelational process. Nevertheless, the individual adheres to professional freedom and individual creativity while she or he remains cognizant of the community's accepted and established forms of beauty. Within the parameters of responsibility to society, she or he can add nuance and the particularity of his or her genius.

The Spiritual

So far we have discussed two of the three components of culture elaborated by Randwedzi Nengwekhulu: *human labor* (or political economy) and the *artistic* (or the aesthetic). We turn now to his final category regarding the *spirit* in culture. Kwame Gyekye of Ghana helps in this effort when he offers an understanding of spirit as inherent to culture: "I use the term 'culture' in a comprehensive fashion, to encompass the entire life of a people: their morals, religious beliefs, social structures, political and educational systems, forms of music and dance, and all other products of their creative spirit."[31]

Consequently, discussions about spirit refer to the creativity that unfolds in culture, a creativity that animates both human labor and the artistic. Beneath or powering all that human beings concoct (both the means of production and the relations of production) and each realization of art (as the classical aesthetic and as good works; as functional, depersonalized, and community-oriented) resides the spirit that weaves throughout the entire life of a community and in its common discourse and historical memory. When one speaks of the creative genius of that which results from human effort, by the work either of human labor or of artistic labor, one speaks of the spirit as a special gift to create.

Gyekye submits that one would be remiss to separate absolutely or draw too strong a divide between the religious and the nonreligious, the sacred and the secular, or the spiritual and the material. Thus we can claim that the spirit inherently dwells in culture. One cannot detach oneself from the ever-presence of some being or force greater than the human self or collective selves.[32] For Christians of all stripes, God fulfills this specification. God is the source of the creative energy of the human psyche, soul, and body—an originative force that allows the human self or the human selves to produce, by way of innovation, products that humans would seem unable to produce. This is precisely what one often calls genius or, in more Christian language, a miracle. True acts of labor (as labor interacts with nature, other humans, and technology) and exceptional products of art (in the representations of the classical, good, functional, depersonalized, and community-oriented) are acclaimed by most communities as work far beyond the ordinary human feat. Indeed, it is often hailed as an extraordinary accomplishment especially because it surpasses the expectations of the everyday, the mundane, or the usual.

If one still assumes that spirit is enmeshed in culture, then spirit serves as engine and fuel for culture's configuration. Claiming spirituality as a universal, Patrick A. Kalilombe writes:

> Spirituality has been described generally as "those attitudes, beliefs and practices which animate peoples' lives and help them to reach out toward the super-sensible realities. . . ." It is the relationship between human beings and the invisible, inasmuch as such a relationship derives from a particular vision of the world, and in its turn affects the way of relating to self, to other people, and to the universe as a whole. In this sense, spirituality is not restricted to any one religion, but can be found

variously in all religions and cultures. It is determined in the first place by the basic worldview of the persons or people concerned. It is also shaped by their life context, their history, and the various influences that enter a people's life.[33]

The outlook, practices, values, beliefs, and attitudes that underlie and animate religion and culture define spirituality. Deepening the question of animation, Kalilombe discerns two sources in the event of spirituality engaging culture. In a word, whence does spirituality originate? Two primary sources, among others, are the past and the present. One cannot track spirit in culture without historical genealogy commingled with contemporary investigation, for culture, which encompasses spirit, mutates and develops. The history of all cultures seems to suggest the prior existence of what one might call indigenous culture. As regional and global interactions process in human history, indigenous cultures become modified, either by absorbing foreign cultures or by suffering from the dominating presence of foreign culture or sometimes by doing both. The original precontact culture (what existed before colonization) does not become entirely obliterated when aggressive alien forces become present. Nor does indigenous culture absorb outside influence without the former undergoing disparate degrees of transformation. Therefore, forms of uniformity and malleable alteration occur in culture and spirituality.

Extrapolating from his own native culture of Malawi (in Central Africa), Kalilombe claims that culture and spirituality change from interaction with foreign pressure (the external encounter) and as a result of the natural unraveling within indigenous culture (the internal exigencies). Thus, on the one hand, people never proceed without a past; history matters. On the other hand, to avoid a romantic conception of traditional culture, one has to take very seriously the impact of contemporary culture and the gifts that arrive from whatever point of origin. The past worldview serves as a lens for interpreting the new contact; the new contact, in turn, interweaves with the traditional to forge something novel that allows for the remainder of some core planks from indigenous spirituality or culture yet synthesizes them with the modern.[34]

Building on Kalilombe's theoretical threads, I propose the following possibilities: (a) indigenous culture and foreign culture coexisting, with each remaining relatively intact; (b) indigenous culture and foreign culture combining to form a new creative syncretism—a third reality; (c) indigenous culture and foreign culture commingling, with indigenous as fluid content and foreign as camouflage form; or (d) indigenous culture and foreign culture enmeshed, wherein one or the other becomes the overwhelming primary determining factor, with the minority aspect retaining remnants of its former precontact status.

For Malawian traditional spirituality, humanity "(individuals and community) is at the center of consideration. . . . African spirituality is based on this centrality of human beings presently living in the concrete circumstances of life this side of the grave. It consists of their attitudes, beliefs, and practices as they strive to reach out toward the super-sensible realities: God, the spirits, and the invisible forces in the universe."[35] The first mark of indigenous spirituality, then, is its anthropocentric nature, human beings' reception of and vivification by divine spirit or super-sensible reality. Such a spirit allows human self and selves to make sense of the cosmic and quotidian struggle between the forces of life and the threat of death. Ultimately, it concerns the pursuit of life worth living as good, harmonious, and meaningful. Traditional culture underscores humanity as primarily the community. Kalilombe, to highlight this point, offers the following aphorism: "It has often been said that where Descartes said, 'I think, therefore, I am' (*cogito ergo sum*), the African would rather say, 'I am related, therefore, we are, (*cognatus ergo sum*)."[36] The second mark of traditional spirituality, consequently, is its profound emphasis on "the value of interdependence through relationships" in contradistinction to individualism and personal independence in and of itself. A submark of this community solidarity is hospitality, wherein family members and nonthreatening strangers are not allowed to suffer, be alone, or go hungry.

A third spirituality mark, flowing from community solidarity, is the outlook, value, and practice of "sharing and redistribution of resources so that no individual accumulates and hoards resources that become unavailable to others when they need them."[37] The individual self and collective selves are obligated by this requirement. The corollary of negative spirituality follows: the sanction against those who oppose the obligations and rights of solidarity and the more likely concomitant spirit of unkindness, unforgivingness, egotism, cruelty, and quarrelsomeness. Communal solidarity also extends outward toward nature and the rest of the nonhuman, created universe. Traditional culture and spirituality, therefore, shun the perception of and active struggle with the universe as an oppositional adversary that one seeks to conquer, destroy, and divide up for utilitarian human purposes. Rather, an indigenous spirituality conceives of partaking in common dependence and shared heritage with all existing ecology and the cosmos broadly construed.[38]

Spirituality originates not only from the *past* (that is, indigenous, traditional, or precontact spirituality) but also from the *present*; this is true both for foreign religions or external spiritual developments and for traditional culture, which experiences internal changes and growth from contemporary factors. Thus the legacies of history and the occurrences of more recent adaptations amalgamate to form existing spiritual realities. For instance, the arrival of foreign culture in Africa included the introduction of a debilitating spirituality that challenged traditional spirituality. Specifically, new values and priorities undergirded a different worldview governing human labor, aesthetic efforts, and the foundational meaning of a communal priority. The contemporary new spiritual thrust

> promises attractive, immediate, and palpable results and has the capacity to validate these promises by offering samples of success that are hard to ignore or pass by. Central to this spirituality is the supremacy of the value of acquiring, possession, multiplying, and enjoying material goods by individuals. This value precedes all others and should not be unnecessarily restricted by other values, such as the consideration of other people's needs and feelings.[39]

In a word, the advent of the foreign derails and shifts the indigenous from a spirit of sacrifice for the whole to a radical accent on the hubris of the individual. Basically, the distortions of the foreign acting on the indigenous exigencies signify two different viewpoints on human beings' relationship to the ultimate or God. One encounters two distinct theological anthropologies resulting from two contrasting notions of the spirit. Clearly, at least in this instance, the spiritual aspect of culture undergoes both a warring between its two sources—the past and the present—while, simultaneously, it adapts from each of the two to formulate something new. Spirit can act as animating force and transformative agent relative to the super-sensible.

Mercy Amba Oduyoye of Ghana reminds us that spirituality as the third and animating trajectory in culture does not remain neutral. It brings normative claims that judge, critique, and correct the traumatic ramifications in the sources of both the past and the present. "Spirituality is a holistic and continuous process of becoming," she asserts. "It enables me to look at others with mutual respect. Spirituality is always coupled with justice. The more I grow spiritually, the more I am concerned with justice and taking action for justice."[40] Through this normative value and worldview, Oduyoye sifts through both the past and the present and discerns the harmful effects of both cultures on the status and role of women.

As typical examples from history and today, she references women's negative part in childbearing, marriage, nurturing, and segregated decision making by sex. Her reasoning points to the disempowerment themes in both modern and indigenous spiritualities. Moreover, traditional proverbs and modern Christian dogma, each containing and teaching definite values and sensibilities about women, are spiritually flawed. "The Hausa [of Nigeria] have a proverb that many African women need to hear. It goes like this: 'They pat the cow before they milk her.' So beware of adulation. For Christian women it is the theology of the cross that they have to suspect. A spirituality of the cross without resurrection is promoted among women."[41] Precontact traditional ways of life already contain deleterious spiritual realities— a sobering fact contrary to romantic sensitivities about pure, positive indigenous cultures. Accordingly, all spiritualities exist as sites of contention between salutary qualities and incapacitating effects.[42]

Oduyoye offers a profound insight when she points to the crucial necessity of situating within culture itself an enduring mechanism of internal self-critique that influences pervasive normative assertions within human labor, the aesthetic, and the spiritual. In a word, we need to avoid the danger of fantasizing cultures, whether they are precontact cultures, a syncretized culture as a consequence of merged indigenous and outside encounters, or some projected eschatological future or ideal earthly utopia. And one of the most glaring red flags signifying harmful culture is the oppression of women.[43]

For my purposes, the goal of internal self-critique, an unending process of normative assertion that adjudicates healthy realities of culture, is the empowerment of the poor among all aspects and vectors within culture. What is the status of the poor and working-class people in human labor, the aesthetic, and the spiritual? When these three definitional components reveal themselves among the discourses of gender, sexual orientation, colonialism, neocolonialism, ecology, and race, where are the poor and working people? Put succinctly, all of culture is dynamic, contextual, contested, and potentially life-giving in relation to the norm of poor people's well-being.[44] A usual litmus test in all societies entails the status of women—the poor of the poor.

As a preview and further elaboration of the self-critique and normative conceptual and practical dimensions of black American working-class culture, bell hooks's work contributes a perceptive perspective. Furthermore, because my later construction of theological anthropology will rely heavily on the pearls of wisdom of black folktales (themselves originating primarily from working-class blacks and African Americans in structural poverty), hooks's analytic category of black folk culture resonates with characteristics of my own theological-anthropological standpoint. Discerning the folk wisdom of everyday black life, hooks analyzes the culture of African American working-class families in the South of the 1950s.

> These were the values taught to me and my siblings by our parents and reinforced by the segregated schools and churches we attended. They were the values that had led to the creation, from slavery on, of a distinct African-American culture, a culture rooted in soulfulness, a culture of resistance where regardless of status, of whether one was bound or free, rich or poor, it was possible to triumph over dehumanization. This soulful black culture of resistance was rooted in hope. It had at its heart a love ethic. In this subculture of soul, individual black folks found ways to decolonize their minds and build healthy self-esteem. This showed us that we did not have to change externals

to be self-loving. This soulful culture was most dynamically expressed during racial segregation because away from white supremacist control black folks could invent themselves.[45]

The taught spiritual values of which hooks speaks are collective solidarity, hard work, self-creation, maintaining integrity, racial uplift, communal love, appreciating the aesthetics of culture, and a voracious appetite for lifelong knowledge. She writes: "Education was the way to freedom. Educated, we would not necessarily change how the white world saw us, but we would change how we saw ourselves."[46] What distinguishes these sensibilities from bourgeois, monopoly capitalist theories is hooks's insistence on and specificity of culture as nourishing one's soul as a spiritual life of service to others less well-off. This distinction of communalism substantiates the nomenclature and normativity of a "culture of resistance."[47] One attends to the sculpturing of the individual self in service to the forging of the collective selves.

Where the Sacred Reveals Itself

In this chapter we have seen how the notion of culture must be taken seriously in our approach to theological anthropology. Therefore, to propose a constructive statement on theological anthropology for today requires a probing into the presupposition of culture inherent to the content of this God–human interacting doctrine.

Encapsulating my own logic, Jesse N. Mugambi's schema of culture clarifies, in summary fashion, what is culture. He establishes what he calls seven pillars of God's house constituting culture: politics (power to decide sharing and distributing of resources), economics (ownership of sharing and distributing resources), aesthetics (dealing with proportions and forms of beauty), kinship (the basic primary relations in society—the family), recreation (relaxation and renewal of self and selves), religion (worldviews and human relations around ultimate visions), and ethics (values of right and wrong).[48] All seven are sacred or relate to an ultimate vision upon which matters of life and death are decided. A qualitative vision or foundational concern transcends the individual self or communal selves, and consequently the spiritual trait appears. And culture is not pristine, neutral, romantic, or statically given. It operates in a flow that is animated by the spirit (for Christians, God's spirit) in contention with adverse spirits (those that harm life and systematize a monopolization of God's creation by one group).

Culture is where the sacred reveals itself. As a result, one only knows what she or he is created to be and called to do through the human created realm of culture. On our own, we are limited to this realm. If we could enter the divine realm by using human efforts, there would be no need for the divine; indeed, such a human capability would restrict divine power to simply the determination of what it means to be a full human being. Because humans cannot create the divine realm, the ultimate vision or the divine spirit must impinge upon and enter the human condition.

Not only does the divine spirit or ultimate vision enter the human sphere, the human being has the presence of the divine spirit or ultimate vision within the human being itself, no matter how smothered or covered over this sacred dimension may appear. All are created with the potential spark to live their lives in service to the least in each social configuration. Through compassionate service for those in pain, we transcend the individualistic spirit of the self. Therefore, culture is sacred insofar as the ways of being human in the world entail some yearning for, belief in, and ritualization around that which is ultimate vision—that which is both part of and greater than the self. Culture is sacred because the ultimate vision is present both in the material (the tangible manifestation inspires humans to keep moving forward) and in the transcendent (the imagination of the ultimate is not limited to the self).

However, though all of culture contains the sacred, the ultimate goal or vision (the divine spirit) of what it means to be human in community is continuously challenged by evil or that which prevents individual full humanity in relation to healthy community. Culture is contested terrain between marks of life and death.

And, finally, the norm is liberation; that is, whatever fosters the freedom of the individual self and the interests of those structurally occupying the bottom of community—in particular, citizens dwelling in systemic poverty as well as working-class people—is good culture because the movement toward practicing freedom for the poor marks the revelation of God.

From the Christian perspective, Jesus announces his sole purpose on earth to privilege the poor—the homeless, the hungry, the thirsty, the prisoner, people enslaved by labor, the abused women, humans lorded over by the powerful, the brokenhearted, the oppressed, the stranger, those without clothing, and the lowly. By removing the systemic structures of human evil while transforming the internal demon of individualism, all of humanity can eventually live together on the same horizontal level. Consequently, the wealthy ultimately cease to exist in culture.

3.

Selves and the Self:
I Am Because We Are

As we have seen, the various contemporary models of theological anthropology all assume that culture is a major factor in defining the human being. Behind this presupposition, the concept of culture assumes a prior understanding and exploration of the condition of selves (communally) and the self (individually).

For instance, a return to chapter 1 finds that progressive liberals take for granted particular selves who are involved in the conversation, interpretation, and understanding dynamic. David Tracy in particular speaks of the heirs of European Enlightenment reason. Postliberals such as George Lindbeck acknowledge certain selves who must immerse themselves in the Christian language and culture. Feminist theoreticians focus on the female selves. And liberation theologians focus on the marginalized selves, especially in their corporate manifestation. Finally, as we move toward a constructive doctrine of theological anthropology using black folktales as the major sources, we will discover that these sources themselves demand clarification of the selves/self in God-talk concerning the divine and human interaction, or what it means to be a human being, singularly and in community.

Communalism: The Notion of the Selves

In sum, the culture discussion of chapter 2 still raises a query about the definition of the human beings who comprise culture (saturated with human labor, the artistic, and the spiritual). Culture does not fall willy-nilly from the sky or emerge from the recesses of our brains when we think about an idea. Culture surfaces from below, from the interaction and creative configurations of the spirit dwelling with real human beings quilted together in the flow of life. But what does it mean to be a self or selves—the ones who fashion the notion of culture?

The Priority of Collectivity

We start with community or with more than one individual self. Throughout this chapter we will claim that community or communalism or the collective selves (all are here deployed interchangeably) is the goal and primary condition in the self/selves problematic. As Ifeanyi A. Menkiti of Nigeria writes,

> The first contrast worth noting is that whereas most Western views of [human being] abstract this or that feature of the lone individual and then proceed to make it the defining or essential characteristic which entities aspiring to the description "man" must have, the African view of [human being] denies that persons can be defined by focusing on this or that physical or psychological characteristic of the lone individual. Rather, [human being] is defined by reference to the environing community.[1]

We of course must still address the vital issue of the individual self, but we should balance this self with a communal emphasis. Indeed, neither self nor selves is viable in a salutary and vivifying manner without the other. One makes the other real. Nonetheless, we argue for the privilege of the common good, in particular the good of the majority of working-class selves and other selves enmeshed in structures of poverty. Only through healthy collectivity can creative individuality arrive at singular being, productive knowledge, and self-consciousness. The human is not defined by frozen notions of memory, will, soul, or rationality; rather, the self becomes a self via introduction into the selves.

The notion of the selves contains several interacting factors. First, each human being within culture is dependent on other people for her or his life and death, sustenance and joy, and survival and liberation. A human being by definition is already constituted by more than the individual. From the simple assertion of parents naturally giving birth and life to an individual, to the necessary reality requiring an extended family, clan, or community to fulfill an individual's well-being and growth, we surmise the priority of the communal over the singular. Beyond the fact that an individual is the offspring of other human beings (that is to say, an individual cannot naturally give birth to itself by existing before its conception), it is a natural process for each human being to be born into a society (that is to say, an individual is not born for solitary existence). People also require sociality for sustenance; that is to say, no person can infinitely provide food, clothing, shelter, and spirituality for himself or herself alone.

Second, the ultimate worth of the individual derives from transcendent legacies already bequeathed to the human person prior to her or his arrival on earth. Not only are the genotypic and phenotypic appearances predetermined by the biological input of the birth parents, but culture, created by collectivity, suggests an imprinted field into which one is born, grows, and has one's very being. One's taste for human labor, the aesthetic, and the spiritual are, in large measure, predetermined before one enters the earth. (We note here that the agential power of the individual is not entirely eliminated by the power of collective culture. On the contrary, the singular self always has the capacity to critique and alter that which already is.) As an atomized self, we are all individually children of a priori material, aesthetic, and spiritual legacies. To be me is to be a result of the existence of a conditional we.

Third, in addition to the collective natural and the communal legacy presuppositions to the self, the self's ontology (that is, its very being and definition) evolves from a spiritual dimension. This spiritual presence, in which we are born and have our being, is comprised of a higher, previously given notion of collective beliefs, values, and rituals. Even from a humanist perspective, bodies of peoples forge intergenerational visions, aspirations, and hopes that carry on in their offspring and into the ongoing communities of future progeny. For example, the pioneering ideas of an individual self emerge from the material left by those who preceded or from the crises of communities. The individual genius creates a cutting-edge proposal or system of thought based on the stuff arising from others outside of the individual. Here, too, genius is necessitated and recognized by community already superseding the solitary self.

Christians term this dynamic and intracommunal transcendent process—that is, one person brings about extraordinary interventions in
the community's situation based on what the community hands the
individual to grapple with—a revealed spirituality. More specifically
and significantly, it manifests as the incarnation of God's spirit of divine
freedom in the singular person Jesus on behalf of the common wealth
of the poor and, through them, all humanity.[2] God, through the individual Jesus, is the author of all of created wealth, and God fashions
the fundamental resources for the flourishing of full humanity (individually and collectively). The abundance of the possible for the corporate human community comes out of the multidimensional overflow of
prior spiritual powers or values gifted to poor and marginalized people
(and through them to all peoples) by way of this spirit taking on the
individual flesh of Jesus.

God is the spirit of freedom for us, with us, and in us.[3] The argument is that God gives us the gift of liberation and by doing so provides
for us before we are able to provide for ourselves. The triple vector of
"for us," "with us," and "in us" designates a web-like flow of trinitarian
enabling power that collective humanity, privileging the well-being of
the poor, can incorporate in the human struggle to be fully human—to
attain and maximize the fullness of the selves' and self's capabilities. The
fact that a transcendent something precedes us and enables us simply
further substantiates my claim that the individual self is conditioned by
a force a priori to the individual person. Spirituality, in this sense, adds
to the prioritization of the notion of the selves.

Community, Communal, and Common Good

Kwame Gyekye of Ghana, from his own theoretical analysis, sums up
this perspective of natural, inherited, and spiritual confluence requiring a look first at the communal. He maintains that "for the individual, community life is not optional—an assertion that follows from the
natural sociality of the person and from the fact that she is embedded
in a set of necessary social relationships." Again, the "we" births, nurtures, and assists the aliveness of the "me." Natural sociality and embeddedness deem the community as the principal entity in itself. Gyekye
resumes by describing what he labels communitarianism, which

sees the community as a reality in itself—not as a mere association based on a contract of individuals whose interests and ends are contingently congruent, but as a group of persons linked by interpersonal bonds, which are not necessarily biological, who consider themselves primarily as members of a group and who share common goals, values, and interests. The notion of shared life—shared purposes, interest, and understandings of the good—is crucial to an adequate conception of community. What distinguishes a community from a mere association of individuals is the sharing of an overall way of life. In the social context of the community, each member acknowledges the existence of common values, obligations, and understandings and feels a commitment to the community that is expressed through the desire and willingness to advance its interests. Members of a community society are expected to show concern for the well-being of one another, to do what they can to advance the common good, and generally to participate in the community life.[4]

Gyekye parses out further the nuance differentiation between community and communalism. *Communal values* inherently contain appreciation for the value and worth of the community. Such values adjudicate the nature of the interactions, including attitudes and behaviors, among individuals in community. Overarching—intergenerational, transcendent, or spiritual—values may include "sharing, mutual aid, caring for others, interdependence, solidarity, reciprocal obligation, and social harmony."[5] Communalism's worldview and normative claims glue the community together and vivify its benefits. The idea of the communal, then, defines the historical trajectory and contemporary substance and helps guarantee (if the communal is consistently adhered to) the conditions for the possibility of the self's and selves' perpetual flourishing. In a sense, communal values offer the highest dynamic state for achieving the full humanity of the natural, inherited, and spiritual community.

A *community*, according to Gyekye, distinguishes itself from a random gathering of individual selves. Rather, it is the interpersonal bonds weaving together strands of common goals, interests, and values—in a word, the possession of an overarching way of life marked by its philosophical and practical qualities (and, I would add, theological qualities, since the way of life transcends the presence and capability of any one entity). Community participants display an advancement of the common good and the individual well-being of the neighbor. In other words, communalism "may be defined as the doctrine or theory that the community (or, group) is the focus of the activities of the individual members of society."[6]

And the forged community, steeped in communal values, centers on crafting the *common good*, based on the starting point that collective selves come before individual self-interest. If the community results not from a haphazard conglomeration of single beings with independent goals, but from a project directed by an overarching way of life, then both community and communalism act toward an ultimate end product, that of the common good. What is materially and spiritually fitting for the collective selves and, therefore, individual participants comprises a sense of the common good. Indeed, this good can be experienced universally in favorable interests to all members of society. At the elemental level, the common humanity of us all requires the basic sharing in that which allows essential teamwork of the one and the many together.

In contrast, the impairment and eventual destruction of the common good originates from civic ties circumscribed and led by perceived individualistic desires. The common good, however, is open to access by all for everything that the entire membership requires for its survival and flourishing. A society's notion of the common good, because of its unique traditions and cultural developments, may exhibit particularized expressions of the good. But we can still argue for some universal traits of the good in common. All community members deserve adequate shelter, food, and clothing; at the same time, the human person needs more than these basic requirements to have a vibrant life in community. The common good, therefore, broadens to include "peace, freedom, respect, dignity, security, and satisfaction"[7] and a feeling of belonging to something greater than the individual self and an individually determined self-identity. The community signifies cultural interaction. The communal provides values to glue together interaction. The common good advances a goal for interactions.

Furthermore, an assertion of universal aspects and the recognition of particularized societies in relation to the common good do not obviate a mandatory norm in establishing the good. The common good is a political and moral notion. "The insistent advocacy and pursuit of such concepts as sympathy, compassion, social justice, and respect of person make sense *because* of beliefs in the common good. The pursuit of social justice is intended to bring about certain basic goods that every individual needs if he [or she] is to function as a human being."[8] Working back from the common good as a final goal, we surmise that social justice is also cardinal for community and communalism.

Values of the Selves

In fact, social justice serves as an indispensable hub for a cluster of additional values related to collective selves. Communal right relations denote mutual interaction particularly in support of one for another. Accordingly, solidarity accompanies social justice. Benezet Bujo of Zaire states that solidarity arises in good and bad situations, a move facilitating a sober discernment of solidarity.[9] Good solidarity is a hallmark of the singular person (to be further elaborated below in the discussion of the individual self). Bad solidarity evinces two negative directions: (a) when one person or individuals actively participate in harmful acts against community, communal values, or the common good and (b) when one person or individuals fail to stand in solidarity in the presence of the good. Failure to comport the self and selves in the right way and at the right time constitutes the bad. Both negative active participation and refusal to participate in the good yield the death of community.

Solidarity gives rise to reciprocity in the notion of the selves. Bujo offers the idea of "continuous flow of life" emanating from God and pervading all of the created order. This "vital force" of life is commissioned by its maker, God, to attain full maturity as it dwells in all living natural and supernatural organisms. Full maturity realizes itself when each member of the collective participates in reciprocity by enhancing the conditions for each person's maturation. At this juncture, reciprocity is key, for no woman or man is an island or superhuman. For a person to reach fullness of the self there must be a mutual interacting process. All peoples embedded and enmeshed in community, the communal, and the common good "must ensure that this initial [transcendent] gift of life reaches full maturity, and this is possible only when people act in solidarity. Each member must be conscious that his [or her] actions contribute either to the growth in life of the entire community or to the loss or reduction of its life."[10] In a word, reciprocity is the close accompaniment of solidarity.

In addition, Kofi Asare Opoku of Ghana enumerates a list of values mandatory for prosperous community. Mutual helpfulness picks up on the notion of solidarity. Solidarity is not merely a verbal attestation of support for the extended family or neighbor. Its realization manifests in actually, practically helping those literally around us or other life-forms at a distance. To help means to cooperate with others. Cooperation presumes generosity, for insufficient help cuts against the grain of building community using communal values for the common good. Opoku cites complementarity and interdependence in his elaboration of his key principles to organize genuine community. In a positive notion of the selves, society's entire membership possesses a worldview of mutual dependence in order to complement one another. The sum of these communal values detests competition as a regulatory norm or a necessary fundamental in community. Opoku thus synthesizes his analysis: "Individuals therefore see their neighbor as their other arm and not as their competitor."[11] In this sense, perception of the holistic selves in community hinges on perceiving collective humanity incarnated in the humanity of others. All humanities thrive when all see their own humanities embodied in others.

When we see ourselves in the very being of others in community, in extended family, and in those at a distance, then levels of harmful friction and damaging anger can decrease. The notion of the selves is then more likely to experience balance and consonance. Hannah W. Kinoti of Kenya explores this intersection by drawing out the implications of cooperation and harmony for society. She critically studied the effectiveness of these values in certain East African civilizations. Kinoti discovered amazing results both at the community level of the immediate family and in the wider environs. "It was this ideal [of harmony], when brought to bear in interpersonal relationships within the family, that did much to minimize domestic violence. When extended to territorial entities it did much to contribute to civil peace on a larger scale."[12]

Beyond the healthful implications of healing and tranquillity among families and between nations, the accent on communal values of the selves expands into nature and the ancestors. What value does the idea of the selves place on the natural creation and those who have died but remain in memory and in spirit? Nature provides the creative sustenance of life for human beings. Removal of nature translates into an elimination of the literal vital force of community. Every material requirement for human selves in social relationships comes forth from the natural world. Nature gives the human community food, air, light, aesthetic awe, and an appreciation of the ecosystem. Nature is so integral to the human family that many Native Americans declare birds, animals, wind, and other nonhuman entities as sisters and brothers and cousins of people. We two-leggeds (in the words of some American Indian scholars) are simply equal to our brothers and sisters who are four-legged or the winged ones.[13] Privileging nature as family clearly broadens the concept of the selves and insists that we humans pause when approaching or (more usually) murdering the nature sectors of our immediate families.

Kofi Asare Opoku agrees with American Indians' sense of worth in their expansive worldview. For him, communal values signify cooperation with and preservation of nature, although he exhibits no naive assumptions about humans' exploitation of the earth for human community's survival and growth. But even the deployment of nature's components for human consumption entails communal values such as balance, harmony, and detecting humanity's life in the life of the nonhuman. Opoku claims that "quite apart from providing sustenance for human beings, nature provides a model, a source of wisdom for the resolution of conflicts in human society. The relationship with nature is often expressed in terms of identity and kinship, friendliness and respect, and this attitude is based on faith in the goodness of the goal of nature."[14] Nature's cycles themselves introduce the importance of conflict resolution and goodness. All living realities undergo a natural ebb and flow that can exemplify normal balance and nonantagonistic difference rather than egotistical conquering for self-serving expressions. As part of the created family, nature, too, presents lessons we need to absorb.

A consideration of the ancestors further opens up a re-evaluation of truncated human interactions. Benezet Bujo proposes the concept of "anamnesis" to clarify the ancestral place among the living human beings. The ancestors are the departed family members, the ones who have crossed over to another realm of living. Their spirits remain and visit those living in body form as long as the earthly living remember the departed names and commune with them in regularized rituals of recognition and supplication. Hence, the living have a huge obligation to consciously maintain an awareness of the physically deceased among extended families and throughout broader community. Indeed, the ancestors are guardians of communal values because they are even closer to the older spirits who died before them. The ancestors, consequently, receive traditions of collective worth and preserve them as well as refine these primal understandings of intergenerational memory. Furthermore, the ancestors represent a lifetime of testing out and living into communal values; thereby, in their material deaths but spiritual life, they harbor pedagogical paradigms of worth. Any people who sever ties with the dead are subject to death themselves—if not literally, then spiritually. There can be no "me" of the remaining earthly family members without the foundational legacy left by the "we" of the family's ancestors.

And so anamnesis is really about remembering the dead who are still alive spiritually. The remembering does not, however, suggest uncritical reflection or inhibitions toward modifications of passed-on values. Nevertheless, by renewing fellowship and sorority with the ancestors, the living renew and reappreciate the status and legacy of communal values. Renourishing communal values of the ancestors, then, facilitates the possibility of a further flowering of those values for those who attend to ritual obligations of remembrance. At another level, groups subject to forgetfulness are more likely to succumb to the adverse spirit of prioritizing individual self-interest. Without ancestral anamnesis, it is more difficult to promote the spiritual embodiment of group worth.[15]

N. K. Dzobo of Ghana substantiates this claim against negative spirituality by detailing the ramifications of individual-first instincts in radical contradiction to other-humans-first compassion: "While the humanistic value orientation derives its origin from [the human's] devotion to the ultimate or the infinite in the finite, market-value orientation derives it sources from devotion to [the human's] economic and social interests well-being, which are believed to be the chief ends of life." Thus the purposes of human beings collectively are to be devoted to that which is beyond the limited self, to embrace obligations to the communal values from the spiritual realm, and to remember the transcendent and embody it in the finite. By contrast, the free-market structure of society succumbs to cutthroat competition over private ownership and eventual inhuman monopolization of wealth, whether it is the material wealth from nature, the wealth and control of human bodies, or the spiritual wealth that defines an entire culture's identity. "Me first" leads to canyons of separation among peoples. Dzobo provides an account of such a market-value orientation: "Instead of being seen as made up of creative humanities, society is viewed as comprising incompatible individual socio-economic interests, divided into groups with opposing socio-economic interests. There is therefore a constant struggle in society to maintain and safeguard privileged socio-economic interests and positions. Life then becomes a struggle for existence and survival of the fittest, with the weak falling by the way."[16] The market-driven society creates antagonistic hierarchies and warring strata fostered by the seemingly obvious, but actually false, assumption that human beings are naturally and spiritually inclined to do for self at the expense of the neighbor. Dzobo opts for what he declares the "we orientation," that is, our observations about community, communal values, and common good surmised in the broad rubric of wholeness.

Thus we can describe the paramount value, inclusive of all attributes of reality, as wholeness. In other words, the well-being of the community is an interlayering or quilting of the earthly human, the spiritual ancestors, family members of nature, the expectations for the unborn to come, and the ultimate transcendent presence, God. Communal values are both worldview and ethical practice oriented toward the common good. They are not only based on an individual stipulation "but realized primarily by means of a relational network that is equally anthropocentric, cosmic, and theocentric."[17]

Communal Political Economy

The notion of the collective selves has implications for political economy. By economics, we posit ownership of wealth and resources, and by politics, we underscore who has the power to determine ownership. Here the Bible will furnish a window into the political economy of communalism.

Kim Yong-Bock of Korea approaches the subject matter with the theme of covenant between God and the poor. More specifically, the new covenant appears in the divine spiritual revelation in Jesus and his relation to those lacking material resources for a wholesome life. Yong-Bock explains:

> The most dramatic expression of the socio-economic dimension of the new covenant is found in the early church, especially in Acts 2:42-47 and 4:32—5:11. This is the protection of the community of the faithful, who are the new people of God: "The faithful lived together and owned everything in common; they sold their goods and possessions and shared out the proceeds among themselves according to what each needed." "None of their members was ever in want." That is, there were no poor.[18]

Young-Bock goes on to infer how in today's human family, established on the monopolization of private ownership of wealth and resources for a small sector of society, the vision described in these Acts passages is dismissed as utopian, eschatological, or hyperbole. That is, Christians and other readers of the Bible have a "me-first" attitude that leads to their misinterpretation of the community, communal values, and common good accent of this sacred history. Yong-Bock asserts that the early church provided a radical paradigm in the hierarchical and exploitative context of the slavery-based political economy in the Roman Empire. Original Christian communities challenged the overall political and economic makeup in the accepted social status quo. Consequently, due to a revolutionary hope offered by Christianity, freed persons and slaves joined the countercultural Jesus movement. Thus, the way (of Jesus) for the poor became a communal calling.

With a closer reading of Acts we see that a sacred political economy yielded collective benefits for all members of the community when the poor were prioritized. The group of believers united in their hearts and souls without monopolizing possessions because all materialities were held in common. This social arrangement left no one wanting; each received according to her or his condition. Moreover, James 2:1-9 amplifies the clarification of the early church: "My brothers and sisters, do you with your acts of favoritism really believe in our glorious Lord Jesus Christ? . . . Has not God chosen the poor in the world to be rich in faith and to be heirs of the kingdom that [God] has promised to those who love [God]?" Prior to the Roman emperor Constantine's co-opting Christianity to serve the wealthy of the empire, the early church lived with a faith that opted on the side of the majority of the people—the poor, the enslaved, the working sectors, the marginalized, those generally without material hope, those "economically destitute—because of their loss of property or their lack of inheritance, or because of their having been robbed by the powerful and rich."[19]

The structure of the early church was thus centered on the poor, the majority, with outreach to the rest of the society, including the wealthy. The primordial gathering of believers experienced the new social benefits of equal ownership and proportional advantage to all. The political economy for the poor, Yong-Bock concludes, permeated the early Christian community as well as the biblical text. Because the God–human covenant defended the poor using covenant codes, legal statutes, and the messages of the prophets in the Hebrew Scriptures (so-called Old Testament) and through Jesus' mission and covenant in the Christian Scriptures (so-called New Testament), the poor became the protagonists in biblical history. A concern for the poor is a central criterion for faithful Christian witness and, some argue, a humanist value system as well.[20]

Theologically, we therefore can reason, the first organized Christian communities and the Bible view God as having a definitive role related to political economy. God stands as the ultimate author, owner, and giver of all wealth and resources found on, beneath, and above the earth. The question of land, air, water, food, space, time, minerals, and the components of technologies derive from the grace or granting of the divine. In broader strokes, the entire creation and ingredients currently harnessed by human beings find their origin before the arrival of human communities and appear as a consequence of some power greater than human capabilities. Creation just is. And we partake of and benefit from it. Mary Getui of Kenya argues that God "does not give us resources and gifts for ourselves alone but that all may be enriched and all may worship [God] regardless of their colour or the part of the world from which they come."[21]

If theology (human comprehension of divine being and acts) tells us something about the nature of God, then theological anthropology brings insight into God's intent for humankind (that is, the relationship between *theos* [God] and *anthropos* [human]). If we then make the claim that God ultimately owns that which God has created and has gifted these to the human family, then God's act of giving is a bestowal for communal use and collective ownership as described by Getui. Young-Bock's interpretation of the Acts passages highlights a historical model of how the first Christian communities or early church understood such a theological anthropology. In addition, Young-Bock provides an insightful interpretation of Genesis:

> The story of the garden in Genesis 1 and 2 reveals the political economy of the sovereignty of God. God has created and entrusted the resources of the earth to humans, who are to cultivate *shalom*, to secure and safeguard life. The production and distribution of economic resources should be seen in this light. Production should be understood as gardening and distribution as sharing (*koinonia*). God has created the world and human beings as a garden.[22]

Consequently, the divine act of giving also entrusts us with stewardship, or a responsibility for that which we have been given. Stewardship obligates the communal owners of the common wealth[23] to cherish wealth and resources for the attainment of group and individual survival and advancement. As recipients and guardians of creation, humans are obligated to participate in active involvement with creation, including sharing and service to the neighbor as signs of thanks for the abundance received from a power greater than human energies. The way, therefore, to ensure community life (*shalom*) is through a political economy of communalism in which the human perspective on wealth is one of gardening or cultivating and distribution's principal criterion is sharing with the neighbor (*koinonia*). *Shalom* and *koinonia* differ from welfare, a concept presupposing that some have privately hoarded wealth and resources and thereby have the power to hand out or distribute from one's monopolized storehouse of goods. In contrast, common wealth and common ownership, symbolizing God's gift of stewardship, enable mutual benefits from and equal use of all that is collectively possessed. The philosophy, way of life, or normative ethic is that every sector of community owns what every other sector has access to. In stratified human arrangements, especially on a national scale, this normative ethic can evolve when the focus is on the bottom of a society—working people, humans in structural poverty, subgroups injured and dying for want of material access, and those shunned and forced to the periphery of corporate life.

An adverse worldview allows for private monopolization of wealth that, in turn, hinders the healthy notion of the selves (community, communal values, and common good). The purpose of private monopolies is "me first": How can I or my family accumulate enough of God's creation for my own personal power to reproduce and magnify additional wealth? Though important welfare acts ensue from a political economy of private monopolization, the immediate and long-term effect of this counter-collectivity is a transfer and redistribution of wealth, income, and tax revenues upward into fewer and fewer hands.

Usually, a massive transfer of wealth is shielded by nationalistic rhetoric implying that the redistribution of wealth is in the best interest of the entire people. All major human institutions gear themselves toward sustaining hypermonopolized privatization. A conscious elite or those paid by the elites necessitate direct and sustained leadership for monopolization. The vast majority of people, however, simply believe that the fact that the wealthy get wealthier and the poor poorer has always been true. The political economy of the me-first monopolies counts on the vast majority of society being either bogged down in mere survival issues, enamored by distracting entertainments, satisfied with what they consider reasonable disposable income, or aggressive in their pursuit of wealth. This last instance, characterized by the attitude "let me get mine as quickly and as much as possible," is the rational thesis and damaging spirit of monopolized ownership of privatized wealth trickled down.

Collectivity on the economic and political level does allow for modified private roles or even the presence of certain types of monopoly, but group interests always come first. In other words, the private sphere must enhance the overall well-being of the whole population, with the status of the poor and working people as the linchpin. Laurenti Magesa of Tanzania explains how communal property itself can be used by individuals or groups based on certain rules that emphasize inclusion. He asserts that communalism seeks a balance between private property rights and public property priorities. Drawing on lessons gleaned from African religion, especially as practiced in Tanzania, he writes:

For African Religion, the ethical task is to establish a balance between exclusion and inclusion with regard to the acquisition and use of material resources; in other words, to establish a balance between the rights to private ownership of property and the human meaning of the resources of the universe. Thus, tradition usually indicates the parameters within which personal ownership may be exercised without harming the common good, which, in the end, is always primary. In African religious thought, the right of personal ownership is situated within the context of joint or public right of access to the basic resources necessary for life. . . . In the moral perspective of African Religion, disharmony must be constantly guarded against, whether it comes from social or economic inequalities.[24]

Ideas of balance and harmony for the common good undergird the parameters for macro-political economy. We might ask, How do these communal values unfold within a nation to the benefit of the common good? Mario O. Castillo Rangel of Cuba provides an insightful answer by introducing four differentiated markets on the macro-level. In line with our embracing the community, communal values, and the common good, the *primary* market that contextualizes and normalizes the activities of the remaining three markets is a nationwide mechanism ensuring that the entire populace (in particular, poor and working people) has ownership of and access to God's gifts of wealth and resources. What has to be satisfied first are the main necessities to survive and flourish in life: food, shelter, education, clothing, recreation, transportation, communication and other infrastructure indispensables, health care, information technology, cultural activities, and land, to name a few. (Ambrose Moyo of Zimbabwe maintains that land can never be personally owned, since it is a general inheritance and sacred trust bequeathed to the progeny of the ancestors who have moved into the spiritual world of memory. All may have opportunities to use land for the benefit of families; still-land possession remains communal.)[25]

Rangel describes a *secondary* market that includes activities for private ownership of goods and services by citizens of the country. A *tertiary* market encourages foreign partnerships from countries with variegated political economies, as long as they adhere to a subordination to collective interests. And a *fourth* market is the informal domestic market, one not formally recognized but still supported so that small-scale goods and services can reach broader populations more quickly. Often spontaneous experimentation and successful innovation in the informal markets are later introduced into the primary community market.[26]

The positing of communal boundaries for macro-political economy, at one level, raises questions about citizens' contribution to the common good in proportion to sharing. If the understood rationale for differentiated markets is for all to receive the basic necessities enhancing material and spiritual well-being, do all individuals put equal effort into the collective pot of society? Kwame Gyekye designates this query as inherent in the communal enterprise. Unraveling this problematic mandates an even heavier reliance on the previously discussed concepts of community, communal values, and the common good, while appreciating the intense prolonged struggle to move from the presently accepted so-called commonsense beliefs that humans are naturally dog-eat-dog creatures whose way of life submerges community beneath individualism. Gyekye accepts that community members diverge in the areas of talents and capacities. The clear consequence is unequal contributions to the common good. The hub of the matter for Gyekye therefore is summarized in the question "Should inequality in contribution lead to inequality in distribution?" which he answers in the negative. Those "who contributed more must have been endowed with greater talents and capacities—natural characteristics and assets for which they were not responsible."[27] Being endowed by nature or a power higher than the individual self does not mean unlimited freedom of self-aggrandizement, but an incentive for the elevation of the neighbor. At the same time, Gyekye soberly and correctly appreciates the persistence of some versions of inequalities despite striving for the ideal.

Furthermore, a novel contribution–distribution orientation flows from a re-evaluation of a unit of the new common wealth: work. Reigning paradigms picture work or labor as survival drudgery, a primary means toward one's sustenance, mechanisms for accumulating wealth and income, a practice to minimize in order to accrue the maximum reward, or even something to be avoided. Here, too, the operative deliberate posture and taken-for-granted ethos is labor serves me first. In contrast, Kim Young-Bock's illuminating intervention into the work debate marks a four-part analysis at the service of the community.

First, work meets physical (health, clothing, shelter, food) and spiritual (cultural life, creativity, and education) obligations of the whole person. Second, recognizing the sacred communal political economy in which God offers creation to total humanity, work brings love of and service to the neighbor. Third, work enables and enhances both selves' and self's penchant for creative expression. Finally, work allows us to secure and safeguard life for people and nature.[28] Consequently, with all-important necessities accounted for, a different (and sober) approach to the contribution–distribution dynamic, and the aim of fostering macro-well-being, new avenues and possibilities emerge for labor.

Relationality: The Notion of the Self

So far our discussion of the selves/self dialectic has centered on the mapping of the collective dimension of this interplay. The anchoring ingredients in the exploration have been community, communal values, and the common good. We now turn toward the investigation of the self while maintaining cognizance of the context of the selves. The self in all of its aspects revolves around the idea of relationality and connections beyond the self.

Self in Whole Community

Archie Smith Jr., postulating liberation ministries and emancipatory struggles, establishes this proposition:

> There can be no true understanding of the self or self-conscious selfhood apart from the web of relations and historical circumstances in which individuals are embedded. This is another way of saying that there can be no true sociology apart from psychology, and no true psychology apart from sociology and history. Communal life and individual biographies stand in a dialectical relation within an ongoing historical process. The structure of social life, and images of the self, may be conceived as an emergence from an ongoing social-historical process.[29]

Who I am as a singular individual embodies the specificity of historical precedents, societal procedures, and psychological makeup. The self is the accumulated negative and positive history of others, the web of contemporary relations among people, and the resulting psychological fingerprint that makes each of us who we are as separate entities. Relationality names the living presence of others in the self and the self in others. Not only is this abiding, indwelling presence true for genotype and phenotype, but the transcendent traditions of the past accumulate into the self's concrete experience. Each self, in this regard, internalizes prior human experiences from a massive span and scale of time and place. Likewise, each day during the self's sleeping and nonsleeping, conscious and subconscious moments, the individual self takes in, through reason, intuition, the five senses, and spiritual avenues, a flood of information from others. Processing history and sociology yields a great deal of the mandatory contours of the self's beneficial psychic identity.

However, all that fashions the psychic self and its agential role does not immediately and necessarily give way to an advantageous psychic identity. That is why Smith offers a crucial caveat for realizing salutary ties between structures and psychology. In the flow of liberation ministries and emancipatory struggles, a profound danger lurks if one fails to adhere to the idea of relationality. Consequently, ministries and struggles necessitate alertness "to the likelihood of oppressive structures being replaced by new structures of oppression. Oppression is both an external and internal reality; therefore the process of liberation must seek to transform the social and political order and to emancipate the inner life of human subjects from internalized sources of oppression."[30] Just as everything from history and society entails mixtures of both ill effects and propitious growth, so too do the ingredients of the self's psychological status.

The historical sifting of enabling traditions, the contemporary sorting of societal contributions, and the continual attention paid to recognizing the spiritual demons of the mind must be congruent in order to unleash the vivifying psychic joys within the self's identity. In other words, the human person as an individual seeks a comprehensive relation between internal and external growth, especially for one who waves a banner of justice, liberation, or freedom. Otherwise, external emancipatory structures will not survive the long haul if the occupants (of whatever theological or political persuasion) shun the nurturing of the inner life. Someone who has a transcendent joy in his or her psychic life accumulated from a practice and orientation of serving the nonvalued strata of society has a better chance of maintaining healthy external selves' structures and internal self's structures. An inner life tormented by jealousy, low self-esteem, a profound obsession with "me first," and a host of other mood-altering negativities not only succumbs to the wear and tear of emotional demons in the self's spiritual and bodily components but also blocks the joy of giving of the self for others' selves. Quality psychological identity can come from sharing with and serving others one by one and from transforming macro-political economies by joining with the least members in the community.

Homer U. Ashby Jr. pursues further the notions of the psychological makeup of the self and its relation to systemic configurations in light of how the self seeks identity formation. Identity, for Ashby, emanates from three vectors intertwined with the micro and the macro: (1) "how one names oneself" and not allowing or enabling others to do the naming; (2) "what one identifies with" relative to a specified goal or agenda; and (3) "living into a vision for the future." The three-dimensional quest for self-identity unfolds within community; as Ashby writes, "clearly identity has much to do with one's connectedness to others. None of us creates our own identity."[31]

Benezet Bujo, in fact, cautions against a definition of the individual person "as self-realization or as ontological act."[32] Self-realization expects a singular self to actualize its identity alone and through the sheer power of initiating force of the self without impingement by the selves. Such an ontological act conjures up the fantasy in which the very nature of a human being emerges from and survives in singular existence. Individualism, too, relies on these false options particularly when the individual strives to adjust the interests of society to his or her own interests.[33] On the contrary, to be a self highlights "a process of coming into existence in the reciprocal relatedness of individual and community."[34] The unfolding of the self occurs through involvements in community. If there is a lack of such participation, in the words of J. P. Odoch Pido, the self resorts to the infamous realm of "a no person."[35] And so with Bujo we would argue that "common action makes the human person a human person and keeps him [or her] from becoming an 'unfettered ego.'"[36] Pulling back the unfettered ego as a way

for robust psychic existence reroutes us to the way of life that emphasizes sharing with and serving the groupings most slighted among the
selves.

Relationality of the self positions one with various but connected
manifestations of identity. The concept of a person involves foundational commitment to the ideals and values of community. Where
appropriate, a person responds to those commitments through practical
engagement with others. Pressing further, commitment and responsive-
ness come about when "an individual, who, through intelligent thinking, judicious planning, and hard work, is able to carve out an adequate
livelihood for himself or herself and family and make significant contributions to the well-being of the community." A responsible society
member comprehends community well-being to mean implementing
conduct with sympathy and sensitivity to adapting self's interests to
selves' requirements beyond the individual.[37]

Moreover, Amilcar Cabral stresses how the social dimensions outside the will of a singular person create and affect identity. He contrasts
the original (that is, biological) identity with the actual (that is, social)
identity. He argues for a leading role for the social identity, explaining
that his model

> shows on the one hand the supremacy of the social over the individ-
> ual condition, for society (human for example) is a higher form of life.
> It shows on the other hand the need not to confuse the *original iden-
> tity*, of which the biological element is the main determinant, and the
> *actual identity*, of which the main determinant is the sociological ele-
> ment. Clearly, the identity of which one must take account at a given
> moment of the growth of a being (individual or collective) is the actual
> identity, and awareness of that being reached only on the basis of his [or
> her] original identity is incomplete, partial and false, for it leaves out or
> does not comprehend the decisive influence of social conditions on the
> content and form of identity.[38]

Cabral itemizes the objective, actual identity arising from economics, politics, sociology, and culture. The economic formative factor
entails human beings' interaction with nature and technology and the
power configurations among human interactions. Politics pertains to

class positionality relative to wealth ownership and labor. Sociology, in broad strokes, accentuates the development, structure, and operations of human society. And culture "is a dynamic synthesis of the material and the spiritual."[39]

Cabral's perspective points to the importance of interrogating the nature of actual identity. We might ask in terms of economics, for instance, Who owns and controls or monopolizes wealth meant for all? In terms of the political, what are the laws and ordinances or policies ensuring such a domination against the majority of peoples forced out of that monopolization? A sociological question might be: How do other structures and developments function in society to preserve such an economics for the elite? And specific to culture we might ask: What material and spiritual resources can the self draw from to act with others on behalf of realizing community, communal values, and the common good? Note that Cabral does not eradicate the requisites of the original identity. Biologically, each unique self cries out for satisfaction of her or his natural operations of the physical body. Yet, in situations of monopolized resources, a skewed wealth allocation, truncated public policies, impaired civic routines, and a warped me-first spirituality determine the ownership, production, and distribution of those central biological staples. One could say, hypothetically, that selves need free health care. But when a me-first emphasis on accumulating wealth for an individual self (or one's family) shapes a society, providing health care for all would appear to cut into the profits of those who are successfully amassing wealth, and therefore a segment of society will not have health care. Such a society denies that "to be human is to belong to the whole community."[40]

Spiritual Source of the Self

Though the self resides within and belongs to the broader community, as an elementary and unique unit of the collective body, it incorporates its own subingredients. The human person gains life from God or a creative force beyond and greater than the singular individual. The Christian interpretation of the book of Genesis describes divine-to-human creation coming out of the dust of the earth but receiving authentic and final animated power from the *ruach*—the divine breath of Yahweh. Kofi Asare Opoku acknowledges the universal theme of this story. As he notes, in many African indigenous religious narratives, the Giver of Life shares life with woman and man through the divine breath. The direct relation between ultimate spiritual presence and material humanity is the breath breathed into the self's body.[41]

Gyekye links transcendental breath with normative claims about the self's worth by drawing meaningful instructions from Akan proverbs of Ghana:

> From the proverb . . . "All men are children of God, no one is a child of the earth" . . . we infer the Akan conception of humans as theomorphic beings, having in their nature an aspect of God; this is what they call . . . soul. This proverb has moral overtones, for there must be something intrinsically valuable in God for everyone to claim to be [God's] child. Man [or woman], being a child of God, would also be intrinsically valuable, and as such he [or she] is an end in himself [or herself] and must not be used as a means to an end.[42]

The Akan proverb deduces the same result without the breath metaphor. Gyekye's instance switches the symbolic schema to parental causality. As self is a child of God, God must be the parent of the self. If God is the parent, then God causes life in the divine offspring. Hence, in the self's nature we discover an energizing aspect of God termed *soul*. God is the first principle, the justification condition for life. Life exists as the paramount good achievement, and whoever possesses the ability of vivification or reviving intrinsically bears value. The self's transcendental aspect or soul derives from the One intrinsically worthy; therefore, the aspect or soul makes the self intrinsically valuable, too, meaning that the self is not to be exploited for the material accumulation benefits of another self or even the larger society of selves. A human being exists as an end in herself.

The self, inherently a spiritual person with a divinely implanted soul, holds a nondepreciating status. Kwame Nkrumah of Ghana submits a controversial challenge to one dominant strand of Christianity that describes the self's moral being negatively, that is, the doctrine of a person's natural subordination. For Nkrumah, the divine gift of endowed internal dignity, integrity, and value dispels any obligatory injunction of mainstream Christian discourse that privileges "original sin and degradation of" the human person. Nkrumah does not exhibit a false naïveté regarding evil. He relegates original sin and human degradation to a secondary status because such doctrinal generalities have proven to be detrimental to the social worth of working-class people amid concrete sin. Beneficiaries of disproportions of economic and political power unleash such harmful Christian doctrines to justify the crushing, laceration, and grounding down of lower social classes. In this theory, a person inhabits a subordinated social stratum because the self retains its debasement through original sin. The result of this doctrine is a fatalism for the poor and oppressed, who give into quietism, resigned to their purportedly predetermined social fate, instead of fighting for the wealth and resources gifted by the divine to all peoples and cultivated mainly by the human labor of working-class individuals.[43]

In Nkrumah's theology, God created every woman and man good. The self, in her or his human nature, is born as an infant with the capacity for goodness and "not depraved or warped by some original sin."[44] The divinely crafted or natural birth does not dictate vigilant chastisement and perpetual restrictions by the immediate and larger communities. One's ontology is good, one can and should do good, and one should have good done to one's self on the part of others. "Can" and "should" speak to woman's and man's moral capacity, thereby highlighting the ambiguity in the self's choice when confronted with sacred and natural capacities. Nevertheless, the clear starting place is goodness, rather than original sin, which operates in the context of social class asymmetries to working people's detriment.

Finally, we ask: What do these spiritually inherent components of the self move us to do? When we see the self of an Other as overflowing with sacred components, we are called to enjoy that self before us.

> To enjoy a human being means you should appreciate his value as a human being and demonstrate that appreciation by showing compassion, generosity, and hospitality. It means you should be open to the interests and welfare of others, and to feel it a moral duty to offer help where it is needed. To enjoy a human being means you should recognize the other person as a fellow individual whose worth as a human being is equal to yours and with whom you undoubtedly share basic

values, ideas, and sentiments. Thus, the main intent of the maxim is
to point out the worth of a human being and the respect that ought to
be given to her by virtue of her humanity. Recognition of the worth of
a human being is, according to the maxim, more important than caring for riches.[45]

This maxim can be summarized thus: enjoy another's self as each of us
would have our self enjoyed.

Note that, in addition to the indispensable spiritual factor, the self
contains other significant traits. J. P. Odoch Pido reasons that a human
being is never a singular activity but one marked by multiple subsets.
To be a person has "physical, social, age-related, productive, emotional,
and spiritual connotations."[46] The singular individual is all of these variegated personalities. Opoku classifies the human person into a bino-
mial relationship of material and immaterial. The self "is a biological
(material) being. It is the material part of [the person] that dies while
the spiritual (the soul) continues to live. Death, therefore, does not end
life; it is an extension of life."[47] Thus the depiction of the ancestors'
spiritual status (that is, the situation of those who have crossed over
to an above-natural world and live via our memory) evolves from an
understanding of a sacredly bestowed soul to the individual self. Prior
to advancing into the ancestors' domain, however, the biological and
spiritual components demand careful balancing and integration. In this
way one recognizes an optimum self when complete harmony manifests
between these two constituent aspects.

For instance, certain West African indigenous worldviews and practices incorporate the belief that it "is the actual bodily or physical behavior of a person that gives an idea of the condition of the soul. Thus, if
the physical behavior of a man conveys that he is happy they would say,
'His soul is happy' . . . ; if unhappy or morose they would say, 'His soul
is sorrowful.' . . . When the soul is enfeebled or injured by evil spirits, ill
health results."[48] Such psychophysical causal interaction echoes Christian tales about Jesus healing marginalized persons possessed by demo-
niacs. Whenever negative emotional or traumatic psychic occurrences
haunt our beliefs, thoughts, fantasies, and actions—the definition of evil
spiritual possession—our bodies and immaterial being cannot begin to

heal. But the actions of Jesus overcame a false division, leading to calmness in the self's mind and body touched by the Healer.

So we observe that if either is damaged, the other suffers ill fortune too. Spiritual malfunction (in the emotional and psychic realms) derails the ongoing health of the physical (in the material and fleshly body). With similar results, weakened physicality lowers spiritual resilience. Opoku questions the use of all medicinal remedies if such efforts separate these two structures of the person.[49] Biomedical, natural, psychological, and spiritual professionals should work together as a team to ensure the reestablishment of an integrated harmony of the self, for the principles of biology and spirituality are most effective when they are in mutual interaction.

A final subset constituent of the self directs our attention: the question of the individual's rational faculty. N. K. Dzobo highlights the distinctive "principal criterion" determining animal and human being in apprehending knowledge and embracing truth.[50] The capacity to acquire wisdom and grasp all of reality is the decisive divide between human person and other created sorts. "A human being is therefore," articulates Dzobo, " . . . 'the being that knows things.'" To have a "live head" describes intellectual alertness about the created textures around the self and comprehension of moving away from or toward correct principles. A self, it seems, experiences an aesthetic morality and a breathing epistemology.

In the same vein, Kwasi Wiredu's philosophical insights are germane at this precise location. Wiredu pulls together culture, the fundamental of mind, and the activation of that mind.

> A human *person* is the product of culture. Whatever else goes into the essence of personhood, mind is a *sine qua non*. But we are not born with a mind, not even with one that is a *tabula rasa*; we are only born with the potential of a mind (in the form of a nervous system). This potential is progressively actualized in a certain way through the barrage of sensory stimulation emanating from the purely physical (i.e., non-social) environment; but the person-making attribute of mentality is not attainable without another kind of barrage, namely, the cultural or socializing barrage of sensory stimulation from kith, kin, and kindred. And this means nothing but sundry forms of communication.[51]

Wiredu confirms these barrages within cultural context (in its labor, artistic, and spirit aspects; see chapter 2) as the larger environment for the self's emergence. Culture molds and nurtures the self. He definitively posits the mind at the core of human ontology. While agreeing in general with Wiredu's view, I would modify his sine qua non of the mind with the additions of spirit and body. It seems to me that the human person succeeds as an integrated fluid organism in a holistic process. Among the other important constituent parts, mind, spirit, and body plumb the depths of human being. Without these three, there is no singular self.

Wiredu clarifies the reasoning self with the nuance of the given and the potential. From the materialist angle, human birth only provides the potential of the analytical mind; the rational bodily procedures are at first underdeveloped. The nervous system encodes the real possibility of critical thinking, yet more is required for potentiality's transformation into actuality. For the mind's logical life to activate (in other words, for the self to achieve its agency status), this "more" originates in external stimulation from the communication of the selves to the imminent, anticipated, critically thinking self. The inherent capacity of coming into being maximizes through a kaleidoscopic nurturing from the community. The stress on selves (community, communal values, and common good) is the condition for the possibility of each individual self's realized ability to think discursively.

This lens on the self and thought aids my argument in support of elevating working people and those in structural poverty to think critically and actualize their genius. The popular conception of the wealthy is that they hold some inherent superior rationality. Wiredu teaches us how external causes operate on and work with the self to attain superior thinking. All things being equal (in internal biology and external sociology), a self of any culture, class, race, sexual orientation, and gender matures her or his internal rational faculty in concert with stimuli from multidimensional selves. A move to a new common wealth of the selves and attention to examining the demon possession internal to each self offer hope for millions of potential geniuses among working people. Repositioning them into direct ownership of God's created and given wealth grants them variegated resources for public use. The only difference between the small powerful elite and the massive citizens at the base of society is that the former has monopolized resources, disposable income, and leisure time to become "geniuses" or can pay someone else to make them appear to be extraordinary intellectual virtuosos. In reality, however, genius is a gift of creation and birth. All carry the agential capacity for reflective perception, abstraction, and inference.[52]

Agential Capacity of the Self

Mary N. Getui notes that "according to psychologists, under normal circumstances, human beings have various needs, namely physiological, safety, love and belonging, esteem and self-actualization."[53] It is to the individual human's imperative for self-actualization that we now turn. Since there is an a priori presence of the selves in the self–selves dynamic, what proactive agency capacity does the singular person have? Archie Smith Jr., with his creative engagement of the relational self as psychosocial self, acknowledges the historical and cultural legacy of the community while recognizing the human being's own initiative: "We are embedded in an underlying and continuous social process which constitutes and reshapes us. At the same time, we can affect the processes that determine the kind of selves we become. If it were not for the capacity for transcending awareness, human subjects would be reduced to nonpersons, prisoners of their own activity and trapped in their biography and history without conscious recognition of their captivity."[54] The human person's very ontology (that is, her or his core identity) empowers it both to receive a given social tradition and avoid passive incarceration in a nonperson limbo. Key to proactivity is the notion of transcendence. Smith claims an active social self continually open to causing significant alterations in the self and the social world. This process hinges on the individual's ability of "role taking"—to take on the role of an Other and then return to the self in order to better observe and address the self. The individual's mature rational faculty sorts through the going out of the self into an Other and back to the self for contemplation. Critical mental reflexivity enables the self to better imagine novel angles on the self and others outside of the self. "People are able to step back," Smith articulates, "and think (i.e., reflect) upon the social process itself. They can *re*-present it through language, synthesize experience in thought and imaginatively reconstruct or construct new possibilities."[55] Consequently, the dynamic effect of transcendence is accomplished by a socially conditioned relational self in rational reflection through communication.

Smith attempts to characterize the nature of resources for transcending the collective causes that constitute the self by focusing on three concrete aspects. The first broaches the arena of the unpredictable. Each person has experienced moments of the thrill and, sometimes, unease of his or her own spontaneity. Spontaneity becomes a liberating virtue because it shows a self, upon reflection, how the person can practically cross the boundaries of the expected and routine. One journeys beyond customary safe limits and undergoes a new height of freedom. Second, reflexivity reveals the power of the self to know himself or herself both as others perceive the individual self (to view oneself as an object) and by pondering how the internal self relates to the social world beyond a person (to view oneself as a subject). The human being attains self-consciousness in both dimensions and frees itself from the given of the group and the given of human nature.

And finally, the self actively participates in the reflexivity of the larger community. The social self can become free when "an intentional community can develop the capacity for self-critical reflection and can direct the collective will of a people toward human emancipation. This third possibility suggests that freedom from domination of structural oppression, Smith insists, "requires collective and revolutionary struggle and the capacity for self-critical reflection upon its own."[56] An authentic self participates in community, with communal values, for the common good inclusive of social segments that are marginalized yet desire a fuller humanity. The struggle of oppressed people together frames the most favorable conditions possible for transformation of the self and emancipation of structures. Smith thereby successfully sustains his psychic (that is, individual transformation) and social (that is, systemic reconfiguration) selves/self.

Still, the person's participation in community will not always go smoothly. Within classes, genders, races, sexual orientations, religious communions, cultures, nations, and other sorts of the corporeal and the metaphysical, we all remain individuals. A person has *individuality*. It contrasts with me-first *individualism*, a smokescreen for a warped self-focus and unethical right to exploit people through maintaining oppressive hierarchy over others. Active individualism pursues selfish perversions of desire. In the individual sense, one-on-one perversion ends in dominating another individual. In the corporate monopoly capitalist sense, it results inevitably in establishing a democracy for the elite at top while massively redistributing wealth upward from the broad base of society.[57]

In an opposite disposition, individuality affirms the *unique identity* of the human person. Each individual has an identity, a will, aspirations, desires, interests, passions, tastes, and thoughts. The breadth of life and the randomness of genetic inheritance produce a variety of distinct units. The stuff of one's distinct identity instinctively searches for self-expression. To be a unique human is to be saturated with the urge to create and create with one's own imprimatur. A woman has a will originating internally. A man brings substance to a name, even if that label is identical to a close family member. Another man bubbles forth with particular interests, tastes, and longings that stamp them as especially his. Another woman exhibits passions and thoughts about that which she considers to be cardinal. These quests for expressive singular identity cannot be quashed by community, except at the cost of violating the self's contribution to the selves, which would directly diminish both the person and the common good. Consequently, the self must stand up and strive for its identity in community. It has a natural inclination for productive and ingenious self-revelations. To be authentic self, one has to struggle and fight to forge one's full, unique identity. Varying categories of community (selves) can only set the external conditions and in a favorable manner so long as the selves remain faithful to their own communal values and common good visions.[58] The self's role is to ensure that selves keep the faith and remain on target.

When one exerts effort for identity, the individual claims the ability of *choice*, an additional measurement of individuality. Each of us is capable of discerning differences and weighing alternatives to reason through and implement options based on one's best judgment at a given moment in time and circumstance. Choice, too, implies intentionality on a person's part wherein the self does not merely or automatically suffer the whims and arbitrariness of mindless group rambling or herd mentality. A human being deliberates on and adopts a conscious intent. Consequently and concomitantly, an individual shoulders responsibility for unique thoughts and decisions. Each is responsible for her or his own actions in a given situation. With intentional choice come responsibility and accountability for the sublime and for the atrocious. Personal initiative dictates submission of choice to public scrutiny, critique, ridicule, and further reformulation of deliberate decision making.[59]

Self-reliance, another feature of individuality within community, instructs the individual to do his or her own work and not naively expect or lazily await a group to labor in the self's stead. An industrious human person perpetually pursues his or her own fortunes and rewards and shuns a lifestyle of passivity or receiving handouts. Thus, self-reliance results in hard work for the self, who strives for a worldview beyond anticipating everything from the collective. In fact, in all endeavors of life, the single being takes the initiative to become a self as long as he or she is able to do so. And the attempt to stand on one's own compels one basically to trust in oneself before turning to the group or community.[60] Somewhat similarly, Jesus demands this self-reliance of those whom he heals. The one who is cured after years of lameness and is enabled to walk is commanded to pick up his bed and travel on. The one forgiven for adulterous acts is commissioned to go and sin no more. In neither case does Jesus anoint the individual to remain in his or her state of pain, want, and guilt. Metaphorically one could say Jesus signifies the internal speck of the divine or the transcendent birth inheritance from the spiritual ancestors through the biological parents. In this interpretive viewpoint, Jesus summons the person to grow the internally given seeds of the self's abilities.

Individuality—clarity of unique identity, fortitude of choice, and ruggedness of self-reliance—presupposes an intact state of the self and a wholesome nature that account for a salutary inner self. Thus we might ask how it is possible to detect one's own individuality if it is clouded over by structural disadvantage and psychological injuries—overshadowing a vitalized *self-concept*.[61] This query is particularly relevant to my ongoing project of engaging sources concerned about the internal liberation and external emancipation of the marginalized self.[62] Toward that end, I harbor no illusions about the profound walking wounded state of the human being encountered in urban ghettos, the Appalachian Mountains, inner-city barrios, trailer parks, depressed rural areas, and government-monitored reservations, and blue-collar jobs.

(The miracle is the number of souls saved from self-destruction and the ones still choosing to fight for freedom beyond mere survival.)

Individuality mandates prior healthy self-confidence, high self-esteem, a feeling one matters, self-respect, and identifying with a positive group. One has to unleash a comprehensive and aggressive process among the poor, working people, and the oppressed to reach these simple elements of an advantageous self-concept. Where they do exist, affirming and institutionalizing public and private rituals can aid further solidity. Where they are absent, intense psychological and material programs must be enacted. We look for "change from within," emotions that then have an impact on the outer world.[63] And so an inner–outer dynamic yields human agency.

Christianity complements secular achievement stories. Even more forcefully, Christianity authorizes and promotes the self's involvement in revolutionary transformation of unjust arrangements. Teresia M. Hinga affirms the idea that the self inherently adopts an agential posture. For her, Christianity, based on what it attributes to God, warrants creative action par excellence: "The Christian belief in a God who transforms things for the better justifies the Christian participation in social change. Christianity is also characterized by hope, an orientation towards the future. It is an eschatological religion. Hope in its turn presupposes desire to change it for the better. This characteristic also makes it theologically legitimate for a Christian to participate in social change, for the better."[64] The authentic Christian helps direct the way to a new tomorrow by vigorous immersion in organizational change today. Theologically, God places alterations of unfair establishments at the center of the dutiful Christian's testimony. In other words, the self's agential stance grows out of a cardinal doctrinal belief linked directly to God's will. It is a pseudo-Christianity that preserves damaging social asymmetries while enslaving itself to quietism and worshiping at its altar. With that fervent reasoning and logical passion, Hinga correctly bridges theological justification, religious conviction, and ritual imperative in the human person's transformative nature.

Officiating Agential Conflicts

The question of the singular person's voice (expressed in multidimensional individuality and vitalized self-concept) sparking friction with another self's communicative lifestyle seeks a response. How does one adjudicate discrepancies of visionary angles and divergences in rules of engagement? What if two agents act dissimilarly? An Akan proverb envisions a potential resolution. There exists a crocodile having two separate heads and one united body. Two separate minds (with different discursive abilities), with two separate mouths (with diverse taste buds) and two sets of eyes (with deviating perspectival lenses), create conflicts. Conflict can be productive with its innovative energies and often iconoclastic challenges to the norm. Conflict can facilitate each individual head's clarifying rationally its stance and identifying its feelings of passion. While the two heads might remain at odds on the surface, their periodic fuss and mercurial fear lead to a common foundational body.

This symbolic pedagogy teaches at least three guidelines for officiating self-to-self debate and discord. (1) Clashes of society's citizens ought to end with each human being's basic needs fulfilled relatively equally and clearly without huge variance in power and privilege. (2) Communal interests contextualize each human being's unique fascinations and contested commitments. (3) Both the singular self and collective selves must participate in ongoing education toward the common good of the new self and the new common wealth.[65]

Under the rubrics of individual rights and individual responsibilities, each human being has the right to care for his or her own individuality and self-concept. The right exists for each citizen to make particular plans for his or her life. She or he can likewise attend to the growth of unique talents, natural abilities, and signature moods. So, too, the person's very self-definition builds upon human rights. However, society's progress evolves out of positioning individual responsibilities and one's group obligations at the head of individual rights and privatized human rights. The self has the responsibility to care for "the well-being of another person or other persons . . . the responsibility to help others in distress, the responsibility to show concern for the needs and welfare of others, the responsibility not to harm others."[66]

Hence, a duty receives priority when it pertains to the least advantaged in community. Individual rights and human rights do not materialize in isolation but diligently strive (sometimes without effort, other times in serious discomfort) to accommodate the forsaken and cast-aside members of the family, extended family, neighborhood, and nation. We can sustain the balance between individuality (rights) and communality (responsibilities) because the exercise of the self's full talents and abilities can serve the overall health of community. As those unique personality traits embellish collective life, the selves, in turn, continually fertilize the soil of the self. In fact, a vital part of the self's right is the inherent right to critique the community, the common values, and the common good. Ultimately, vigorous collective reappraisal and renewal engender the longevity of both self and selves. In sum, individual and privatized rights exist within group needs, and they exist to serve those needs.

The Gender Critique of Selves/Self

A gender critique facilitates shoring up the honesty and durability of community. Even though we have deliberated over general selves and self and touched on the specific divide between sectors of the wealthy and poor, women selves/self occupy a sector of caste domination within every stratum of corporate living. And if the criterion for a healthy, congruent relationality between selves and self reflects in the elevation of the very oppressed or disregarded peoples, then a look at the male and female gendered selves is in order.

Gender hierarchy subverts the affirmation of community, common values, and the common good. As Anna Mary Mukamwezi Kayonga of Uganda writes, Gen. 1:27 unveils the divinity fashioning "a crystal clear indication of the fundamental equality of the sexes. Each is the image of God, and equally so this divine image is complete only as reflected in both man and woman, not in the man alone."[67] Equality rewards the overall community when the male gender and the female gender are allowed full play in their unique individuality. One could also make a similar argument from nature and intelligence. In biology and sagacity, both genders live on par. Genotype and brains do not prescribe male prerogative.

Perpetrating male privilege delays one part of the human complement from being her full self. Abbreviating female self restricts it from adding even more resources, talents, abilities, imagination, and joy to the entire storehouse of total humanity. Curtailing female gender in particular forces a bright spotlight on how fracturing communal values (by suppressing equal individuality and enhancement of self-concept) not only structurally positions woman at the bottom but also deprives man of the fruits of what woman contributes out of her sacredly created purpose in life—to be a complete self for the common good. If woman were aided in her individuality and self-concept, man, children, and nature would all benefit. A new self and new common wealth will have to alter the values of privilege, power, and monopolization of wealth by elite men in addition to transforming the accompanying norm of "me first" at the expense of an Other. Here the other is woman.

Philomena N. Mwaura of Kenya examines the nature of patriarchal legitimization of woman's subordination. Antifemale values allow man to work and explore independently, while woman's ontological identity is subsumed "naturally" and by "divine" intent under motherhood and wife. Man leads and decides. Woman bears his children and nurtures him upon his return from the public domain. The asymmetrical gender perception and false role-playing bring definite consequences: "inequalities along gender lines"; "non-participation of women in leadership"; "unequal gender power relations"; "inculcation of feelings of inferiority within the girl child, older girls and women"; "apathy in women leading to few women aspiring to leadership positions in church and society"; "women's occupation of low decision making positions"; "low self-esteem"; "poverty and lack of economic empowerment"; "women's lack of legal and human rights"; and "girls' and women's inadequate access to education."[68]

The denigration of women is widespread. Nyambura J. Njoroge of Kenya paints a comprehensive portrait indicting patriarchy in all spheres of human creation: government, society, African (and other) indigenous religions, theological scholarship (inclusive of liberation theologies), and Christianity. She then recounts many women's acceptance of and participation in misogynistic systems resulting in violence by women against other women.[69] In fact, Christianity and its interpretations of the Bible are marked by steadfast justifications for woman's exploitation. From several Hebrew Scriptures prophets' rhetorical use of maiming, raping, and murdering women[70] to describe Yahweh's relation to a wayward Israel to Paul's insistence on the Christian Scriptures' injunction against women, from the Christian tradition's burning and impaling alleged Salem witches in New England to contemporary doctrine against women in the ministry and assignments of women clergy to toxic congregations, the "Word of God" and the "People of God" have left quite an abundance of damning data. In the poetic and cogent words of Mercy Amba Oduyoye, "women should not have a monopoly on the servant role. . . . We cannot assign the cross to half of humanity and the resurrection to the other half. Our theology of cross and resurrection must remain together."[71] Because female gender and male gender, motherhood and fatherhood are cultural and social concepts crafted by common consensus among the selves, the human community can recast them to resurrect one of the most oppressed among the oppressed and one of the most oppressed even among the nonoppressed segments of society.[72] The gender question exceeds the woman question. It challenges the very equilibrium between all selves and self.

The Self in Community

God-talk or human-talk about the human person's nature and condition must take into account the matrix of culture. According to Christian doctrine, a gracious divinity gave the gift of liberation to the poor and marginalized by way of human culture. Consequently, today's theological anthropological dialogues are helped when each interlocutor does not take for granted any meaning of culture, but instead enunciates her or his own definition.

These conversations likewise proceed with the understanding of real bodies doing and developing culture. Specific self and selves live out labor, the artistic, and the spirit. From that line of thinking, a fuller explanation of the self and selves flows. Due to Christian beliefs, nature, reason, and justice concerns, we prioritize the selves before the self. The selves, in turn, include the community, communal values, and the common good. We are all associates of some gathering beyond just the one person of the individual self. So community is a given. Communal values guide us into a theory of community. And both community and communal values project a future that features a converted individual self and a new common wealth. Along that journey, we struggle to balance the selves and self dynamic. Ultimately, we must ask: How do we forge life-giving relationships for the majority of oppressed people? Jacquelyn Grant provides insights to help us answer this question:

What we've learned recently from various expressions in liberation theology is that the recognition of the humanity of people must be a basic part of our search for the reigndom of God. Components of this sense of humanity are: (1) an affirmation of human dignity; (2) the practice of justice in human relationships; (3) the establishment of equality among human beings—men and women, differing racial and ethnic groups, etc.; (4) self-affirmation as a necessary category of human reality; (5) self-reliance, self-definition, and self-control as components of humanity; and (6) economic empowerment for historically oppressed peoples. Individual, social, economic, and political relationships are the focal points in determining the perceived humanity of individual persons and groups of people.[73]

4.

Race: Nature and Nurture

In the United States an obsession with race is deeply embedded in the concept of a human being. The 1607 Jamestown, Virginia, and 1620 Pilgrim, Massachusetts, arrivals of white Christians from Europe created a ranking in which human beings were placed on a racial scale in the so-called New World. This racial hierarchy inspired the Christian genocide of and land removal from American Indians, and the Christian enslavement of millions of Africans and African Americans in North America. These movements were marked by their color-coded aesthetics and power. Consequently, every single American, as well as those who visit the United States, receives a racial status within the anthropological hierarchy. And in the historical definition of the God–human interaction, race seeps in and out of the doctrine of theological anthropology.

Ideas of an individual self-identity and corporate designation acquire racial trappings. Despite perceptions of an individual's self-understanding, group demands and biases box in individual differences within color grids. The selves/self dynamic takes on the criterion of the uniquely American cultural fantasy of the one-drop rule: any person with "one drop" of African or black blood automatically becomes not white—or Hispanic/Latino(a), Native American, or Asian—but a black self. Whites have enforced this rule to police the boundaries of European American identity, aesthetics, and power. Blacks accede to the rule in order to increase their numbers within the public sphere of contested racialized human-made hierarchies.

Even when an African American person is white phenotypically, the black racial self emerges within human-fashioned definitions of colorized selves. Similarly, when a white person with one drop of "black" blood[1] volunteers for or is forced into blackness, one can only conclude that the concepts of selves/self, shrouded in race, result from culture. Therefore racial investigations flow from selves/self analyses after these analyses evolve out of theoretical considerations related to culture.

Moreover, any objective scholarly discussion of the contested voices among contemporary models of theological anthropology will uncover the explicitly or inexplicitly stated claims to racial privilege or the lack thereof. At all times, within these models, we encounter evasion or acceptance of this fact. The overwhelming majority of European American men rarely confess their racial identity in religious scholarship, yet that color trait determines their approaches to theological anthropology. In contrast, the progressives among white female theologians are quite comfortable in naming their culture as white women's culture. And blacks, Native Americans, Hispanics/Latinos(as), and Asian Americans are most readily willing to address the rainbow races of America. One reason derives from their celebration of racialized selves in order to embrace the beauty of their cultural particularities as contributions to a universal well-being. An additional reason is that failure to do so could yield psychic and physical harm if certain white phenotypical spaces are violated. Contemporary paradigms of theological anthropology, inherently and inevitably, drip with presuppositions about race.

Theological anthropology debates today occur because they already suppose beforehand an understanding of culture, self, and race. However, this understanding needs to be made explicit, for definitional clarity of the three component parts facilitates the construction of a theological anthropology.

Consequently, this chapter tackles the final, but not exhaustive, condition of possibility for a constructive statement on theological anthropology. To build a positive, normative, and instructive position on the God–human connection, especially in the U.S. landscape, necessitates a theoretical and historical engagement with race. Race presents, perhaps, the superlative overarching mark of what a human being is in the United States. At first glance, one can observe communities differentiated by simple racial categorizations with transparent indications accompanied by ideological and theological justifications. But in fact many communities struggle to claim the right to explicate race in their own terms. Theories abound. Historical narratives proliferate. And today the usage of race for societal and political leverage is ever more explicit.

We turn now to the foundational question: What is race and its variegated representations? To that end, we advance into the theories of race. In the reconfiguring of contemporary debates and the configuring of something new in theological anthropology, culture situates itself in the specificities of particular selves/self processes. Likewise, just as culture is bounded by selves/self interactions, these interactions in the United States, at least, always appear as racialized selves and self and colorized culture.

Theories of Race

Divergent but intersecting discourses on race persist. They are not simply the stringing together of descriptive words located in the superstructure or ideologies of human social interactions. But in their word connections they do signify a complete view of the world and a method of accumulating intellectual theories about diverse colored human beings. Furthermore, along these lines, the ideological or superstructural meaning suggests an entire way of knowledge allowing us to see a period of history, the textured analysis of human interaction, and a fixed but fluid approach to systems of ideas. Complementing the superstructural and ideological dimensions, theories of race adumbrate ethics and the material world. These theories can help or harm people.

First, we encounter the *rational* theory of race. Here the theorist assumes that all human beings inherently harbor an intellectual faculty capable of sorting out differences via reason. Thus, with conversation and argumentative logic, any reasonable person would arrive at an antiracism posture. Furthermore, and closely related in this argument, is the belief that racism follows a rational course. For instance, Kwame Anthony Appiah intimates that racism contains its own logic and its own inherent structure of thought.[2] Humans are rational creatures, and race pursues a rationality. Consequently, reasonable discursive rituals of engagement saturate both the analysis of interlocutors and the autonomy of the racial phenomenon.

The *psychological* theory of race offers the psychic dimensions in the race debate. In particular, according to this theory, white people embody a deep need for and rationalization of human phenotype differentiations.[3] Whites create a world or a culture reflective of their inner fantasies. Their inner desires give way to cultural formations that meet their psychic needs. The ego urges the self to fashion symbols complementing the repressed impulses of the ego with tangible acts of material results in a racialized hierarchy of human communities. The ego's fantasy drives and symbol-making allow people with power to craft inequitable systems in culture that incarnate the powerful's psychological visions.

The *political* theory of race welds notions of racial connections to the wielding and distribution of power within the civic and public spheres. White supremacy, like a demonic multipronged policy, monopolizes political power over Third World people domestically and internationally. The U.S. government and its rule over the affairs of its citizens (and increasingly over other nations' citizens in its role as political global empire) are anchored fundamentally in a racial political contract. The establishment of the United States at the 1787 Constitutional Convention in Philadelphia and the attendant American civil religious documents of the Declaration of Independence and Bill of Rights do not serve as objective, race-free enterprises, according to the political theory of race. Instead the theory posits that white supremacy itself is the racial contract upon which the nation stands.[4] The United States is a white political democracy whose coded public policies presuppose an understanding of white racial solidarity in matters of government. At its core, the U.S. government does nothing to radically alter the power of white privilege. The (white) racial contract fulfills its mission to take material resources, self-esteem, and land from Third World people domestically and abroad. The making of the white race is, in fact, by legal fiat. Race is a legal construction in America.[5]

An *economic* discourse in racial theory takes on the ties between monopolization of wealth and disproportionate possession of income on the part of white citizens. The concentration of great wealth belongs to a very small group of exclusive white families who influence, if not dominate, every major institution in America.[6] Thus, the majority of white Americans lack control of wealth. However, even in matters of income, white citizens, in total, control income out of proportion to their abilities if there were not a skewed, racialized economic playing field. In other words, one of the unstated public criteria for access to wealth and income is being a white person.

Furthermore, wealth and income differentiate into two distinct but complementary arenas. The reality of wealth means control of materialities such as huge farms, factories, land, banks, military businesses, buildings, airplanes, monopoly capitalist corporations, oil and other natural resources like gold, and so forth. By contrast, income results from one either selling one's labor or reaping proceeds from one's investment. For example, just imagine a man who owns an oil field and a man who works in a factory. When the first man retires, he still owns his oil field, which is wealth. When the second man retires, he might receive income from Social Security (if the federal government has not abolished it) and from retirement investments (if those elites who control the investment of working people's monies have not stolen their clients' retirement funds).[7]

Other race theories revolve around a cluster of concerns—that is, *geographical* origin, climate, melanin quotients, and essences. White and black races face a seemingly insurmountable wall of absolute divergence because white being comes from cold climates and certain land-masses of the earth, while black being originates from the opposite climate and very different continents. Consequently, melanin presence, due to geography and climate, is linked to race and is sometimes seen as marking the essence of the races. White and black people, and societies in general, arise and thrive relative to location or ontological differences.[8]

Certain *biblical* theories of interpretation provide explanations for diversified racial origins. Those who look to the Bible to explain race typically refer to Genesis 9, the so-called curse of Ham. Noah, as the story unfolds, is a drunkard and naked. His son Ham sees the father in an intoxicated hangover, and Noah curses Canaan, the son of Ham (and Noah's grandson) and his progeny to be slaves in perpetuity. European Christians subscribed to this conceptual posture during the Middle Ages and the Renaissance. Likewise, white supremacist Christians in the United States during slavery and American apartheid trumpeted this theological rationale for the subhuman creation of the black race.

Finally, in the *cultural* claim related to race, the ways of white folk and their system of white supremacy are merely part of a white racial reality derivative of European and European American cultures.[9]

These disparate theoretical voices on race attest to the ruminations of the different authors rather than objective scientific data. While theories supply intricate conceptual approaches, the scientific community, through objective investigations, lends additional credibility to race-talk. In other words, we can more deeply appreciate racial theorists' insights as long as we acknowledge one human race. And so we turn to the origin of the one human race for two reasons. First, the establishment of one biological race highlights further the cultural createdness of races in the U.S.A. Second, we document that objectively the entire globe is genetically African peoples. The fact that this knowledge is hidden from popular propagation is further proof of how individuals and groups with power can manipulate cultural inventions of current phenomena called "races."

One Human Race

Mounting evidence from archaeologists, geneticists, anthropologists, biologists, geologists, philologists, and paleontologists establishes the fact that the oldest precursors to the human race and the origin of what we understand as the human race come from the continent of Africa. In fact, the discussion and debates revolve around which regions or areas in Africa are the exact locations for the beginning of all humans who live on the earth today. Spencer Wells, previously connected with the Welcome Trust Centre for Human Genetics in Oxford, England, substantiates these claims in his book *The Journey of Man: A Genetic Odyssey*.[10] His findings clarify in a scientific and rational manner that genetic analysis indicates how all human gene pools evolved from Africa some sixty thousand years ago. Moreover, he argues that Y chromosomes in males prove the historical trace of African origins, because the Y chromosome remains intact as it is passed down through male offspring. Therefore he names Africa as the location for generating a "genetic Adam" for all peoples across the globe. The genetic Adam produced offspring who migrated throughout the world. To document his

conclusions, Spencer Wells collected blood samples from men throughout the planet.

Wells explains how the first African global migrations began sixty
thousand years ago and, even previous to this exodus, the first human
beings existed in Africa for 150,000 years before venturing out. Eventually, human beings departed from Africa and traveled to the east, cling-
ing to the southern coast of India and Eurasia. By fifty thousand years
ago, they had arrived in Australia. Wells goes on to argue for a second
exit wave from Africa, but now moving inland to Central Asia, where
one group broke off and began to settle in Europe thirty-five thousand
years ago. Another part of the East Asian migratory population, fifteen
to twenty thousand years ago, crossed the Bering Strait and colonized
North America. A male migratory ancestor from Africa forty-five thousand years ago left and settled in the northeast African peninsula (the
so-called Middle East).[11]

Complementing the genetic Adam research, other geneticists argue
for an "African Eve" as the mother of human beings. These scientists
explored mitochondrial DNA, which only the mother passes down
through her subsequent generations. Dr. Sarah Tishkoff, a biologist
at the University of Maryland, spearheaded a team of researchers who
reached this assessment. According to Dr. Tishkoff's study, the mitochondrial genome acts as the basis for all subsequent and current varia-
tions in genome types. Thus we all relate back to an African Eve as the
mother of the one human race. In a related research effort, Dr. Lynn B.
Jorde at the University of Utah and his colleagues at the University of
Helsinki and Pennsylvania State University likewise examined critically
mitochondrial DNA, the fundamental carrier of human DNA. Their
method was to study groups of Asians, Africans, and Europeans. Similarly, they discovered that Africans are the oldest human population on
the earth.[12]

In contrast to this "out of Africa" scientific research, a few theorists had offered China as the seat of the origin of humanity. However,
the scientific community in China has apparently made these claims
moot. Dr. Li Jin, a professor at the National Human Genome Center in Shanghai, the Institute of Genetics of Fudan University, and the
University of Texas, worked with other Chinese scholars and found that
Africans migrated about sixty thousand years ago to Southeast Asia and

then divided into two migratory patterns. One went north to China, and the second headed to Indonesia and eventually on to Oceania.[13]

The debate among the scientific community therefore seems not to be mainly over whether Africa is the origin of the one human race, but to be about where in Africa this beginning took place. Archaeologist and anthropologist Dr. Albert Churchward maintains that humans evolved two million years ago in the Great Lakes region in Central Africa. In 1963 Mary Leakey, a paleontologist, discovered human fossils approximately 1.75 million years old in East Africa. Just two years later Dr. John Martyn, a geologist, uncovered human skull remains in Kenya's Great Rift Valley. These remains were 2.4 million years old.[14] And Dr. Eric Higgs, from the University of Alberta in Canada, investigated the migration patterns of ancient humans and surmised that the first European had migrated from east or central Africa.

Furthermore, two British Museum of Natural History anthropologists, Christopher B. Stringer and Peter Andrews, have presented compelling evidence for the single origin theory. According to their theory, *Homo sapiens* developed from an African *Homo erectus* population roughly two hundred thousand years ago. The latter then moved on to Asia and Europe around a hundred thousand years later. By way of comparison, the two scientists substantiate the fact that the oldest Western Europe human fossils are a mere thirty-five thousand years old.[15]

Other scientists offer the Ethiopians as the ancestors of the East Africans, thereby positioning the start of humanity in northeast Africa, while still another camp has proposed the oldest archaeological digs in southern Africa as proof of a southern African prehistoric start. More specifically, the anthropologist Raymond Dart found the skull of a human predecessor in South Africa in 1924. Furthermore, a 1997 skull and skeleton discovery in South Africa was dated at 3.5 million years old, and French paleontologist Michel Brunet of the University of Poitiers found in Chad fossil remains of a human ancestor dating over 3.5 million years.[16]

Thus multifaceted theories of race operate within the larger biological reality of one human race. The crucial caveat for any investigation of racial conceptual constructs is that theories have explanatory power insofar as one is aware of an objective biological fact of human unity.

The Garden of Eden

To further our discussion of the human being's origin, Christian discourse, if taken seriously, can advance the point of one human race. Faith claims on the God–human interaction could open up additional analytical takes on the human race's beginning. At this juncture of explaining Africa as the parent of all humankind, we argue for science and religion complementing one another.

For that purpose, let us now move to the notion of the Garden of Eden. Within the American Christian narrative, the Garden of Eden suggests an important place for how and where God consciously chose to reveal the divine self to humankind. And whether Eden's location is mythology, theology, or science, Christianity privileges the story of the Garden because the entire religious understanding of God's revelation to humankind hinges on the origins of the human race coming directly from divine manufacturing.

The biblical narrative provides a picture of the divinity directly offering an image and likeness of the divine self in the soul and body of woman and man. If we can ascertain insights about what type of individuals were the original people in the Garden and where the Garden was most plausibly located, then we might draw conclusions about the intentionality of God's fashioning the one (biological) human family.[17]

Genesis 2:10-14 mentions four rivers in connection with the Garden of Eden: the Pishon, the Gihon, the Tigris, and the Euphrates. The Gihon River flows in the land of Cush (today's Ethiopia and Sudan). The Tigris and the Euphrates bodies of water run through Syria and Iraq, two countries joined to Africa prior to the building of the Suez Canal.[18]

Dr. David Adamo of Nigeria, professor of biblical and religious studies and author of several works on the Old Testament, believes scientific evidence aids in situating Eden in Africa. According to Adamo, the possible African location of Eden is supported

> by modern science in their discoveries. . . . In 1984, the American Shuttle (NASA), through its powerful microscope was able to penetrate beyond the earth land surface while in space. The result was a

startling discovery of "an old river system complete with valley and channel and channel and gravel and sand bar that had been covered with sand sheet" in the southern portion of Egypt. This system, according to the Sir-A-Images, was as "large and as complex as the present Nile river." . . .

In cooperation with the Geological Survey of Egypt and U.S. Agency for International Development, Cairo, and U.S.G.S. [U.S. Geological Survey], scientists have visited the location of the ancient river and have dug test pits in the ancient river and stream beds for verification of the Sir-A data. Along the radar detected river were hand axes and ash layers which are the evidence of the presence of pre-historic people who "migrated to Europe following the river path."[19]

Therefore, it seems that a likely location for Eden is Africa. However, Dr. Modupe Oduyoye of Nigeria, a philologist, raises questions about the existence of a factual Garden of Eden because he wants more proof of how the four rivers connect. (Oduyoye's opinion was written thirteen years before Adamo published his research. It would be interesting to know Oduyoye's response to Adamo's later evidence.) Whether or not the rivers connected in actual history is an open question for Oduyoye. But he does sense the power of linking the four rivers for theological purposes or Christian mythology.

Despite his request for additional proof, Oduyoye implies that Africa's presence is linked to the Garden of Eden. Philology proves key for him. Oduyoye offers two reasons for Africa's presence. First, the book of Genesis specifically cites the names of regions of Africa where some of the rivers flowed. Second, Oduyoye claims that the Semitic language (the system of sounds and symbols connected to Hebrew and the original Israelites) is part of a larger family of African languages. Thus the language used to describe the four rivers is an African-related discourse.[20]

If Africa is the location of a paradise where the first humans received divine revelation, then perhaps it can lead us to some clarity on God's creation of one human race. Even if one believes Eden is mythology, still the writers of this Bible story included several of Eden's rivers as being in Africa geographically or linguistically.

We might now ask, if all people around the world originate from one race out of Africa, how did the notion of one common human race transform into the normative definition of a white supremacist racial hierarchy globally? To answer this question, we must address the concept of race within American culture historically and today.

Race in the United States

Clearly, scientific and theological theories have countered the societal construction arguments about race with the claim that, in the biological sense, only one human race inhabits the world *Homo sapiens* family. In my analysis, combining both perspectives brings us closer to the correct understanding of race.

Within the parameters of the United States, culture and the selves/ self dynamic are greatly determined, if not over-determined, by race. Race results from combining both *biological* and *sociological* traits. Certain biological phenotype attributes are given by nature (or created by God) and have been societally labeled as black in the United States. Yet these same features in another country and culture would not be identified as black. For instance, some American blacks with light skin would become, in the global dispersion, Algerian, "coloured" (in South Africa), mulatto (in Brazil), brahmin (in Asia), or Samoan (in the Pacific Islands). Yet because of the unique sociohistorical and politico-cultural power of white Americans (descendants from Europe) and the subsequent move on the part of black people (descendants from Africa) to embrace that which was considered evil (that is, blackness and Africanness), race evolves from both natural, God-given phenotype and accepted social designation.

Science provides further insight into the varieties of global racial designations: "Geneticists have shown that 85 percent of all genetic variation is between individuals within the same local population. A further 8 percent is between local populations or groups within what is considered to be a major race. Just 7 percent of genetic variation is between major races."[21] There exists, therefore, more genetic variation among black/African persons than between white/European persons and black/African persons. Race, in a cultural matrix, is a social construction. White Americans initiated the dynamic of racial categorization to maintain white supremacy.

The black American philosopher Charles W. Mills underscores the contrived nature of race revealed in the categorized constituents of racial definition. Mills lays out seven criteria invented for defining race in contemporary U.S. society; these elements usually overlap. He cites bodily appearance, ancestry, self-awareness of ancestry, public awareness of ancestry, culture, experience, and subjective identification.[22] These attributes substantiate my definition of American racism as a syncretism of biological phenotype and social designation.

In addition to conceptual clarifications, theological anthropology must take on the discourse of race because God interacts with human beings through culture in specific collective selves and the individual self. The single self and corporate selves receive transcendent spirits in the existing racialized preoccupation and obsession in U.S. racialized culture. I define these spirits[23] as a contested terrain occupied by a spirit of liberation of the poor versus a demonic oppressive spirit.

And so, on the one hand, God has created the phenotypes of race. Biologically and naturally, some are born into the world with distinctly identifiable appearances. No human engineering can erase completely these given racial characteristics. On the other hand, in the cultural configuration of the United States, human beings live out the spoken and unspoken omnipresence of predetermined racial classification all the time. The color line permeates the broad and the narrow, the major and the minor, the space and the time dimensions of what it means to live in North America. In fact, an American, by definition, is a racial being. The God–human connection (that is, the created definition and vocational sacred purpose of what it means to be a full human) centers on racial selves and self.

In my theory of race for the American reality, not only is race reflective of a combined phenotype (that is, biological traits) and cultural givens (the one-drop rule), but a theory of race also presupposes a spirituality of white supremacy. Such a demonic spirit consists of three component parts: racial *identity* ("free, white, and twenty-one") is linked directly to *aesthetics* (beauty) and *power* (who has it and who does not). "The 'spirituality' of a people," argues Peter J. Paris, "refers to the animating and integrative power that constitutes the principal frame of meaning for individual and collective experiences. Metaphorically, the

spirituality of a people is synonymous with the soul of a people: the inte-
grating center of their power and meaning."[24] The spirituality or soul
of a people has both positive and negative dimensions. The structural
manifestation of the soul of white power has been white supremacy.
Fortunately, within that systemic and meta-daily reality, one discovers
race traitors—those of European descent who consciously risk opting
out of the larger racist spirituality in favor of liberation of working-class
people, the poor, and the oppressed of all colors globally and domestically.[25]

The spirituality of white supremacy was crafted out of history and
created into something new in the United States. This spirituality burst
forth from materiality but transcends each individual white person and
subsequent white generations. It is immanent and immediate and lives
on across time and is fed by its own rapacious internal drive for more
power, privileges, and perks. Consequently, to be sane in America is
to simply agree that white people's perpetual position at the top of the
racial hierarchy is normal. Of course, only the mad would dispute this
normative assertion.

The first of the three components of a white supremacist spirituality,
racial identity, is a conscious and unconscious sense of self that affects
how one views oneself, others, and the world and how one goes about
participating in one's relation to wealth, health, and personal relationships. *Aesthetics* is a perception of value, a normative judgment resulting in a hierarchical ranking, thereby attributing goodness and badness.
And *power* highlights the ability to bring about desired results through
a monopolization of the military, money, missionaries, and the media.
Any objective observation of the U.S. system will conclude that white
identity, aesthetics, and power are norms. Even more so, now that U.S.
white supremacist spirituality is the sole imperialist superpower across
the earth, under the sea, and in space, one can feel immediately its
unchecked performance in the Third World and even in its unilateral
operations independent of its (supposedly) European allies' wishes.

Now that the Union of Soviet Socialist Republics no longer exists
and so cannot criticize[26] this spirituality's heinous violations against
black, brown, red, and yellow peoples, tax dollars and wealth are rap-
idly being redistributed upward to the elite (white male) monopoly
economic barons. Similarly, lacking a countervailing superpower pub-

licizing U.S. domestic human rights violations, this adverse spirituality has intensified violations of the rights of citizens whom the federal
government deems as circumventing a patriotic act. The structure of
the nation has been altered, appearing to override the contested claims
of both Democratic and Republican Parties' explanatory propaganda
departments. Epoch-structural shifts have unfolded while the official
political parties execute distracting chatter about surface issues.

Today's reigning status of race (with its biological-sociological syncretism and white supremacist spirituality) heralds from a historical trajectory and complex genealogy created by the evolution of imposed
values on black and white, dark and light colors. The tracking of this
process, therefore, is warranted. As we pursue this mapping, we must
remember the following fact: in the United States, because an asymmetrical system and warped morality persist in positioning whites at
the apex, American "races" are human creations. The good news is that
whites will not monopolize normalcy ad infinitum. Just as humans created the system and the morality, humans can participate in totally dis-
mantling it and establishing a new individual self and common wealth.
The practice of freedom for all comes to fruition by training color-des-
ignated individuals away from selfish interest and toward enhancing the
humanity of those who differ, especially the marginalized, the poor, and
the working class.

Race: The History of an Idea

Today's understanding of races as biologically determined comes from
the modern debates and refinements occurring during intellectual developments in seventeenth-, eighteenth-, and nineteenth-century Europe
and the United States. Prior to this decisive historical era, race was preceded by observations of color contrasts that took on a fluid variety of
incarnations from the thirteenth century BCE until the modern period
in Europe. Therefore, while tracing the origin of race classifications in
European narratives, one has to make a distinction between the beginnings of simple racial dissimilarities of ancient times and the more
refined white supremacist writings of white male intellectuals from later
Europe and their elite offspring in the United States. The purpose of
looking at race, the history of an idea, is to observe an ancient soil that

provided the historical seeds out of which European men of European modernity could then reach back in tradition and point to past human differentiations to justify racial hierarchies that still affect us in the present. A genealogical review of race can facilitate a comprehension of that idea today.

Robert E. Hood terms the thirteenth-century BCE stance on color as the "beginnings of a Greek black aesthetic."[27] "Figures with Negroid (Africanoid) features appeared in Greek art as early as the thirteenth century B.C.E.," writes Hood.[28] And Greek mercenaries settled in Egypt in the seventh century BCE. Consequently, a heightened contrast between Greeks and Africans ensued from the sixth century BCE on.

At this time, Greek mythology conjured up half-human and half-beast figures called satyrs. Most peculiar, for our purposes, are the Negroid features—"thick lips, broad noses, and wooly hair." Moreover, Greek cosmology consistently portrayed these African human–beast creatures as engaged in various forms of lustful, erotic acts. Whether Greek thought in the thirteenth to the sixth centuries BCE merely described Greek psychological fantasies projected onto African peoples or whether the painting of the Negroid features signified a pejorative slight against African peoples remains contested. What is clear is that the Greek exposure to and mercenary settlement among African peoples in Egypt led to a categorization of contrasting phenotypes linked to a reputed African primal craving for ongoing sex. Aesthetically, one surmises the beginnings of Greek beauty in contrast to African/Negroid primordial instincts (according to the Greeks' classification of Africans).

After the Greek conquering of the Persians in the fifth century BCE, ethnocentrism and racial concepts emerged. For example, Euripides (circa 485–406 BCE) became one of the first to advance a Greek racial supremacist ideology when he labeled all foreigners as slaves and servile by nature and all Greeks free persons and superior by virtue of being Greek. With a minor caveat, the biblical scholar Gerhard Kittel acknowledges the possibility that blackness was positively symbolized during ancient times. Yet he also underlines the emergence of a negative moral dimension associated with blackness, which "meant or at least implied negative qualities in the sense of sinister, dreadful, terrible, unlucky."[29]

Here ethnocentric differentiation allowed for Greek identity to assume elevated texture over all non-Greek ethnic groups. At the same time, we must be careful to note that ethnocentric hierarchy and Greek racial discriminations do not equate ancient Greek arrogance with the modern European white supremacist cementing of permanent distinctions among races based on divinely or naturally created phenotype of superiority-inferiority. The Greek conceptions maintained a much more dynamic stance on black and white contrasts. Rather than simply always linking black to dark-skinned peoples and white to their opposites, the two colors represented light and dark relative to the day and night.[30] Ambiguous color categorizing manifested in other instances. While Herodotus (480 BCE) praised the military prowess of Ethiopians, other Greek scholars, such as Ptolemy at a later date, constructed a typology of shades of blackness found among different African communities. In addition to crafting a classification, they also invented new words to describe the variety of black skin colors they encountered among African peoples.[31]

On the philosophical front, both Greek thinkers Plato (427–347 BCE) and Aristotle (384–322 BCE) laid the basis for future racial hierarchies. Plato's *Republic* shifted the subject from one involved with the world in which she or he lives to one who approaches the world and others as object, resulting in the need to control that which is different. Previously one attained knowledge through intimate involvement and sympathetic participation with that which was studied. Now the one studied becomes objectified in order for the one studying to control the object. Moreover, Plato splits the human person into reason, appetite, and emotion. Obviously, as the tradition of dominant European male history of ideas bears out, such a division privileges the anointed male Greek philosopher with his self-normalized faculty of reason. Elite free males embody, writes Plato in his *Republic*, "the desires that are simple, measured, and directed by calculation in accordance with understanding and correct belief only in the few people who are born with the best natures and receive the best education," in contrast to the majority of the people filled with "diverse desires, pleasures, and pains, mostly in children, women, household slaves, and those in the inferior majority who are called free."[32] Dichotomies give rise to hierarchies that give rise to normative valuations.

Plato's method was also part of Aristotle's thought. Ancient Greek writings had portrayed the world constituted by two extremes—the white, straight-haired, blue-eyed Scythian in the northern hemisphere and the black Ethiopian with woolly hair in the south. But Aristotle (in his *Politica* and *De generatione animalium*) deepened these opposites when he argued for the superior intelligence of the white, straight-haired, blue-eyed Scythians by disparaging Ethiopians' woolly hair and brains.[33] Furthermore, according to Aristotle (in his *Physiognomics*), "Egyptians and Ethiopians possessed a character trait of cowardice . . . because of their black . . . complexion."[34]

These ambiguous ideas of color contrasts reflected in an asymmetry of aesthetics, ethnocentric distinctions seen in identity formation, and racial superiority symbolized in power distribution would lay the basis for white supremacist intellectuals of the European modern period to argue for ancient justification for a permanent white supremacy. Future centuries' perspectives on race could draw on and nurture the seeds of racial superiority elements from as far back as the thirteenth century BCE.

An examination of Rome in the first century BCE and first century CE uncovers a continuation of upper-crust thinkers demarcating black Africans from the given status of Roman superiority. Though ambiguity persists here and though male white supremacy of European modernity does not obtain, still ancient Romans maintained an impulse of difference between them and Africans. One example indicates the usage of African pygmies as servants and entertainers for the Roman ruling classes. Latin poets, in another instance, portrayed "white as a sign of divinity and [good] luck while black was a sign of dread and bad luck."[35] And, like Greek ideas, Latin culture perceived an inordinate amount of sexual potency and pervasive eroticism associated with Africans because they were Africans, even to the extent of accusing African men of seducing Roman women. In sum, Roman intellectual elites (such as Virgil [c. 70–19 BCE] and Cicero [106–143 CE]) posited and developed a superior aesthetic over African peoples that both aided the formation of Roman identity and eventually justified Roman use of power to colonize northern Africa as a result of the Punic Wars in 146 BCE.

With the rise of Christianity in the first century CE, a rigidity of paralleling color with character set in. Ancient Christianity adopted the surrounding Greco-Roman cultural symbols. Gay L. Byron,[36] cognizant of this broader ethos and studying Christian documents from the first through the sixth centuries CE, argues that Egypt, Ethiopia, and blackness were rhetorical figures of speech deployed by some early Christian writers to separate Christian orthodoxy from heretical identities stained by bodily passions, lustful sex, and other sins. And the denigration of blacks, Egyptians, and Ethiopians was not exclusively associated with race or ethnicity. In other words, the negative implications of blackness and African countries (such as equating them with demons, evil, general licentiousness, specific temptations of Ethiopian women, and ugliness) were used by some authors of Christian literature not only to subordinate blackness but also to mark any deviations from the Christian status quo. Still, interesting is the fact that *black* was chosen as the color for all non-Christians without favorable features.

During the European Middle Ages (roughly 400 to 1400), three fundamental factors enhanced the rise of the Christian community's negative association of blackness with people of darker hues. The first was the Muslim military victories over Christian lands and colonization of holy sites during the seventh through the fifteenth centuries, but especially during the early twelfth century. The dark complexion of the Muslim conquerors indicated to the Christians that the former's God had cursed them. Particularly irksome was the loss of Jerusalem. Similarly, the Moorish victory over and control of Christian Europe (that is, Rhodes, Cyprus, Sicily, southern Italy, and seven hundred years over Spain) further added to the Christian mythology of dark phenotype resulting from supernatural condemnation. The Islamic or non-Christian "infidels," because they opposed the true and only representatives of God on earth, had to be emissaries from Satan. Thus theological discourse justified both Christian loss of land and wealth and religious identity. By rallying against and demonizing another religion, the church filled in the textures of its own self-understanding. Only with the potency of the Devil could the nonfaithful overpower and rule Christian space. Accompanying the process of identity formation and struggle for material power were the growing European Middle Ages' iconographic and aesthetic depictions of Satan, demons, and the Antichrist (a title focused on the Moors) as black or displaying African features.[37]

The Plague or, as European Christians came to call it, the Black Death spread throughout Europe between 1347 and 1349; 30 to 50 percent of the population was lost.

The European slave trade in African bodies stands as the third formative factor influencing demeaning perceptions of black people. In 1441 the first group of Africans left the West African coast bound for Portugal. Upon the ship's return to its home port, the Africans were given as trinkets to Prince Henry, sovereign of a Christian country. Portugal held the first slave auction in 1444. Subsequently, other Catholic states (such as Spain and France) and Protestant countries (such as England and Holland) joined in the physical hunt for the sale of black skins. Consequently, popes blessed the European slave trade, and both Catholic and Protestant clergy accompanied the slave vessels that went forth to do the work of Jesus in Africa.

The first boat of enslaved Africans to reach England arrived in 1555. Initially, Queen Elizabeth looked with disdain on the enslavement of black flesh, but she relented once she calculated the immense profit to be made.[38] Thus we note that the appearance of enslaved Africans in England and the heinous attitudes of the English toward blackness can be established well before the two colonial English settlements in Jamestown, Virginia (1607), and Plymouth, Massachusetts (1620). For example, the Oxford English Dictionary provides the following understanding of *black* in the fifteenth century: "deeply stained with dirt; soiled, dirty, foul. . . . Having dark or deadly purposes, malignant, pertaining to or involving death, deadly; baneful, disastrous, sinister . . . foul, iniquitous, atrocious, horrible, wicked . . . indicating disgrace, censure, liability to punishment, etc."[39] So white Christians in the seventeenth-century colonies in Virginia and Massachusetts came from a culture and society in which enslaved Africans and associations of blackness with evil already existed. The first English colonies were not, therefore, innocent adventurers who automatically accepted the first group of Africans as indentured servants or possessing equality with whites.

Thus different religious countries in the Middle Ages underwent increasing negative stereotyping of Africans and darker-skinned peoples. At the same time, Europeans began to associate black with chaos, evil, sin, madness, and disorder.[40] The virulent racism created by elite men of the European modernity (by way of philosophy, anthropology, and missiology, among other things) should not be confused, how-ever, with the wicked and atrocious associations with African phe-notype in the medieval period. The Middle Ages created part of the aesthetic, identity, and power basis for the modern creation of racism, but its demeaning treatment of blacks did not equal a sustained body of knowledge around, conventional practices against, and wealth reaped from modern notions of racism. Even in the Middle Ages there existed some instances of paralleling blackness with sanctification. This sweep of time did harbor disparate forms of ethnocentrism, xenophobia, and beliefs in cultural superiority. But at that time Europe had no con-sciousness of or term for race as we know it today.[41]

With the rise of European modernity, signified by late-fifteenth-cen-tury voyages to the so-called New World and the subsequent Christian conquest of the Americas, genocide against the indigenous populations, and institutionalization of the European slave trade in black people from different African empires,[42] human history changed forever.[43] Certainly by the beginning of the sixteenth century, race had definitively replaced religious and ethnocentric markers as the dominant human categori-zation. Specifically, the aesthetic shift appears in Hieronymous Bosch's *Garden of Earthly Delights* (1500), in which color symbolism not only links the color white with moral purity and black with evil, but likewise correlates color and morality with absolute racial differences.[44]

It is no accident, therefore, that massive wealth was systematically stolen from the darker peoples of the Third World with the rise of mod-ern white supremacy in Europe. "At the start of the nineteenth century, Europe had colonized 35 percent of the non-European world, yet by the beginning of the First World War, after a century in which racism spread into the academic disciplines, Europe had colonized 85 percent of the world."[45] Elite white men (who claimed objective, rational, calm, and detached reason) provided the intellectual justification for the ter-rorist removal of dark indigenous people's land, human bodies, water, cultural artifacts, ancestral bones, inventions, and natural treasures. More specifically, *philosophy, anthropology,* and *missiology* (that is, intel-lectual, scientific, and Christian grounds) are three conditions for the possibility of modern racism: the conscious and consistent belief in and ritualization of the subordination of darker-skinned people to demar-cate permanent differentiation between the polar extremes of white and black. Dark skin color now inherently reveals mental, genetic, and moral deficiencies.

Philosophy

The European Enlightenment produced privileged white men who expounded extended opinions on the nature of being and the world. Usually ignored or covered up are these thinkers' views of Africans and darker-skinned humans. The key issue here is to realize that all of these writings by the so-called brilliant philosophers of Europe privileged upper-class white men. Others, such as women, blacks, the indentured, workers, and so forth, could partake of bourgeois democracy once a select group of white men secured their place as owners of wealth and other people's labor. Drawing on their ancestors and, in some cases, blood kin, North American white men used the lessons from their counterparts in the European Enlightenment and wrote the American Declaration of Independence and U.S. Constitution also for white elite men. These two bourgeois-democratic documents have been modified subsequently by way of interpretation and amendments. But the fact remains that, just like their Enlightenment brethren, the founding fathers founded the United States of America for white wealthy men. Women, blacks, the indentured, workers, and others come into the picture and are placed into an already-existing asymmetrical framework after the wealthy white men secure their status. Philosophical opinions on both sides of the Atlantic worked to this end.

The German thinker Immanuel Kant waxed on in his work about religion, reason, moral imperatives, and overthrowing authorities restricting the advancement of people's thought and being. But Kant was talking primarily about himself and other privileged European men. In his 1764 *Observations on the Feeling of the Beautiful and Sublime*, he wrote:

> The Negroes of Africa have by nature no feeling that rises above the trifling. Mr. Hume challenges anyone to cite a single example in which a Negro has shown talents, and asserts that among the hundreds of thousands of blacks who are transported elsewhere from their countries, although many of them have even been set free, still not a single one was ever found who presented anything great in art or science or

any other praiseworthy quality, even though among the whites some continually rise aloft from the lowest rabble, and through superior gifts earn respect in the world. So fundamental is the difference between these two races of man, and it appears to be as great in regard to mental capacities as in color.[46]

Kant drew on the work of David Hume, an Englishman, to craft a male white supremacy philosophy. Hume's own theoretical abstractions lend further credence to the development of modern white racism. In his 1748 and 1754 essay "On National Characters," Hume wrote:

I am apt to suspect the negroes and in general all other species of men (for there are four or five different kinds) to be naturally inferior to the whites. There never was a civilized nation of any other complexion than white, nor even any individual eminent either in action or specu-lation. No ingenious manufactures amongst them, no arts, no sciences. On the other hand, the most rude and barbarous of the whites, such as the ancient Germans, the present Tartars, have still something eminent about them, in their valour, form of government, or some other partic-ular. Such a uniform and constant difference could not happen, in so many countries and ages if nature had not made an original distinction between these breeds of men. Not to mention our colonies, there are negroe slaves dispersed all over Europe, of whom none ever discovered any symptoms of ingenuity; though low people without education will start up amongst us and distinguish themselves in every profession. In Jamaica, indeed, they talk of one negroe as a man of parts and learning; but it is likely he is admired for slender accomplishments, like a parrot who speaks a few words plainly.[47]

Both philosophers offer a stark conclusion. By natural development or biological creation, white folk are superior in their intellect, their aes-thetics, and their right to power over darker-skinned peoples globally.

Similarly, the English thinker John Locke advanced rational opin-ions on "race, slavery, property, the just war, and their influence on the emerging Enlightenment" with the effect of justifying the European slave trade in Africans and the racial system of bondage in the English colonies in America. Locke was more than a scholar; as the secretary to the Carolina Proprietors of South Carolina, he "played a key role in drafting both that colony's Fundamental Constitution of 1669 and the Instructions to Governor Nicholson of [colonial] Virginia." This white supremacist thinker was a white supremacist colonial administrator. And Locke looms large among elite male thinkers of that historic intellectual turn toward modern racism; indeed, his personal speculations pervaded the entire Enlightenment era and decisively affected many notables, including David Hume.[48]

The Frenchman Charles-Louis Montesquieu wielded immense influence on the thirteen British colonies with his treaties regarding (bourgeois) democratic government and political liberty. Nevertheless, his stances dripped with racial bias, exemplified in his 1784 *The Spirit of the Laws*. Advocating freedom for European elites, Montesquieu argued in favor of personal and political slavery for Africans and Asians. He perceived a direct connection between intelligence and climate; he believed there was "reasonable" evidence that hot climates produced races obsessed with "bodily pleasures and sloth" while cold climates yielded races of high intelligence. Moreover, the *Laws* decried the black body as ugly, and Montesquieu speculated whether his rational Christian God would have inserted a soul into such a dark being. He thereby questioned whether black folk were even humans.[49]

The French writer Voltaire likewise thought about equality and democracy; he has been considered white elites' paragon of modernity. But he, too, prioritized his race and accented the males in that race. In 1734 Voltaire opposed the prevailing ecclesial doctrine of biological monogenesis—the church's claim of human oneness from creation. Likewise, John Locke asserted polygenesis. Whites, blacks, and yellow races, in his view, originated from different ancestors and hence signified completely separate races. And whites, in his words, "are superior to these Negroes." David Hume was also a polygenesist.[50]

In sum, philosophy helped to engender modern racism in various ways. First, eighteenth-century male thinkers revived notions of aesthetics from their intellectual ancestors in classical Greece. Aesthetics, in Greek experience, deemed the beautiful as that which exhibited proportion and symmetry. In addition, the perfect subject who embodied these values actually revealed ontological value. Therefore, aesthetics existed not as an objective, neutral discipline or worldview. On the contrary, it denoted a hierarchy of value, with free Greek males at the top.

Eighteenth-century theoreticians glued ancient Greek thought on essential beauty to a hierarchy of race. Europeans possessed the supreme phenotypical proportions and, hence, naturally occupied the superior heights among the diversified global anthropologies of humankind. One's very being was constituted by an already given definition of what it meant to be fully human. The philosophical notion of symmetrical appearance from ancient Greece was wedded to a fixed notion of asymmetrical social races. Whites stood for perfection; blacks stood for deformity. In a similar manner and toward the same end, nineteenth-century male thinkers in Germany drew on ancient Greek and Roman ideals to fashion a contemporary aesthetics of cultural purity known as German romanticism.[51]

In addition to natural aesthetics, philosophy fostered modern racism in the domain of identity. Here, too, modern men drew lessons from their Greek male ancestors to forge a white identity. How does one assess the white and the nonwhite? What personality traits offer themselves? What underscores advanced white civilization? What justifies this inherent superiority? For the racialized reasoning of the philosophers, Aristotle offered a response to these queries in his *Politics*:

> The races that live in the cold regions and those of Europe are full of courage and passion but somewhat lacking in skill and brainpower; for this reason, while remaining generally independent, they lack political cohesion and the ability to rule others. On the other hand, the Asiatic races have both brains and skill but are lacking in courage and will-power; so they have remained both enslaved and subject. The Hellenic race, occupying a mid position geographically, has a measure of both. Hence it has continued to be free, to have the best political institution and to be capable of ruling others given a single constitution.[52]

Modern theoreticians took these speculations as warrant for European countries to enslave darker-skinned peoples. However, they had to devise convoluted conceptualizations to achieve this conclusion, since Aristotle, in his parochial but honest attempt, actually limited perfected identity to Greece and even relegated northern European disposition to a lower position in the human hierarchy. Nevertheless, the moderns deployed their objective, calm, and rational thought in such a way as to situate all of Europe at the pinnacle of human personality. They resurrected and reconstructed the ancient world for modern white supremacy.

Enlightenment philosophers combined aesthetics and identity with power. The three factors yielded absolute racial superiority of white Europe against the darker peoples of the world. Dissertations and essays on white beauty and sense of self did not merely reflect an abstract history of ideas stretching back to Greece and Rome. An aestheticized identity served to undergird the political and economic power Europe squeezed out of the black bodies in the European slave trade in Africans and the subsequent raping of Africa, Asia, the Caribbean, Latin America, and the Pacific Islands for prime land and precious resources. Elite white (Christian) men in Europe, starting with Portugal's 1441 West African coast contact and Columbus's 1492 unplanned arrival on the American Indians' continent, seemed to have received a boost in their rapacious appetite for global raw materials and workers. The eighteenth-century Enlightenment philosophical ideology of conquest provided that boost.

In fact, elite white men did form a conscious conspiracy at a conference in Berlin in 1884 and 1885 at which these same types of capitalist regimes carved up Africa into false states and negotiated which European "democracies" owned which African territories. The centuries surrounding and inclusive of the Enlightenment symbolize the largest transfer of international wealth in the history of humankind. The philosophical aesthetics of perfected identity accompanied and rationalized the stealing of bodies and materials from the darker peoples of the Third World into the coffers of Europe and the thirteen British colonies and subsequent United States of America.[53] Perhaps a divine spirit had indeed fashioned the world in the image of Europe and North America. And the remainder of the globe, which comprised the overwhelming majority of the earth's citizens (a majority that happened to inhabit darker skin), had been left out or left behind in this spirit's theological anthropology.

Indeed, talk of the spirit flooded the analytical musings of another sacred cow of European and North American aesthetics, identity, and power. Georg Wilhelm Friedrich Hegel (1770–1831), a German philosopher of history, combined the "transcendental speculative with the racialized historical" to situate once again the white spirit/intellect at the peak of human creation, thought, and activity. Each of the world's people, for Hegel, marks a dialectical process of their spirit/reason moving through history. Therefore, world history reveals spirit/reason traveling through history to fulfill its (spirit/reason's) destiny. Progress results from spirit/reason traversing sequentially across various levels of human development. "History passes through despotism and error as it ascends towards freedom, religion and absolute knowledge. Consciousness also passes through intellectual despotism (the master/slave and priest/penitent relations) as it travels that same dialectical path towards freedom. Consciousness and history go through the same stages of development, in the same order," wrote Hegel.[54]

Both spirit/reason and history merge into an inevitable conclusion from the primitive social encounter to the superlative civilization. In Hegel's feelings, the so-called Orientals occupy stage one with their despotic tyranny immersing reason in nature. Next comes Greek-Roman infancy with imperfect freedom; that is, exhibiting the consciousness of freedom where freedom separates from nature. But only with Hegel and his Germans (via their experiences of Christianity) does human growth attain perfection. Here one discovers universal freedom when the spirit of reason becomes self-conscious of its essential nature as freedom. A transcendental spirit and reason journey through a racialized history from Asia, through lower stages of Europe, to German philosophy as king of speculative humanity. From Asian lack of freedom (that is, despotism) to Teutonic absolute reason (that is, authentic freedom), history evolves from the barbaric to the advanced. Thus both spirit/reason and history are racialized across the materiality of time, space, and place.

But where is Africa? Hegel, in line with the theoreticians of his day, assigned Africa outside of human history. Africans were even below a primitive human definition. Africa, for Hegel, had no reason or spirit or history because the continent did not feature any history, civilization, or rationality. In a word, Africans were not fully human beings and could not be subjects of theological anthropology. They were savages.[55]

Anthropology

Reason/spirit bestows a historical mandate on Europe to bring its freedom and civilization to the rest of the world. (Later on, David Livingstone would deem this ethical imperative of imperialism as the three Cs:
Commerce, Christianity, and Civilization.)[56] To that end, the science
of anthropology assisted the speculations of philosophy in the attitude
toward and conquering of darker-skinned peoples globally.

Throughout the eighteenth century and echoing Enlightenment
claims, elite white men in Europe who studied the particular differences
and commonalities among races, concurred that distinctions among
races resulted from climate and environment. Nurture seemed to tri-
umph over nature. Consequently, all peoples maintained the potential for improvement through alteration of climate and environment.
Though the general agreement spoke to one human species, at the same
time, the foundational perspective held that a hierarchy still existed,
with Europeans standing at the top, above the world's darker-skinned
peoples.[57]

The first essay on racial arrangement belongs to a French physician,
François Bernier (1684). Surpassing previous classifications by region
and geography, Bernier offered the category of race, specifically the face
and the body representing the primary proper scientific analytical mea-
surements of human communities. Consequently, biology now replaced
space and place.[58] And even with the move to biology, the majority of
the eighteenth century adhered to the monogenesis stance: all peoples
arose from one divine biblical narrative or through a singular natural
creation.[59]

Still, nuanced arguments ensued within overall consensus. In the
1730s, Carolus Linnaeus, a Swedish botanist, argued for human biological races, and his scientific views set the standard for future comparisons and contrasts of whites and blacks.[60] Georges Louis Leclerc, Comte
de Buffon (French naturalist, mathematician, and biologist) assumed
human difference was a product of manners, food, and climate. While
supporting the idea of the unity of humankind, he felt the white biological race was the norm. Johann Friedrich Blumenbach, a professor
of medicine at the University of Göttingen, likewise touted the one
human race theory. But he, too, in the 1770s took a normative position on the aesthetics of differentiations. Blumenbach was the first to

introduce the notion of "Caucasian" and hailed it as the most beautiful race of all time, based on surface traits of color, hair, face, and skull. Conversely, blacks and other non-Caucasians were mere degenerations. Historians bestow Buffon and Blumenbach with the honor of being the joint founders of anthropology.

Despite the dominance of the monogenesis thesis, other male scientific thinkers in Europe held the minority position of polygenesis; that is, they proposed that black and white contrasts derive from two divergent Christian or natural origination points and not from one environmental factor or one God. John Atkins, an English physician, decried common ancestry among peoples when he theorized that savage blacks and civilized whites emerged from divergent primal parents. Dutch naturalist and medical expert Pieter Camper analyzed human skulls to ground his polygenesis racial hierarchy, with the ancient Greeks' facial angle proving their intellectual superiority over the blacks, the absolute bottom of racial asymmetry. A German physician, Franz Joseph Gall, equated head shape with human character to display the rigid divide between white and black.

However, even though sharply contested views of the natural world and nuance within common camps existed, prevailing historical wisdom recognizes *Essays on the Inequality of Races 1853–1855* by Joseph-Arthur, Comte de Gobineau, as the groundbreaking writings inaugurating modern racism. Gobineau, French ethnologist and racial theorist, claimed all history as the struggle between the races, where the white race prevails over the black. Concomitantly, the strength of a civilization lies in the forcefulness of that dominant race. Black and yellow races did not create anything significant; hence human history becomes only that of the white race.[61]

The first half of the nineteenth century in Europe saw the rise of the "new science of man," the call for an objective, materialist, evidentiary examination of the classification of human races. In order for elite European men to achieve this innovation, a series of novel scientific breakthroughs were necessitated. Thus the broader framework entailed research that privileged a "teleological view of history" (that is, the historical ascension of human development from the lower to the higher), "continuity of the human and the animal world" (that is, further highlighting the evolutionary basis of racial categorization as natural), and "mental abilities related to physical characteristics" (that is, further evidence that humanity resulted not from culture but from nature).[62]

Consequently, the rise of the "new science of man" and the establishment of anthropology substantiated Europe and whites in North America as the logical peak paradigms of aesthetics, identity, and natural power holders on the world stage. And this fact was embedded in biological inheritance, in contrast to eighteenth-century monogenesis opinions on climate and environment. Unlike in the eighteenth century, nineteenth-century anthropology conflated and therefore identified social inequality with natural inequality; social differences followed the laws of nature in the new racial science of "man." Scientific polygenesis (multiple human origination points) and biblical pre-Adamism (comprised of nonwhites) had become by the 1850s delectable alternative explanations for the inherent racial inferiority of blacks, Africans, and other dark-skinned peoples globally. Clergy and scientists in the United States played a prime role in promoting this view.[63]

By the end of the nineteenth century, anthropological theory had concocted a sophisticated biological determinism in the social realm. Human race speculators had modified the English scientist Charles Darwin's *The Origin of Species* (1859) to match natural biological distinctions among humankind. Biological survival-of-the-fittest thought easily morphed into Social Darwinism. The eugenics movement likewise grafted nature's purview onto human relations and concluded intelligence linkages to racial classification with the intent of eliminating the black race. Another Englishman and Darwin's cousin, Francis Galton, the father of eugenics, produced his seminal work *Hereditary Genius* (1869) that "definitively" correlated group skin color (heredity) with brilliance (genius). Again, as in the overwhelming majority of anthropologically related research, black folk and white folk occupied extreme opposites in nature's preference. With scientific authority Galton wrote, "The average intellectual standard of the negro race is some two grades below our own." His eugenics solution, therefore, demanded forced sterilization.[64] Lewis Henry Morgan, a U.S. ethnologist, lent further anthropological credence to this prevailing scientific ethos with his *Systems of Consanguinity and Affinity of the Human Family* (1870), a text expounding on seven stages of human development from lower savagery to civilization. With its advanced writing abilities and accomplishments, Morgan asserted, only European American society earned the status of civilization.[65]

In fact, the parallel white supremacist perspectives held in common between elite white males in Europe and their North American brethren can be traced back to the original English colonial occupations of Native American lands. From Governor Winthrop of the Plymouth Colony to Thomas Jefferson to Samuel George Morton, Josiah C. Nott, Louis Agassiz, and Theodore Roosevelt at the beginning of the twentieth century, North American philosophers and anthropologists were perhaps even more brutal in their intellectual musings on Africans and African Americans because blacks were enslaved.[66] Amid such intellectual white power, the last ten years of the nineteenth century in the United States witnessed the complete professionalization of anthropology, now a public, mainstream scientific field that studied race in specialized journals, university departments, and academic organizations.

The year 1896 is a case in point. The first professor of anthropology in the U.S.A. and president of the powerful and prestigious American Association for the Advancement of Science (AAAS), Daniel G. Brinton, wrote these words in the January 1896 edition of *Popular Science Monthly*: "the black, the brown and the red races differ anatomically so much from the white . . . that even with equal cerebral capacity they never could rival its results by equal efforts." Three months later, the first director of the Bureau of American Ethnology housed in the Smithsonian Institute, John Wesley Powell, echoed Brinton with his own interpretations: "the laws of evolution do not produce kinds of men but grades of men; and human evolution is intellectual, not physical. . . . All men have pleasures, some more, some less; all men have welfare, some more, some less; all men have justice, some more, some less."

Three weeks later, Melville Fuller, both a U.S. Supreme Court justice and the chancellor of the Smithsonian Institute, agreed with the majority opinion of his colleagues in the infamous *Plessy v. Ferguson* legal decision, which argued, "if one race be inferior to the other socially, the Constitution of the United States cannot put them upon the same plane."[67] Constitutional law drew from the objective science of racial anthropology. And both philosophy and anthropology assisted and, thereby, engendered the broader worldview of inevitable manifest destiny: monopoly capitalist democracy, rational manners, and advanced religion—hence commerce, civilization, and Christianity as God's gift to the darker-skinned peoples of the world. Globally, black was seen as evil (a religious aesthetic), the opposite of white (in human identity), and naturally subservient (not deserving power). Consequently, the white races of Europe and especially North America bore the burden of lifting up the lesser races throughout the earth. In a sense, God had ordained it that way. White supremacy's manifest destiny was the Great Commission of Jesus Christ.[68]

Missiology

In addition to philosophy and anthropology, a third body of knowledge grounding the possibility for modern racism is missiology—white men from Europe and North America, fulfilling their missiology calling from God, employed the Bible to educate and subordinate, if not exterminate, quite a number of the darker peoples of the world. The writers of the Gospel of Matthew claim that Jesus commissioned his eleven disciples with this injunction: "I have been given all authority in heaven and on earth! Go to the people of all nations and make them my disciples. Baptize them in the name of the Father, the Son, and the Holy Spirit, and teach them to do everything I have told you. I will be with you always, even until the end of the world" (28:18-20). Christians took this passage as a universal commission. Actually, Jesus only gave instructions to eleven of his male friends. Still, with these political orders of making the entire world Christian, European and North American white men set sail to turn blacks (that is, dark-skinned peoples) into good Christians. The infectious spread of Jesus' gospel of absorbing the Other called for dominating the earth with one truth and one belief.

The resulting missiological revelation of racial supremacy from the Northern Hemisphere was violent colonialism of darker-skinned peoples in the Southern Hemisphere. Christianity only crossed the oceans because missionaries had access to the privileges of colonial empire and the Christian injunction to take over other peoples' indigenous religions.[69] These energetic pioneers of the Father, the Son, and the Holy Spirit brought a cross and the flags of their respective countries. The manifestation of the aggressive spirit of Jesus Christ was the materiality of white Christian imperialism displayed in missiology as bellicose colonialism.

As Jean-Marc Ela from Cameroon has discussed, race in missiological endeavors consisted of the crown (colonial governments), the cannon (the military), commerce (the growth of capitalism in Europe and North America), civilization (the supremacy of white culture), and the cross (the imposition of the noninclusive truth of Jesus Christ).[70] As it tore down barriers and seduced its victims, the power of colonial Jesus violently attacked the religious identities and cultural aesthetics and ancient powers of indigenous peoples throughout the globe.[71]

The Roman Catholic nation of Portugal brought the first group of enslaved Africans to Europe in 1441.[72] Subsequently, the first European missionaries were from that country and labored tirelessly for the Roman church and with and on behalf of the Portuguese government's commerce in Africa. Catholic priests routinely sailed along with colonialists, adventurers, businessmen in the slave trade, and the military and worked as the religious authorities in new African coastal settlements of trade communities. This crafted the paradigm for later nineteenth-century missionary flourishing. In fact, religious workers used trading-military forts for launching pads into Africa's interior to establish evangelization for recruitment. On the African west coast, as Gwinya H. Muzorewa of Zimbabwe comments, slave-trading companies, European commercial establishments, or colonial governments often had clergy on the payroll.[73] Similar patterns played out in East Africa. Jesse Mugambi of Kenya concludes:

> Christian missionaries in East Africa between 1885 and 1918 endeavoured to prepare their converts to accept the colonial situation which had become inevitable, following the Partition of Africa by European leaders conferring in Berlin [Germany, 1884–85]. . . . The missionaries served as the link between the rulers and the ruled, between the powerful and the powerless. They provided literacy and other skills to the people who were later to become interpreters, clerks, teachers, evangelists and artisans when colonial administration became established. The mission stations became centres of westernization. The converts became like extension officers in the process of Europeanization. Evangelization was defined in terms of acculturation.[74]

Indeed, we observe a similar global missionary strategy repeated throughout Africa, Asia, the Caribbean, Latin America, and the Pacific Islands. Some schools are built; a few medical services are provided. But the black populations are offered these social services and converted to Christianity to remove them from their indigenous religions and traditional cultures, and to "civilize" them into European culture. Educational and medical resources, in too many examples, have been granted only as privileges to a small group of the dark-skinned peoples. For example, David Livingstone epitomized a nineteenth-century British model of religious outreach to Africa. Explorer, trader, colonizer, and missionary, Livingstone asserted, "If we call the actual amount of conversions the direct result of missions, and wide diffusion of better [Western cultural] principles the indirect, the latter are of infinitely more importance than the former."[75]

White Christian men looked at the black bodies of Africans and wondered whether or not they were actually human beings. Were they really created in God's image, thereby allowing them a God–human connection? Ogbu U. Kalu of Nigeria explicates this relegation of Africans to the realm of the nonhuman by quoting a white missionary's feelings about West Africa in 1917: "'I arrived at Bende to attempt anew the dredging and purifying of that ugly jungle pool of heathenism, with its ooze-life of shocking cruelty, reptilian passions and sprouting evil, spreading itself broad in the shadows amidst the most fruitful land on earth.' . . . Thus Christianity views her domain-to-be, lifting herself high above the secret springs of paganism's turgid streams below."[76] Were African peoples akin to the orangutan or perhaps the boa constrictor? It is this subtextual doubting, suspicion, and theological query that pursued Africans and their descendants around the world. Mercy Amba Oduyoye of Ghana describes the nineteenth-century British Christian Missionary Society encroachments in Africa. The Society referred to the West Africa mission field as a space "where barbarity and cannibalism reigned undisturbed" and to South Africa as "the hardest of all fields, the borderlands of native barbarism and European civilization," with the implication that the entire continent was inhabited by "superstitious barbarism . . . [of one] who seeks to appease the evil spirit."[77]

South Africa, unlike the majority of the continent, was a European missionary settler colony. White folk decided to remain there in order to sunbathe by the heavenly vistas conjured by the beautiful area of Cape Town. In 1652 the Dutch Protestants arrived at the Cape and stole land from the original African peoples. They announced themselves as the divine providential unfolding in the elimination of the "Canaan-ite" African majority. Moreover, terrorizing the preexisting population, these missionaries of Jesus perceived themselves as God's chosen people of conquest and as preservers of Afrikaaner identity.

In 1806 the British took the South African Cape area from the Dutch (now self-transformed into Afrikaaners with their Dutch Reformed religion). Like the white male Dutch settlers, the Anglican church aggressively endorsed and practiced racial supremacy and theft of land from the indigenous Africans. The advent of the British signaled an increase of white missionaries from both Europe and the United States. As a result, the nineteenth century saw the establishment of churches for blacks. The Dutch Reformed Church (Afrikaaners) and assorted English missionary churches felt compelled to house their black servants but did not desire to worship near their dark bodies. Hence, prior to the white settler government crafting a public policy of apartheid, the Afrikaaners and the English Christians had already established a model that was later followed directly by the government when it created apartheid.[78]

Latin American indigenous peoples were another first wave of communities to be the objects of Christian missiological efforts. José Míguez Bonino of Argentina proposes two phases to this encounter, "Spanish colonialism (Roman Catholicism) and North Atlantic neocolonialism (Protestantism)," and the ensuing utilization of "Christianity as a tool of oppression."[79] Christianity established a beachhead in Latin America during the sixteenth century with conquest and colonization and during the nineteenth century with modernization and neocolonialism. "In carrying out the enterprise of the Indies," Columbus asserted, "it was not reason, or mathematics, or charts that helped me; the discovery was simply a fulfillment of what Isaiah had said."[80] Isaiah, the Hebrew Scripture writer, referred to God's promise of guiding ships to capture treasures for God's own sanctuary. The missiological first phase of sixteenth-century Roman Catholicism equated the lord-king of Spain with the Lord-King of heaven, and genocide and slavery with evangelization. The darker-skinned indigenous owners of the land in the so-called New World were the objects of Christian beneficent outreach.

Spain's attempt at planting Christianity among the indigenous land-owners duplicated the semifeudal class relations in Spain. God occupied heaven, the king straddled the throne, and the landlord held court in his manor. As the gradual extermination of the original peoples unfolded along with the theft of their land, the crown gifted the European adventurers and bold missionaries with large tracts of land for the purpose of profitable commerce. Even as the overwhelming numbers of missionaries served the interests of colonial imposition, one or two of them did raise queries about the decimation of the Native peoples who worked the land as slaves for colonialists and the Roman church. Still, the dominant scenario was missionary submission to the crown's authority. Indeed, the Spanish king nominated the bishops and enforced papal proclamations in the New World. The Roman church compromised its independence with dual subordination—one to the government and the other to the small group of colonial landowners. If any resistance bubbled up from missionary proselytizing, the military stood ready to enforce a truer interpretation of Jesus Christ. In this fashion, the cross, the crown, commerce, and the cannon were dominated by an elite fraternity of white men from Europe.

Trumpeting democratic civilization, freedom, science, and capitalism, Protestantism made its debut in Latin America between 1870 and 1890. It brought a few medical facilities and education for the exclusive strata. And though the enslavement of Africans and their exportation to the New World began under the hegemony of Roman Catholicism, the intensification of black bodies moving for capitalist profit emerges under the watch of Protestantism. In 1871, for example, blacks from Jamaica were imported into Costa Rica as forced laborers in the banana industry. This violent exploitation of black labor power materialized simultaneously with an attack on both black workers' memory of African traditions and their emergent syncretized Afro-Caribbean and Afro–Latin American cultures.[81]

Costa Rica and other Central American countries were dominated by Protestantism, and black laborers were eventually allowed to be part of that religious tradition. With blacks in Brazil, however, Roman Catholicism maintained its hegemony even as Protestantism and its capitalism affected the remainder of Latin America. The European commerce of Africans in slavery reached Brazil from 1530 until

1850. Here, too, like Costa Rica, enslaved blacks worked in mining, stock raising, and farm plantations. The same missiological formula unfolded: African and black cultures were persecuted and attenuated. The Roman church eventually assumed a definite negative ideological and theological posture toward black Brazilians by arguing for the policy of *branqueamento*, in which the "human ideal is being white," as the black Brazilian Mauro Batista writes, "or being human and being white are completely equated." Perhaps the most sinister effects of this religious doctrine are the manifold internalizations of self-hatred on the part of black Christians.[82]

Logically, this white supremacist theological anthropology cast anathema and aspersion on Afro-Brazilian religions, various forms of both African religiosities and syncretic African–Roman Catholic expressions. The missionaries condemned black faith as Satan's work and the revelation of black savagery and superstition. European civilization, orthodox Roman church teachings, and white culture would, white religious leaders felt, eventually supplant black heathenism.

Within the ethos of a *branqueamento* theological anthropology, missionaries advanced two primary theological trajectories. Black Brazilian Silvia Regina De Lima Silva posits the following: "The theology of *transmigration* was based on the assertion that the black community needed to pass through successive migrations as a process of purification in order to obtain the salvation of their souls." Christian leaders justified this white supremacist fantasy on the so-called curse of Ham. Africans descended from this curse, and their forced removal from the reign of Satan on their continent signified the first transmigration. The European slave trade was mandatory to get blacks to Latin America, where the enslaved Africans would meet Christianity and be saved and the second transmigration to heaven would follow.[83] The second trajectory, Lima Silva continues, entailed the theology of *retribution*, which necessitated specific virtues on the path to eternal happiness. For enslaved Africans, eschatological bliss resulted from patience while enduring whippings, in work, and through other forms of Christian torture. Submission to their lot in life accompanied patience under pain, for God had brought Africans to Brazil according to sacred will and divine goals.

The indigenous and enslaved Africans in the Caribbean islands were forced to undergo a similar aesthetic, power, and identity dynamic dictated by European and U.S. missionaries in Latin America. The European Jesus continued to be a white supremacist in the so-called West Indies. Indeed, the 1492 accidental contact on the part of Christopher Columbus actually took place in the Caribbean. He never did "discover" the future United States. Nonetheless, Columbus planted the Roman Catholic banner of Spain in the islands.

In 1513 one Spanish religious leader, Martín Fernández de Enciso, echoed the familiar refrain that white men deployed throughout the Third World, including the initial encounter with American Indians' land. De Enciso claimed the Caribbean in the tradition of Yahweh granting the promised land to the ancient Hebrew peoples. Therefore, the king of Spain would be justified in killing "those idolatrous Indians" if they refused to grant the crown their lands. Did not Joshua do this in the land of Canaan? To mollify such brazen Christian arrogance, the monarchy suggested constructing schoolrooms and training the Amerindians to wear European clothes. But, as Patrick "Pops" Hylton of Jamaica documents, the initial Spanish conquistadors focused on accumulating gold and land and did not implement the words of their king. Furthermore, leading members of the Roman Catholic Church received huge amounts of wealth as profits from enslaving the indigenous peoples to work in the gold mines.[84] For instance, the Jeronimite Order of Monks forced the Amerindians to work in the gold mines in Cuba. Throughout the island, the Roman church's religious orders enslaved thousands of Amerindians and Africans, who labored on plantations and fought against rival European colonial incursions.

The eighteenth century witnessed increased Protestant missionary fervor in the Caribbean islands. Anglicans and Presbyterians, Dutch Reformed, and Lutherans taught the inherent incapability of enslaved Africans to comprehend religious instructions. Black people were unintelligent. Because they were not full human beings (subsisting below humanity or constituted as half humans), they could not receive Jesus, for "Christian religious instruction was intended for humans (which Africans were not) and that if African slaves were to gain knowledge of the principles of Judaeo-Christianity they would be misled into believing in the social and spiritual equality between themselves and their white masters." Moreover, being "savages," argued clergymen, Africans "were in fact closer to the simian than to humans (whites)."[85]

The missionary enterprises of the Moravians, Methodists, and Baptists followed suit by portraying Africans as the descendants of Ham and the inherent carriers of the Hamitic curse. Missionaries controlled land, and some even owned thousands of enslaved Africans. The Baptists and Methodists, although they failed to subscribe to the curse myth, propagated a Jesus fable that separated the necessary enslavement of the black body from the freedom of the spiritual soul. For instance, an Anglican rector in Jamaica signified the general white Christian consensus. Winston Arthur Lawson of Jamaica summarizes the Anglican rector's perspective: "Blacks [were] imperfect in their faculties, strange and barbarous, restless in spirit and indolent, operating by instinct, not reason, all alike savage [*sic*] and nearer to animals, serviceable, stupid and squalid."[86]

Perhaps one of the most dramatic shifts in missionary outreach to the Caribbean manifested in Cuba. For a couple of centuries Roman Catholicism and Spain dominated the island. But when the United States violently took Cuba from Spain in 1898, U.S. Protestant missionaries commenced to flood the colony and challenge the Catholic hegemony. Specifically, the U.S. government and its military thought it wise to facilitate the conquering of Cuba by working with white Southern Christians as they came in droves to Cuba. Consequently, Southern white supremacist attitudes toward blacks began to spread like a virus along with the Bible and U.S. culture.[87]

Australia and the Pacific Islands likewise bore the brunt of eighteenth- and nineteenth-century Christian missiology projects. The English Crown commissioned lieutenant (later captain) James Cook to take the land of Australia from the Aboriginal nations in 1768. Two years later, Cook simply stated that eastern Australia had become the private property of British royalty. Beginning in January 1788 the English invaders settled in Australia. The political rationale for occupying hegemony revolved around the spurious notion of *terra nullis*—empty land. Subsequently, England proclaimed official sovereignty of the "empty land" of Australia, even as indigenous blacks continued to wage armed self-defense for their sacred lands in 1788, 1824, and 1829. The colonialists then granted huge tracts of Aboriginal lands to their English missionaries and Christian churches. Not only did clergy and adventurers steal land, in the analytical investigation of Guboo Ted Thomas (an

Australian Aboriginal writing in an anthology on black theologies from the Southwest Pacific), there "are Christians among the racists, who somehow reckon Jesus to be a white man."[88]

And by the beginning of the nineteenth century, white male Christian missionaries had enslaved Aboriginal peoples through employing, among other things, a system of kidnapping black children and splitting up families, often separating mothers and fathers from each other. Slavery, in the spirit of European land-grabbing, provided the best situation for converting indigenous people from savagery to a more refined way of life. As Anne Pattel-Gray, an Australian Aboriginal writer, documents, English men in colonial, commercial, and religious authority perceived indigenous blacks as pre-Christian animals.[89] Therefore, to better serve the divine conversion demands of Jesus Christ, blacks were forcibly removed from the land of their nations and deposited and, in many instances, chained in Christian missionary compounds. Moreover, to pacify the population and their resources, government and church colluded to terrorize the indigenous woman. Representatives from church and state beat the female, participated in gang rapes, poisoned her water holes and sugar and flour, resorted to shooting women "down like dogs," and, in other instances, "shoved spears into her vagina until she died."[90]

Christianization, civilization, and commercialization forged a distinct worldview and purpose: to force black folk to wear European clothing and adopt white culture (hence, the aesthetic accent), to educate Aboriginals into speaking English and adopt "Christian" names (hence, the identity move), and to imbue them with a Protestant (capitalist) work ethic to remake them into laborers on their stolen lands (hence, removing their power by revoking their land-ownership and mandating a Christian necessity to surrender their labor power for the priest, the property owner, and the politician).

Native Hawaiians endured similar results of the gospel of salvation spread throughout the remaining Pacific Islands. Initially, the Hawaiians literally welcomed James Cook with open arms in 1778. They boated out to greet him and his men with "food, water, garlands of flowers," and openness to intimate relations. The crew accepted this traditional religious hospitality and returned these kind acts of healthy humanity by eventually introducing alcohol and giving the indigenous peoples gonorrhea and syphilis.[91]

Beginning in the 1820s, the United States had dominated the sandalwood industry in Hawaii, and American missionaries soon followed close behind. Capitalism and Calvinism enjoyed a profitable marriage. "The fertile field of conversion," in the writings of Haunani-Kay Trask, a Native Hawaiian, "was littered with the remnants of holocaust, a holocaust created by white foreigners and celebrated by their counterparts as the will of a Christian god. By the 1840's, Hawaiians numbered less than 100,000, a population collapse of nearly 90 percent in less than seventy years."[92]

Indeed, American missionaries negotiated with indigenous chiefs to educate the chiefs' children in U.S. culture, language, values, and clothing and the doctrine of sin. Moreover, these followers of Jesus acquired large tracts of land, in one example actually owning one of the Hawaiian islands. Missionaries facilitated white capitalist men's receiving long-term land leases from kings and queens in order to establish sugar plantations. Eventually, white American missionaries and their Christian capitalist cohorts gained economic control of the Hawaiian Islands. With the aggressive support of the U.S. military, the descendants of settlers and missionaries captured the Hawaiian legislature. White Americans had found their paradise and successfully conquered their promised land with privatization of property, enthusiastic biblical proclamation, the closing of Hawaiian-language schools, and decisive political control of government toward the latter part of the nineteenth century.

Suliana Siwtabau of Fiji writes about the legacy of globalized racism for dark-skinned peoples of the Pacific:

> 1. Recognizable socioeconomic changes are transforming our communal societies into individualistic ones; participation in these changes entails the rapid exploitation of our natural resources, the desecration of our environment, and absorption into the expanding capitalist network [marking a spirituality of individual accumulation and privatized hoarding].
>
> 2. Our cultures are evolving into new forms with the introduction of new beliefs, new ideas, and new value systems [initiated by Christianity].
>
> 3. We observe the growing militarization of our region, with accompanying subtle political dominations by those who wield both

economic and military power [thus a shift from God to a belligerent idolatrous faith].[93]

Unlike other regions of the world, the basis for racism existed internal to the communities in India long before the conquering of European and North American Christians. James Massey describes how the dark-skinned indigenous peoples of India (ancestors of the present-day Dalits, formerly the Untouchables) were invaded and subdued by Aryan aggressors between 1500 BCE and 700 CE.[94] During these centuries the caste system became normative, and, as a result, the Dalit peoples suffered a near lethal decimation of their land, history, religion, culture, and, most profoundly, a sense of being fully humans. Outside and beneath the caste system, the Dalits endured excruciating oppression symbolized by, in the words of V. Davasahayam, "the stigma of untouchability due to their 'polluting' professions such as leather works, skinning, moving carcasses, carrying night soil on their heads and so on," a status of landless agricultural workers, and intense poverty.[95] Dalits wore containers around their neck in which to spit so that their saliva would never touch the ground and thus pollute members of the upper castes. Dalits hung leaves from their buttocks to the ground to sweep up their footprints so no upper castes would walk in these imprints. Dalits could only enter a town around 9 AM so as to keep the sun from casting their shadow on the earth, and they had to shout out that they were on a road if they saw a non-Dalit approaching.[96] Thus their status was subhuman or nonpeople. From K. Rajaratnam's perspective, Dalit caste suffering, among other things, is pure racism.[97]

Hence, when the Roman Catholic Francis Xavier arrived on the west coast of India in the middle of the sixteenth century, caste had been entrenched without signs of reversal. The Roman church accepted caste based on familiarity with Christian hierarchy already existing in Europe, dominated by the pope and the king (that is, power concerns), based on European white racism (that is, identity issues), and based on superior European culture (that is, aesthetic prioritizing).[98] The increase in Protestant arrivals took place in the nineteenth century. To a degree, they verbally condemned caste as antithetical to the gospel of Jesus. Yet both the Roman church and Protestants adhered to the existing caste system by supporting it inside and outside of the church.

Initially, all denominations commenced conversion attempts with the upper castes and the wealthy Indians. They provided Western education to these elites while the millions of Dalits and members of other low sectors of society suffered. Whites from Europe and North America, in particular, cursed Dalit history, beliefs, and practices as evil. Only after the Dalits approached the missionaries to join Christianity did the foreign proselytizers feel pressured to attend to and ratify the "mass conversion" movement that the Dalits and the oppressed populations were already carrying out among themselves.

Alien missionaries did offer some important relief for the marginalized communities during the great famines of 1876–77 and 1896. Furthermore, they taught some children trades such as carpentry, tailoring, masonry, and blacksmithing. Jacob S. Dharmaraj nevertheless argues:

> Under the pretext of civilizing and modernizing the colonized lands after the model of Europe, the conquerors expanded their territories around the world, particularly in India. The missionaries subscribed to the view that "civilizing" the Indian people would prepare the "primitive religious people" to embrace Christianity. In the nineteenth century, Christianization and civilization were considered two sides of the same coin. . . . The Indian people's social and religious life was portrayed as culturally inferior, intellectually backward, and religiously superstitious.[99]

Made in God's Image

We have pursued this conceptual journey through the nuanced textures of race because white supremacy is perhaps the most egregious material revelation of how dark-skinned peoples in the United States and globally and their passionate relation to God are demeaned. All peoples are involved in a healthy theological anthropology. They are made in God's image (*imago dei*) and are equally called to pursue the *missio dei* (mission of God). Unfortunately, certain physical traits typologize peoples so that some interpret Christianity, unleash capitalism, and define the notions of civilization at the expense of the majority of the world's dark-skinned peoples and their connection with divinity.

Despite the objective scientific data for one worldwide, biological human race, theories and practices of race persist with a syncretism of nature-nurture and creation-culture. Despite the rational fact of all the world's populations hailing from an African "Eve" and "Adam," today the United States and its historical homelands in Europe have relegated Africa and blackness to the bottom of the human hierarchy. Africans, blacks, and dark-skinned communities suffer the sorrowful and stereotypical status of weakness in rational capabilities, lacking in effort, narrowness in vision, vibrancy in sensuality, truncated in civilization, and wanting in theological importance. It is as if God has fashioned these sectors of the human population for an enormity of suffering and perpetual second-class status.

One amazing reality—or miracle—of the human–divine interaction is the persistent creative genius of global dark-skinned peoples. Millions have, in the midst of a damning definition of white skin privileges, appropriated both racial categories and a reinterpreted Christianity to model a theological anthropology of individual renewal and structural transformation toward the practice of freedom—that is to say, a new self and a new common wealth.

5.
Conclusion as Introduction

We now must ask: How does the discipline of black theology outline the indicators of a theological anthropology? Here discipline means both the rigorous study of an interdisciplinary body of knowledge with its traditions, authors, audiences, writings, sources, and so forth and the practical ways of self-conscious and critical reflection on the unfolding revelation of faith for African American people.

The black community undergoes a complex, revelatory experience with transcendence, a spirit greater than any one person or subsegment of African American people. Various sources of the folk express a multiplicity of occasions when the spirit's presence makes itself known. Noting the diversity within African American discourse, we can look for the liberation markers and ascertain lessons for the Christian goal of practicing freedom for the poor and, through them, all female and male humanity and creation.

Theological anthropology interrogates what people are created and called to be and do. How does spirituality connect to the human reality? What is a human being from a healthy spiritual perspective? Particularly for Christians, the question persists in this fashion: If Jesus symbolizes humanity's embodiment of divine spirit and material flesh, then how does that confluence implicate an individual's interaction with transcendent reality? Before one can respond with intellectual honesty and create a constructive theological anthropology, we argue for a prior step, the imperative to think through the notions of culture, selves/self, and race. Moreover, we assert that these concepts, among others, require conceptual clarification because they so heavily determine, if not over-determine, the doctrine of theological anthropology. Yet representatives of contemporary theological anthropologies lack sustained definitional entries into the fields of theory or abstractions on such crucial terms undergirding the construction of today's discourses on the God–human relation. Thus, we must examine the notions of culture, selves/self, and race and their interconnections prior to an extended statement on divine–human connections.

Contemporary Models and Presuppositions

The progressive liberal theologian believes the authentic person is committed to the ultimate significance of human lives in this world. Moreover, Christian faith and the faith of secularity are one. Faith, from this vantage point, reveals itself in the rational powers of the modern and postmodern human person engaged in (a) civilized and reasoned discourse based on Greek philosophical logic; (b) European Enlightenment bourgeois democracy (that is, individual freedoms of speech, religion, press, assembly, and so forth to serve the capitalist class); and (c) solidarity with the oppressed within the parameters of and subordinated to bourgeois democracy priorities. For this claim, one discovers how the progressive liberal theological anthropology explores human reasoning from the *culture* of the European Enlightenment genealogical ethos. Also, such a theological anthropology presumes that the heirs of the Enlightenment are ever-present (but, I would add, unclarified) *selves* and *self* in progressive liberal God–human interactions. And most, but not all, progressive liberals remain silent on the decisive dimension of *race* in their God-talk.

Similarly, these three notions lurk just beneath the surface of the conscious opinions of postliberal theological anthropologies. For this trajectory, the authentic person immerses oneself into the uniqueness of Christian language and culture to then confront and change the non-Christian culture. One relearns the language of the Bible and absorbs non-Christian culture and philosophy into that divine language. As a result, one hopes to Christianize secular culture. Here one observes a direct deployment of the notion of *culture* in theological anthropology. There exists a distinct Christian culture called to wage war against secular culture inebriated with liberal and philosophical elixirs. And postliberals assume a fixed *selves/self* status saturated in revealed Christian culture–secular culture cosmic battles. Yet *race*, from the postliberal vantage point, hardly registers on the critical, self-conscious Richter scale. Postliberal thought suggests a universal, abstract group of soldiers for Christ who battle secular culture. In fact, however, the silence on race underscores the particular elite white male's experience in postliberal theological anthropology.

Contrasting progressive liberal and postliberal theological anthropologies, feminist theoreticians demand the development and promotion of the full humanity of women as authentic reflection of or relation to the divine. Because the majority of negative dualities and harmful hierarchies in society are based on oppressive woman–man dualities, woman's divinely intended genuine self can model more healthy human relations among people, between people and nature, and with the sacred. Woman's relational culture portends a salutary selves/self proposition for the universal humanity. And feminist theologians critique male academic thought as theological speculations cemented in the anthropology of exclusive male culture. An additional contrast resides in women intellectuals' alacrity to name their sexual and gendered selves/self in racial descriptors.

Compared to other models of theological anthropology, the ideas of culture, selves/self, and race are more present among people of color or Third World communities within the United States. Black, womanist, Hispanic/Latino(a), Asian American, and Native American perspectives on the human–God interaction point to poor and marginalized peoples' cultures and the selves/self of citizens oppressed in societies and quite willingly offer race for theological interrogation.

We began this book with extended comparisons and contrasts among contemporary models of theological anthropology. Likewise, we conclude this book with black theology constructing another contemporary model of theological anthropology by using African American folktales. In this sense, we have come full circle to the initial concern for discerning what we can say about the human condition and human nature today. What have woman and man been called to be, think, believe, and do? Before we re-enter the realm of grammar and principles strictly applied to developing a contemporary theological anthropology from black folktales, a brief recapitulation of the presuppositions—culture, selves/self, and race—is warranted because they are the requisite *conditions of possibility* for all contemporary musing about God, the human condition, and human nature.

Three Conditions of Possibility

We have argued that culture (the first condition of possibility) consists of three central components. Culture is the totality of *human labor*, a fluid dynamic of mutual effectivity between material base and ideational superstructure. Human labor influences greatly other cultural dimensions. But so too is labor affected by cultural aspects such as emotions, intellect, and religion. In addition, the *aesthetic* or the artistic comprises the notion of culture. We found that a person's inner characteristics and ethical practices, adjudicated by community, determined the quality of one's outer beauty. We then proceeded to explore the aesthetics of the human, the natural, and the human-made. While acknowledging the creative genius of the individual, all aesthetics, at some level, have functionality for and favor from the collective will. Basically, the aesthetic has to be life-giving and community-building. The third element of culture, the *spirit*, agitates the two previous constituents. Healthy spirit, in contrast to demonic spirituality, is the creativity unfolding in culture and vivifies both human labor and the aesthetic. God fulfills this function in Christianity. Finally, spirit in culture denotes contention between a sense of service to those on the peripheries of the world and a sense of hyper me-first individualism.

Specified *selves* and *self* craft culture out of the human mix (infused with spirit). We claim the priority of plural selves due to their formative status regarding the individual self. The idea of the selves brings together communal values (that is, sharing, mutual aid, caring for others, interdependence, solidarity, reciprocal obligations, and social harmony), community (that is, interpersonal relations), and common good (that is, the end product or goal defined by what is materially and spiritually fitting for the collective selves and individual participants). In ongoing dialogue with the selves, the notion of the self privileges relationality (that is, naming the living presence of others in the self and the self in others; emancipating the self from inner psychological demons and oppressive external constraints; and defending the uniqueness of the self, revealed by its own individuality, self-concept, and agency).

Race, the final but not exhaustive required condition of possibility for a contemporary doctrine on theological anthropology, has been delved into from an assortment of analytic angles. We paused to review multiple racial theories: the rational, psychological, political-legal, economic, geographical, biblical, and cultural. I then asserted my own definition. Race localized in the United States (though having global implications, given the hegemony of U.S. monopoly capitalist empire) means explicitly combining biological or God-given phenotype with malleable sociological characteristics. And, concomitantly for me, race breathes a white supremacist spirituality, interrupted by occasional exceptions to this demonic spirituality.

Having sorted out conceptual options, we come to the objective scientific understanding of one human, biological race. The interdisciplinary, international scientific community has proven how the global human race evolved from a woman and man out of Africa. Race in theological anthropology has to take seriously this rational fact because it underscores further how contrived the popular notion of race actually is. Human beings through their cultures and selves/self configurations create definitions of races beyond the one genetic earthly human race. Therefore, race is a shifting signifier based on cultural contexts and the power to define.

The evidence for Africa as the cradle of the human race is germane because it further underlines the dangerous but spurious popular and scientific emotions about Europe as the land of human origins. In unpacking the concept of race, we have verified its mutability and discerned how Europe underdeveloped Africa, its diaspora, and all darker-skinned peoples throughout the world discursively and physically. We might ask, If Africa founded humanity, then how did the white leaders of Europe and their offspring in the United States conquer the racial world?

We encountered the stirrings of racial differentiations and hue hierarchies in ancient Greece and Rome. Still, modern racism with its God of white supremacy triumphs in intellectual language and ethical imperatives during the seventeenth, eighteenth, and nineteenth centuries in Europe and North America. Elite white men from Europe and North

America subjectively constructed the disciplines of philosophy, anthropology, and missiology to convert the world. And the result was the globalization of race.

One of the by-products of massive displacement of Africans in this religious quest to convert the world was the creation of the African American phenomenon. Prior to white Christian profiteers' transporting tens of millions of black bodies via the European slave trade in Africans, one imagined no such thing as black Americans or African Americans or Africans in the Americas. Consequently, the novel race of black people, a rather new concept in worldwide human history, grappled with forms of resistance to their loss of African free status before their High God and crafted an unprecedented invention syncretizing[1] memory of African religious culture, reinterpreted Christianity, and everyday, commonsense folk wisdom. Black folktales surface from this deeply developed hybridity of New World cultures, selves/self, race, and religious cosmology. To outline a constructive theological anthropology for today, we turn now to lessons from black folktales.

The Spirit and the Poor

From strong indications within African American religious traditions, God tabernacles especially among the African American poor and affirms the positive cultural and political traditions and practices of this sector of community. The creative and rich realities of the black poor and their contributions, real and potential, to the rest of humanity, especially to the rest of working and poor people in the United States (and the world's poor), exhibit exactly the God–poor encounter. A universal hopeful gift to all humanity is how black folk living in poverty are able to sustain the ultimate vision of liberation in the midst of excruciating external circumstances. And even as they experience the negativities initiated by themselves within their own communities, the least in society somehow maintain their eyes on the final goal. A survivalist quest for liberation amid the twists and turns of ever-present storm clouds shows the empowering notion of an ultimate vision of liberation. The optimistic and ultimate vision of a better day of equal and just human interaction (that is, the perspective of final attainment of full humanity or practicing freedom) resides in numerous life-giv-

ing sources from the African American tradition of poor and working folk. The almost infinite kaleidoscope of human–sacred practices
entails political movements, cultural groups, women's activities, social
analysis and social visions, and the complex intricacies of enslaved black
lives before the 1865 emancipation.

Out of the prophetic and priestly wings of these sources, God has
created and called humanity to be *full* human beings—to attain the
maximum level of their God-given human capabilities at every human
level in service to the least in society. In opposition to this universal
human harmony, and in an overwhelmingly and radically disproportionate manner, whites with power have established a system that ren-
ders affirmative action to whites primarily because of their whiteness
(the American combination of phenotype and cultural determination).
This negative affirmative action (negative because it promotes white
racial mediocrity) underscores the unspoken racial edge that whites
have relative to nonwhites simply because they are white.

Consequently, in the American civic fabric, there inheres an unspoken prerequisite for success: the requirement of whiteness. Power and
wealth ownership reside in white hands. This contradicts the purpose of
theological anthropology. Hence, the created goal has been thwarted due
to human hubris and arrogance. Nevertheless, God has called human
beings to continue the struggle toward the original created understanding of what it meant to be a full human being. The created meaning and
the vocational mandate remain the same.

Even as one pursues the meaning and mandate, the sinful, white
asymmetrical structure (sinful because it denies healthy theological
anthropology) has produced and continues to replicate an increased
impoverishment of black folk economically and politically. Likewise,
the structure polarizes white at the extreme top and black at the lowest
rung in society, even within racial and ethnic groups. Thus this fore-
grounds how black people themselves make decisions to *participate in*
and help perpetuate oppressive ideological, psychological, material, and
theological systems not in their interests or humanity's interests. Other
colors (yellow, brown, and red) within this white structure dwell in
between the two poles.

In order to achieve full humanity for all classes beyond a sinful asymmetry, the vocation to live out the fullest human capabilities hinges on

liberating poor and working-class people from this harmful configuration that reproduces unbalanced social relations, deleterious emotional states, and wounded human personalities. Because far too many African Americans are forced into the negative end of this system, they can play a vital role in the struggle to liberate all humanity into the vocational goal of full human beings. When the bottom rises to alter fundamentally social arrangements, it not only liberates itself but also liberates the oppressor group by removing the system that allows oppression. In the United States it means, to a large extent, democratizing ownership of wealth and technology and allowing equal wealth ownership to foster healthy political processes on behalf of the majority; that is to say, it means a rising standard of material and spiritual prosperity, a correct relation with nature, and the healing of wounded emotions and damaged personalities among all peoples.

The foundational presupposition to liberation posits the following nonnegotiable *theological* principle: all human beings are created with a spiritual purpose (or transcendent or ultimate vision) to share in the material resources of the earth. Therefore the earth and human relationships do not belong to any one group or community. To hoard these resources or monopolize these relationships is to act as a god and forces an individual or group to be outside the definition of what it means to be a wholesome, relational human being. In order to foster a sanguine human family, humans work with the earth's resources and in human interactions toward the goal of serving those marginalized in a community. And, thereby, people not only facilitate the crafting of the collective humanity but also participate in further fashioning themselves as individual persons. Pursuing this end reconstructs the individual. Thus the individual self materializes through starting with the most disenfranchised voices in community. Here we should underscore "broken community," because as long as there are the disadvantaged, the understanding of the collective and individual human person is weakened and distorted.

The individual matures by service to others, those outside of and beyond the individual. This is the crossroad of the transcendent and personal dimensions. The self tied to community realizes a spirit of liberation. In sum, a human being is one involved in service to the least in any society, while all community members have equal access to the communal resources to forge the fullest and most wholesome individual and communal practices possible. Moreover, this response to sacred vocation means that a spirit of liberation vivifies a human being toward the goal of practicing freedom, starting with the compassion for the those at the bottom of social relationships.

To develop further my constructive statement on theological anthropology, I draw on black folktales—a prime paradigm for the bottom of social interactions. In particular, black folktales (as cultural indices of the positive encounter between the black poor and the sacred vision) illustrate a multiplicity of life-affirming indicators as gifts to the rest of humanity. Four models stand as potential examples of and lessons for theological anthropology.

First, the black *trickster* type deploys the discourse of *reversal* as linguistic sign and as ethical play and reveals a spirituality of *human flourishing*. Second, the black *conjurer* figure works with *nature* to manipulate spiritual powers *of all creation* for human advancement. Third, the black *outlaw* type commands an array of diffused *ambiguity*, with a spirituality of *individual desire*. Fourth, the *Christian witness* figure most consistently yields *empowerment* for the most vulnerable, thus a spirituality of *compassion for the poor*. All characters or archetypes display some dimensions of healthy theological anthropology—what God has created humans to be and what humans are called to become still today: individuality serving equal identities, shared spaces, and mutual ownership of wealth in community.

My argument is largely determined by the definitions given in the four folk sources themselves. Consequently, by *culture* I mean a total way of life (at minimum, circumscribed by human labor and the aesthetic and animated by the spirit). This lifestyle is religious insofar as the ways of being human in the world entail some yearning for, belief in, and ritualization around that which is ultimate—that which is both part of and greater than the selves/self. Culture is religious because the ultimate vision is present both in the material (tangible manifestation) and in the transcendent (the imagination of the ultimate is not limited to the selves/self). Thus, in this book, culture refers to religious culture as a total way of life.

By *folk* I mean nonelites—working people, communities living in structural poverty, the marginalized, and the unrecognized voices in our society. According to this description, the folk believe in and practice a sacred way of life from the bottom of society. Moreover, this view and ethic of the folk, as they pertain to a sacred reality, includes life-and-death questions about the ultimate values, meanings, and actions for the least sectors in society.

By "theology" I emphasize Christian theology—the revelation of a spirit of liberation through Jesus Christ, yet informed by lessons from non-Christian expressions of this same spirit. In the four cultural types, I have discovered that the normative characteristic of God or an ultimate vision is a transcendent will that all of creation be liberated and practice freedom. Jesus Christ, in many of the sources, is an authoritative manifestation of that revealed characteristic. However, though a decisive embodiment, Jesus Christ is not the only or exclusive incarnation. African American folk culture, I contend, substantiates the claim that theological anthropology includes a transcendent and human connection showing a spirit of liberation that empowers humanity through diverse media. Because this spirit or transcendent reality or ultimate vision lacks narrow boundaries, human beings have more ways of attaining their full potential. The key is a spirit of liberation, and there is no great divide between the so-called secular and sacred. Indeed, such a view, alien to the types of black folk culture that I am engaging, would limit the freeing power of the spirit.

In other words, my Christian theological anthropology is enhanced by different expressions of how the spirit works, especially with the least in community. One can be a Christian and still learn from the freedom emphases in the conjurer, the trickster, and the outlaw types.

Using an inductive method, I draw my constructive conclusions about theological anthropology by questioning the primary sources of the four folk literary types and reading them as texts. Indeed, the multidimensionality of these texts suggests at least four levels at which theological implications are found. The first level concerns the authors or the tellers of these tales. What meanings did they intend? This requires, as much as possible, grasping the contexts and the content of their voices. A second level is the meaning found in the stories themselves. Though the original authors intend to have an impact on the readers, in a sense the stories leave the authors and take on a life of their own. Here, too, we bring in the role of the context found in the stories, which discloses further the stories' significance. Third are the readers' own interpretations of meaning. Likewise, the contexts of the readers influence greatly how they determine the stories' theological meanings or conclusions. The fourth level arises from putting into conversation the previous three levels of analysis. What do these levels of investigation, separately and together, say about how the spirit of liberation for the bottom in society fosters the individual and communal dynamic?

A theological anthropology will result from comparing different versions of the four literary genres in black folk culture. The approach here is inductive—beginning with the primary texts and weaving a process of critical comparison into a larger whole. It is this embeddedness of the spirit of liberation in various texts, contexts, and times that prevents the norm of liberation from becoming a jaded, generic mantra.

Folk Culture Paradigms

The trickster, conjurer, outlaw, and Christian hero folk figures signify stories primarily told by poor and working-class blacks among themselves. These understandings of human createdness and purpose for living emerged in a specific culture in a highly racialized communal context. From slavery in the South and North before 1865 until de facto segregation in the North and South today, black folk archetypes have served as surrogate space and mythic identities enabling an African American marginalized individual self and corporate selves to transcend their immediate predicament in order to venture, at least metaphorically, into a "what if" reality of freedom.

The trickster acts out the notion of human reversal in which usually the weak character (that is, poor and working-class black folk) deploys the weapon of wit to outsmart the physically strong owner of material resources (that is, elite whites with power).[2] This dynamic produces a spirituality of human flourishing. Restated, the trickster character suggests a spiritual environment in which the disadvantaged majority can flourish and have abundant life by tricking the arrogant powerful few. Such tricking yields a human flourishing spirituality characterized by creativity, cunning, and balance. Brer Rabbit or Buh Rabbit is the paramount trickster protagonist in this black folktale genre.

In the Tar Baby story line Brer Rabbit constantly takes or repossesses water or crops from Brer Fox or Brer Wolf. These strong creatures possess and occupy the best land. And, in narratives about water from a well, the weak creature waits until the strong completes the necessary digging to tap into this life-giving liquid and, under the blackness of night, the weak animal takes water freely. Eventually, the stronger animal sets a trap by situating near the well or garden a female-looking character constructed of tar. As usual, Brer Rabbit comes late at night to take water or food. Rabbit addresses the black Tar Baby figure several times. After receiving no response, Brer Rabbit becomes angry and physically attacks the object and inevitably becomes stuck. The next morning, the stronger animal finds the weaker one intertwined with the Tar Baby. When Brer Fox or Wolf threatens to kill Brer Rabbit by burning, drowning, or hanging him, Brer Rabbit pleads with abundant joy that all of these lethal alternatives were agreeable. However, the greatest punishment, Brer Rabbit articulates, is to be thrown in the briar patch. Of course, his captors toss him there because the rabbit has feigned extreme fear of this location. Once he lands, Rabbit runs off laughing and announces that the briar patch is where he was "born and bred." Instead of succumbing to torture and death, Rabbit has tricked the stronger animals into returning him into his natural habitat, where he was born, survived, and flourished.

Here the definition of human interaction intimates that the strongest should perform most of the work because they have monopolized most of the survival sustenance and technologies. And this skewed act has upset the balance of community within the jungle or the woods. Therefore one encounters a clash of cultures and world outlooks pertaining to what it means to be created as and called to be a human being. Within the broader culture of the animals, Wolf and Fox understand humanity normatively divided into gradations, with their ilk on top and the majority of the people on the bottom. To think differently, in their eyes, denotes lawbreaking or anarchy (and perhaps heresy) in accepted and assigned human stations.

The weak, on the other hand, are called to perceive reality differently. They imagine a vision of society in which the bottom strata have natural access to all that is healthy in life. The move to think and see from a more inclusive posture empowers them to pursue whatever they need by using their instinctual mother wit and intellect to overcome the inequitable circumstances created by the strong's focus on the individual self. Such reimagining enables one to risk a new present in order to have a better tomorrow. Despite the apparent overwhelmingly superior force exhibited by the strong, the weak, once overcome with a spirit of the potentially new, boldly enters the culture and environment of those with sharper teeth and bigger paws, continually democratizes the land by acquiring whatever is needed, and, even when captured, turns the mind of the powerful upside down so that the weak are returned to their natural cultural habitat where they were "born and bred." In the midst of dire circumstances, entangled in the tar of life, the weak pursue hope to flourish and live in abundance.

Brer Rabbit and the Tar Baby tales also relate how the trickster character is not always consistent in its theological anthropology; that is, the figure at times operates against the vocation of symbolizing and working for the weak. For instance, in the footrace between Buh Rabbit and Buh Frog, both creatures attempt to quickly complete a five-mile course in order to marry a Miss Dinah. Whoever crosses the finish line and jumps into her lap becomes the new groom. Buh Rabbit perceives, on the surface, a slow physical and dull intellectual opponent in the frog and, accordingly, already assumes himself victor. In the meantime, the frog positions several identical-looking relatives at each of the mile markers while Buh Frog waits at the finish line. At each one-mile marker, the rabbit calls out to the frog to see if he has arrived. Of course, one of the frog's relatives steps out ahead of rabbit at each of the markers. Rabbit approaches the finish line, and Buh Frog leaps out into Miss Dinah's lap and wins the race. In this example, Buh Rabbit fails to win due to his denial of the healthy traits of what it means to be human. Indeed, by not taking seriously the humanity of the seemingly invisible and insignificant people in society, he imitates the worst dimensions of the strong animals such as Wolf and Fox.

Sometimes, the trickster attempts to trick the other weak creatures by mirroring the dominating and stronger animals and succumbing to arrogance, overconfidence, underestimation, and a failure to perceive the equal humanity of the little people in society. Therefore the role of the story here is to offer self-critique of the black working people who are the immediate audience of the narrative.[3] The liberating art of the trickster—through reversal, offering hope to the weak with superior wit over the strong and thereby suggesting a human flourishing—is not automatically inherent to the oppressed sectors of the human family. It transcends them. But because of their weak social location in the structures of power and privilege, they are relatively more open to the possibilities of transforming both the individual self and collective selves.[4]

Another significant archetype in African American tales, conjure doctors are folk characters who call on elements from nature to perform either good or evil against another human being. Some claim that they receive their powers from association with the Devil; others cite the grace of God's direct revelation. Still others credit their natural extraordinary gifts to the fact that they were born the seventh son of a seventh son with seven cauls covering their face or claim that wisdom was passed on from a person long deceased.[5] In any case, the conjurer introduces a spirituality of all creation.

Conjure doctors can bring about psychological, emotional, and physical healing or sickness in communities because of their openness to, knowledge of, and co-laboring with nature. Along with an insider's knowledge, the doctor uses roots, leaves, herbs, hair, pins, needles, salt, pepper, a silver five-cent piece, fried and powdered jellyfish, insects, and snakes. Various combinations of ingredients are mixed and placed, in most cases, within a small red flannel bag or jar. Less complicated natural formulas include positioning a horseshoe over a door, storing a smooth stone in one's shoe, hanging silver around the neck, or wearing a goose quill below the knee.

The conjure doctor can cause two people to love each other (the matchmaking role), keep a lover faithful (as moral police), win back a husband, kill someone (carrying out an execution), help free an alleged criminal (as a lawyer), hurt an enemy, drive a woman crazy (intensifying psychological demons), bring about various types of deaths, cause revenge on a woman, make a woman drown herself (here exhibiting almost hypnotic power), locate buried treasure, discover freshwater in the ground, and deal with haunts (ghosts).[6]

In one tale, a male suitor visited a conjure doctor to ask for instructions on how to make a certain woman his wife. The doctor sold him a "French Love Powder" (sugar of milk) and prescribed the sprinkling of this substance on all gifts for the woman. Another case finds an unhappy wife receiving a "bottle of medicine" (lemonade) from a conjurer in order to transform a husband's quarreling nature. And an Aunt Mymee always carried her "luck ball" comprised of rags, ashes, and a chicken's breastbone. Periodically the ball was given a drink by sprinkling whiskey on it. "An old Negro cook" was never without her conjure, a good-luck charm consisting of a dime with a hole in it, a beetle, snakeskins, a lizard's tail, a fish eye, and a rabbit's foot.[7] Conjure can even cure a swollen foot and enable the jobless to obtain employment.[8]

During American slavery conjurers were consulted to shield a black worker from punishment, to evade the roadside white patrollers out looking for black "lawbreakers," and to avoid the master's wrath when a runaway decided to return to the plantation.[9] In one story, an enslaved man named Solomon became distraught after his girlfriend had been sold away from the plantation. A conjure doctor gave him a ground-up root power that the cook later put in the master's okra soup. As a result, not only was the girlfriend returned, but the master became much more lenient with all of his black workers.[10] The potency of nature and its esoteric wisdom allow the conjurer to facilitate a balance of ethics and morality among the folk as well as have an impact on the structural powers of domination outside of black culture. Conjuring works on the individual within a racial culture and has the potential to reconfigure the stubborn minds and callous hearts of oppressors.

Conjuring depicts a humanity for whom equilibrium and disequilibrium are key to creating a comprehensive social interaction within culture. As an aspect of theological anthropology it draws on human mystical ties to the supernatural powers derived from nature and from the strength of the spiritual (associated with God or the Devil) worlds.

Fundamentally, it instructs us to tune in to the latent and too-often underutilized resources offered by nature to the human realm. Conjuring intimates that human daily survival is a consequence of the presence of animals, plants, air, water, and the earth. To be human, in the fullest sense imaginable, derives from attending to the gifts of nature or all of creation. Ecological endeavors, therefore, enhance the quality of penultimate and ultimate visions of what humans are created and called to be. Both on the level of the individual self and in the realm of collective selves, wholeness and health (physical, spiritual, emotional, sexual, and mental) or brokenness and morbidity result from tapping into the living physicality surrounding the human community.

Here, too, the status of a subordinated community based on race, class, gender, and sexuality allows that community to open itself to possibilities usually shunned as superstitions and ignorance. Within black folk culture the power of the conjure doctor operates as a viable option. The folk are the most removed from ownership of and benefit from wealth and privileges. Consequently, they seek out whatever healing and potency are within their reach. While pursuing standard remedies of socially accepted norms and conventional scientific medicine, they readily explore the transcendental gifts from nature and comprehend the necessity of revering and fearing the awesome personality of the natural world. Not to heed nature as a protagonist in what it means to be a human could lead to the destruction of the individual's psychic and bodily health and an end to the community. At the same time, the folk appreciate how the struggle between sacred and demonic in human cultural and social interactions connects directly to a parallel battle on the plane of nature. All of creation becomes a witness to and actor in the process of visioning and realizing the imagined new human relations.

Foundationally, conjure works because of faith in the supernatural and natural remedy. Based on years of observation and partial initiation, one scholar observes:

> *The Power of Faith.* It is hard to convey to the modern materialist the intense reality of voodoo beliefs to the average illiterate Negro. The astonishing thing to those who are not acquainted with the almost unbelievable actuality of the spirit environment to the primitive people is the fact that voodoo so often works. Reputable physicians everywhere recognize the power of faith in human affairs, and it is due to this overpowering belief in conjuration that the hoodoo-doctor so often accomplishes what he sets out to do, whether it be witching things into, or witching things out of a person.[11]

Furthermore, many conjure practitioners and followers perceive a consonance between Christian belief and the conjure-nature outlook on life. "We believed God's hand was in everything, but that there were certain things you didn't ask God for. Just like you didn't ask God for revenge, that's what [the conjure doctor] was for."[12] Hence, conjuration requires, in theological anthropology, a realignment of sophisticated notions of good and evil, repudiation of sacred and secular dichotomies, and reformulation of narrow rigidities in the understanding of scientific reason. To be holistic selves and self means to see and enjoy nature, for individual and collective sanity depend on the nonhuman population.

At first glance, perhaps, the outlaw folk character seems to be the most unlikely example of what it means to be a healthy human self. Usually a male protagonist, this folk hero kills seemingly innocent bystanders, relates to women in a utilitarian manner, and, in general, creates chaos in community. Yet these surface marks obscure the deeper appreciation that black working people and those living in structural poverty often derive from the ambiguity of outlaw or bad-man toasts and ballads. The ballads are crafted by and acknowledge a spirituality of individual desire.

The Shine cycle of tales embodies the most concentrated notion of the human person underscoring the absolute rejection of everything normative in upper-income culture, especially that of privileged white communities. As the narrative tradition unfolds, Shine is the only African American allowed on the ship *Titanic*. In fact, folklore has it that not only were no other blacks allowed passage, but even Jack Johnson, the renowned black heavyweight boxing champion of the world, was denied travel. So Shine is emblematic of the one entire race and culture of African American people. Moreover, his humanity is that of the marginalized and working sectors of the black community: Shine labors at the very bottom of the ship as the lone stoker in the engine room. When the *Titanic* hits an iceberg, three times Shine emerges from below and warns the white captain that water is rising. But the captain confidently tells the lowly worker that this ship can withstand anything. After the third warning, Shine jumps over board, and before the news of the *Titanic*'s sinking reaches shore, Shine is "half drunk" and enjoying himself on land in a black neighborhood, thereby refreshing and renewing himself in his natural habitat.

Shine teaches outsiders and outcasts how the potential to pursue their own sense of self and become an "outlaw" dwells in each of them, despite the dominant society's mores that claim to define an authentic self. Shine transforms from a normal black worker into an outlaw or bad-man trope. An outlaw person suggests defiance of all oppressive realities. Shine fractures all racial and class rules, conventions, desires, and rewards. From his bottom-of-the-boat example the lowly might perceive a new way of claiming one's desire. Shine has solid faith in his own knowledge and common sense, along with compassion for the above-ship white passengers, who are depicted as the superrich elite on the ship's maiden voyage. Yet the captain (signifying race, gender, and class privileges) arrogantly believes that the most advanced and wealthiest technology known to humankind, in the form of the *Titanic*, is far superior to threats from nature (the iceberg and the ocean). And certainly he believed his rational sensibilities and scientific background, combined with such a technological marvel that Western culture had produced, would prevail. More fundamentally, Shine's notion of the self, the community's well-being, the threat of nature, and working-class know-how was insignificant to the man who commanded the helm of the great ship.

Having failed to project his own voice into the stubborn—and thus doomed—path of the captain, Shine avoids classical temptations from powerful cultures and swims for life and against death to reach higher ground. As he jumps overboard, the captain's daughter and wife scream out to Shine that they are his if he would only rescue them. But he remains focused on his goal. A millionaire offers all the money Shine can imagine, but the latter continues to swim. A pregnant woman cries hysterically for assistance in hopes of perpetuating, through her surviving to give birth, the prevailing social and emotional configurations. Again he ignores this plea. And a baby on the ship wails frantically for Shine's help; still the black worker heads toward, and thereby pursues his desire for, dry land. In the course of traversing rough waters, both a shark and a whale, at different times, defiantly announce that they are kings of the ocean. Shine retorts that they will have to exhibit adept skill at out-swimming him before he would become their meal. In a word, for certain cultures, communities, and individuals to be human is to turn toward a higher vision of firm land and a goal of refreshment and rest. The satisfying consequences can result in shattering conventional seductions of success that actually contain even more debilitating restraints over a free self.[13] Contextually driven, one has to pursue individual desire.

If Shine represents the lowly worker transforming into an outlaw, Stagolee (also referred to as Stackolee) bursts on the scene as the epitome of "bad" (read "good" to marginalized blacks and read "criminal element" to upper-income communities). Though highly problematic, Stagolee offers a redefined sense of courage, quasi-superhuman feats, bravery, and an internally centered self. Like Shine, Stagolee shows contempt for any hypocrisy inherent in civilized society's etiquettes.

Stagolee was reared in the backwoods, where his father raised a bear, and Stagolee had three sets of jawbone teeth and an extra layer of hair. At the age of three he sat on a barrel of knives, and, around the same time, a rattlesnake died after biting him. As an adult he enters the most criminal section of the black community, is dissatisfied with a meal from a bartender and kills him, becomes intimate with a woman he does not know in the business establishment, curses out the mother of the deceased bartender, and kills the bartender's brother who comes to avenge the death. Because of his legendary reputation, the police department mounts a massive army to capture him. Standing before the judge, Stagolee claims his ninety-nine-year sentence to be insignificant time. Most striking is his unfettered attitude toward the authority of the white police and judge. Because he has always been his own self and followed his own desire, the police fear him.

Likewise, he carries an independent and uncommon sense of time. Neither the criminal justice system nor the threat of one form of the temporal deters him from the perception and peace of another comprehension of immediate and long-term time. Stagolee operates in a space where race and a hierarchy of privileges are configured differently. Furthermore, he has attained a dimension of living in which death emerges as an extension of life. In some versions, Stagolee goes to hell, enjoys all of the women, sexually threatens the Devil, takes over hell, and stands on its head the symbol of the worst-imagined torment of humanity. Indeed, the Devil cries out for help to expel him. Hence, Stagolee is free of the ultimate human deterrent, the eternity of hell after death, highlighting his own alternative ultimacy.[14]

While blatantly flaunting all accepted civility of the larger community of power, Stagolee poses questions for the nature of the self and community within the black culture of the poor. In this sense, one discerns a self-critique about what type of spirituality exists among the oppressed. Specifically, the folktale raises challenges to respectable, stable family ties and parenthood. Similarly, some of Stagolee's dubious antics toward his peer group are his highly misogynist practices (for example, his derogatory female labels and utilitarian approach to black women) and his destruction of businesses in his own community.

Yet, despite the profound ambiguities of the likes of Stagolee, the community extends compassion even to seeming misfits and potentially harmful characters. Where the larger culture disciplines (even to death) such folk figures, the tough love of the folk, in contrast, embraces them and thereby manifests a certain practice of realistic and sober compassion. Here the paradigm of "badness"—the outlaw—suggests a gray area (and a thin line between heroic acts and criminality) in the understanding of human nature; that is, the complexity of defending both an individual desire and healthy collectivity within black folk culture requires a more focused norm in order to pursue a higher standard more consistently: individuality in service to collective well-being.

The fourth and final model for theological anthropology appears in the Christian witness that effects empowerment and thereby yields a spirituality of compassion for the poor. Two historical figures speak to this paradigm, and, though factual persons, folklore legend has jettisoned them into the realm of quasimyth. Harriet Tubman, deemed the Moses of her people, escaped slavery on a Maryland plantation and, despite a $40,000 bounty posted for her arrest, returned nineteen times to the South to successfully free more than three hundred fugitives. She personifies the essential Christian witness for human beings dwelling in forced circumstances. In Christian perspective, the vocation of a full individual human self is to risk and sacrifice one's own privileges in order to fashion the possibility of freedom for the least selves in one's culture. Furthermore, both Tubman and Denmark Vesey contended with a highly charged racialized Christian culture in which discrepancies in status saturated the very notion of what it meant to be a Christian.

Additionally, Tubman's journey highlighted the necessity of prayer. "She literally 'prayed without ceasing.' ''Pears like, I prayed al de time,' she said, 'about my work, eberywhere; I was always talking to the Lord,'" even when she washed her face or picked up a broom. 'Oh, Lord [she would groan], whatsoebber sin dere be in my heart, sweep it out, Lord, clar and clean.'"[15] Christian witness involves active prayer and contemplation within the mundane context of daily life. Tubman "talked with God, and he talked with her every day of her life." Such a witness indicates, among other potentialities, a continuous focus on and constant conversation with the self's ultimate vision about one's intended role in life.[16]

And this ongoing seeking and critical reflection disregards false or unnecessary separations between esteemed sacred and demonized secular spaces. One broaches the theological topic of the final new humanity at all times and in varied arenas. Instead of the quotidian dominating one's thoughts of the self, the hope of the ultimate new human being (that is, conclusions about created and called purposes) surfaces within and permeates daily culture. Christian witness materializes as the leading factor in webs of the everyday. Prayer, contemplation, and meditation call on the spirit of the ultimate vision or hope to cleanse one's self as preparation for implementing that which one is called to be, think, believe, and do as a paradigmatic human self in service to others in all spaces and at all times.

Tubman cites a created notion of Christian rights defined as inherent to the self's constitution, an endowment with the optional goal of liberty or death. One chooses to activate this gifted proclivity for freedom in the human situation as a consequence of pursuing the ultimate nature of what is a human being while defining oneself already living into the future. In other words, a witness for the future beneficent vision grows out of witnessing already to the vision now. One submits oneself to utter dependence on that longed-for status in order to experience an energizing foretaste of the eventual in one's daily witness. "'For,' said she, 'I had reasoned dis out in my mind; there was one of two things I had a *right* to, liberty, or death; if I could not have one, I would have de oder; for no man should take me alive; I should fight for my liberty as long as my strength lasted, and when de time came for me to go, de Lord would let dem take me.'"[17]

In a similar Christian witness, Denmark Vesey correlated individual rights and privileges with the liberation of group status and communal empowerment. Vesey purchased his freedom from a slavemaster in 1822 on a Charleston, South Carolina plantation, pursued an enviable trade as a carpenter, and enjoyed the admiration of free blacks, the enslaved, and plantation owners. Yet, like Tubman, he felt estranged from his self due to the languishing of other Africans and African Americans laboring for the slave system. Indeed, he surrendered his lucrative profession (that is, lucrative for a free black) in order to cease "working himself at his trade, and employed himself exclusively in enlisting men, and continued to do so until he was apprehended."[18] Vesey and his intimate confidants organized more than six thousand enslaved Africans and African Americans for insurrection against plantation patriarchs. (One informant betrayed the plans and, thereby, aborted what would have probably become one of the most democratic moments in American history—the abolition of hierarchical racial structures.)

Vesey's view of the Bible was that blacks paralleled the Israelites of the Hebrew Scriptures and their encounter with the faithful promises of Yahweh. Thus slavery subverted the Ultimate Will. The religiosity of authentic Christian witness called on oppressed strata in society to assert their created (that is, ordained) human rights. "His general conversation was about religion which he would apply to slavery, as for instance, he would speak of the creation of the world, in which he would say all men had equal rights, blacks as well as whites—all his religious remarks were mingled with slavery."[19] For Vesey, such a grand interpretive method required a global perspective on the righteousness of his Christian understanding of theological anthropology. Throughout the endeavor to achieve a reconfigured practice and community of healthy social interaction, Vesey informed his colleagues that once they commenced their democratic revolution, they would receive reinforcements from the independent black republic of Haiti and supportive forces from Africa.[20] Therefore, part of his self-perception entailed a universal concept of healthy human being that urged his outlook beyond the empirical limited numbers in his locale. Such an expansive mind-set ushers one in to global affinities with similar theological anthropologies found among black religions in Africa, Asia, the Caribbean, Latin America, and the Pacific Islands. To be human is not to succumb to classifications of immediate adverse structures, but to be guided by lofty notions beyond a restricted predicament.

Finally, Vesey's theological anthropology forecasts a novel ecclesiology, or understanding of the institutions that carry out religion's practices. Apparently, during four years of planning the insurrection, strategy sessions unfolded within the African church. In fact, the majority of the leadership and the remainder of the Christian conspirators had been or were members of the African church "from the country to the town."[21] In this instance, the organizational gathering of adherents shared an ultimate vision to link the theory and envisioning of new humanity with the practical witness of Christianity. No doubt, Vesey and his collaborators participated in conventional trappings of worship (preaching, singing, testifying, and conversions). Yet, with the success of the uprising, what was customary would have been transformed into living out the content of the normal ritual forms of Christian discourse and doctrine in radical ways more appropriate to Jesus' life.

In a word, institutional formation fused with ritualized familiarity would be the vehicle toward the realization of what it meant to be truly created and called into an economically democratized, human communality of shared life. Church witness adumbrated a reorganized future structure in which both the formerly lower and higher sectors of skewed community relations would have the conditions to forge a level playing field of humans interacting as coequal humanity. Christian witness is human empowerment.[22]

The Spirit of Liberation

As a Christian theologian—a conscious pursuer of the revelation of the spirit of liberation through Jesus Christ with working-class people and those in structural poverty and consequently all of humanity—I am simultaneously informed by non-Christian theological anthropologies working with a similar spirit. In the four folk paradigms, a normative characteristic of God or an ultimate vision is a common quest or journey on the part of the poor for communal life in place of capitalist restrictions. This spirit of liberation (as well as a spirit opposed to liberation) comes upon the human condition and in human nature through diverse means. Spirituality, therefore, is that which transcends the self, particularizes in a concrete (while extending beyond the specific), and carries positive and negative dimensions. God is the specific spirit of liberation for the earth's majority (that is, working people and the poor, and, through them, the remainder minority populations of the globe). Co-laboring with God's spirit, liberation becomes a move beyond harmful restrictions on the self and the poor. A liberation from harmful restrictions moves the poor and the working class into a humanized spiritual realm directed by freedom.

The practice of freedom is love. Indeed, black folktales teach us how the four themes of reversal, nature, ambiguity, and empowerment coupled with the corresponding spiritualities of human flourishing, awareness of all of creation, individual desire, and compassion for the poor embody love and the practice of freedom. Moreover, both love and freedom intimate a healthy theological anthropology that directs us to live out the image of God (*imago dei*) and to carry out the mission of God (*missio dei*).

To be in a state of freedom, then, is to love the unrestricted creative humanity of the poor as God loves the poor. Healthy collective and individual human creativities mirror God. This is the *imago dei* incarnated in real flesh. It stands for human efforts to open up space for those once chained internally by psychological sin and externally by structural sin. More specifically, the first aspect of the image of God means awareness of who we are as human beings. This form, likeness, essence, or fluidity in divine image means to know the self as a community comprised of individuals who can create in the image of God's inaugural creative act found in Genesis. Yahweh creates humans, nature, and life with abundance and not limitations. To be made in that image is to have the capacity to create healthy life with restrictions removed from inside and around the poor and working communities.

Freedom as awareness of who we are, the first aspect of the image of God, not only entails the capacity to create but also models God's collective ownership of all wealth. Hence, freedom in theological anthropology means that human beings act as stewards with equal collective ownership of all wealth and technology. Genesis, again, shows God bestowing equal communal ownership onto human beings (as stewards) in the Garden of Eden. Still, to achieve the ultimate vision of freedom (on earth as it is in heaven), creativity and equal ownership must include poor and working-class peoples. The greatest Fall or sin in human history was the individual's choice to accumulate personal capital (in contradiction to God's gift to all) as private ownership (the primordial wickedness of Adam in the Garden). The Fall—the rise of monopoly capitalism—gave birth to and marginalized the majority of the world's population in the modern period. The historical turn away from collective property and toward individualism intensified the exploitation and oppression of fellow humans and nature by a minority cohort in the human community. At this point, healthy theological anthropology became untethered from its root. The remainder of the entire Christian Bible is a drama (or "lies") about how to move the oppressed out of spiritual and material slavery, individual and corporate sin, and back into freedom—loving the poor and working people, and the rest of humanity, into a state of balance affecting each person's spirit and involving the ancestors who are dead, the unborn to come, and our plant, animal, and other natural family members. Capacity to create and collective ownership facilitate the love and balance within ourselves and among all of creation. Here, too, living into this type of love is the practice of freedom.

In conjunction with knowing who you are—a child of the spirit's gift of creativity and equal ownership—being made in God's image is accompanied by a second aspect, knowing whose you are. Saturated with knowledge of whose you are, you know that you are possessed by a spiritual calling to subordinate yourself to the service of others. Jesus walked this earth with that purpose in life. Emmanuel (that is, God-with-us) continues to dwell in that garden with us today, despite the seeming weaknesses in all humanity. The spirit of liberation moves us to freedom consistently even at times when we fail to love ourselves and the rest of creation.

Freedom, furthermore, flowers beyond acceptance of one's *imago dei*. A holding pattern of mere acceptance eventually withers the spirit's gift of God's image. Rather, the divinity works with us, persuades us, and loves us into carrying out this good news. In other words, the *imago dei* unfolds outward into the *missio dei*. We are called to exhibit healthy humanity by recognizing this divine image and sharing this liberation evangelism with others. And the four paradigms with their related themes and spiritualities help us to put more flesh on the bones of what we mean by freedom. The notion of freedom in a constructive theological anthropology draws on lessons from the spiritualities of these four paradigms and themes. The diversity of "lies" (that is, black folktales) constitutes what humans are called to be, believe, think, and do. Within these four models, we discover the positive dynamic of being human: to be human is the synonymous relation between love and the practice of freedom. Love is to live out the image of God and the mission of God. Likewise, the practice of freedom is to live out the image of God and the mission of God.

Specifically, the Christian witness incorporating empowerment gives us a spirituality of compassion for and service with the poor. These types of "lies" show us a spirituality that requires a self-love, love of others (including the stranger), love of God, and a love, based on justice, of the oppressor. The conjurer with nature teaches us about a spirituality of all creation. We therefore need to be attentive to revelation of power in directions (north, south, east, and west), elements (air, water, earth, and fire), animals and plants (our family members), and time dimensions (past, present, and future). The outlaw with ambiguity gives us a spirituality of individual desire, urging a direct assertion of our unique identities, space, and voices. Such a spirituality travels beyond the boundaries of dominating norms and keeps an eye on the vision at all costs, even sometimes seeming to harbor a ruthless pursuit of the goal. Such a spirituality of human desire opposes the philosophical maxim *cogito ergo sum* ("I think, therefore I am"), because this abstract formula rips apart mind and body. As an alternative, individual desire embraces sensuality and sexuality of the body, where one also finds the attached brain. Finally, the trickster, using reversal, embodies a spirituality of human flourishing that leads to creativity, cunning, and balance.

In the four folk culture types, the presupposition for building community is equality of access to the earth's resources, the assertion of self as a bearer of ultimate vision for realization of one's potentiality, and the same status within human relationships for all people regardless of race. As a result, the condition that makes this theological anthropology possible is each person's having the ability to determine his or her own true identity and his or her own space relative to accountability within community. At the same time, the accountability of the individual to community unfolds with the community's obligations to help the individual reach her or his full human potential. The community, therefore, uses the resources of the earth and of the collective body for individual identity and development (as it enhances the advancement of the least in community). The collective body nurtures the requirements for the individual to gain voice, space, identity, and material resources within the group. In this manner, an ultimate view of and quest for liberation assists in bringing about this practice of freedom for both the individual and the collective.

The achievement of the goal of individual and collective liberation is complicated by the diversity of theological anthropological themes in folk culture. For instance, the conjurer works with the spirit of liberation exhibited in nature, yet conjuring as a human purpose can entail benevolent and malevolent ramifications for the human realm. Similarly, the trickster ordinarily stands between the powerful and the weak and, through reversal, brings about social interactions of justice. But the trickster can "trick" even the weak. The outlaw, by definition, includes ambiguity—an outlaw to the norms of the dominant society, but bordering on individualism within the oppressed community. And though the clearest example of a liberating spirit is the Christian hero, this figure, as it pursues empowerment, has to guard against a triumphant, narrow, and exclusive Christocentrism. Among diversified paradigms, I argue for a liberating spiritual presence as the thread. And this normative thread takes seriously the emphasis on those at the bottom of society as the measure for the health of the entire community of human beings, the oppressed and the oppressor.

Theologically, my project contrasts with several conceptions of theological anthropology. The first is illustrated by the thesis *cogito ergo sum*—"I think, therefore I am." This perspective can suggest an "I" separated from a "we." It also imagines a mind disconnected from the body (that is, sensuality) and compassion (that is, feelings). The second perspective involves a laissez-faire, free-market approach to human well-being. Here each individual in society uses her or his self-centered will, and, through the survival of the fittest, individuals who are "stronger" reap honorable rewards and those who are "weaker" are selected out "naturally." The third view reduces people to commodities. Here the purpose of humanity is for one sector of society to exploit others for profit. In today's churches, furthermore, another negative definition of humanity is growing. It combines conservative, otherworldly doctrines and ethics with a mixture of evangelical fervor, a "name it and claim it" immediate prosperity focus, and a privatistic healing/recovery/spiritual presence expectation.

The theological presupposition of the four folktale genres (with their themes and spiritualities of humanity's relation to conjurer-nature-all creation, trickster-reversal-human flourishing, outlaw-ambiguity-individual desire, and Christian witness-empowerment-compassion for and service with the poor) is that all human beings are born with a spiritual purpose (or transcendent dimension or ultimate vision) to collectively own and partake of the abundant material wealth. No elite families have a natural, moral, or divine mandate to possess creation. Exclusive privatization of God's gifts to all communities makes one a nonhuman being. In order to nurture and sustain healthy people, we collaborate with nature to engender flourishing of the oppressed, the window into the entire *Homo sapiens* world. Today's United States of America results merely from human culture and can be transformed by human re-creation, commencing with altering the status of the bottom of society.

When a society's priorities are redirected radically to alleviating the majority of its members' plight through phasing out the super-elite's privileges, genuine democracy results. In the reconfiguration of an obsessively racialized society, we develop both collective selves and unique individuality. In this way, all people enjoy the grace of possibilities inherent in full human potential.

Notes

Introduction: Who Are We?

1. Linda E. Thomas, ed., *Living Stones in the Household of God: The Legacy and Future of Black Theology* (Minneapolis: Fortress, 2004), vii.

2. Dwight N. Hopkins, *Black Theology U.S.A. and South Africa: Politics, Culture, and Liberation* (Maryknoll, N.Y.: Orbis, 1989); *Shoes That Fit Our Feet: Sources for a Constructive Black Theology* (Maryknoll, N.Y.: Orbis, 1993); and *Down, Up, and Over: Slave Religion and Black Theology* (Minneapolis: Fortress, 1999).

3. On black theology, see James H. Cone, *For My People: Black Theology and the Black Church*, Bishop Henry McNeal Turner Studies in North American Black Religion 1 (Maryknoll, N.Y.: Orbis, 1984); James H. Cone and Gayraud S. Wilmore, eds., *Black Theology: A Documentary History*, vol. 1: 1966–79 and vol. 2: 1980–1992 (Maryknoll, N.Y.: Orbis, 1993); Harry H. Singleton III, *Black Theology and Ideology: Deideological Dimensions in the Theology of James H. Cone* (Collegeville, Minn.: Liturgical, 2002); Bruce L. Fields, *Introducing Black Theology: Three Crucial Questions for the Evangelical Church* (Grand Rapids: Baker Academic, 2001); Dale P. Andrews, *Practical Theology for Black Churches: Bridging Black Theology and African American Folk Religion* (Louisville, Ky.: Westminster John Knox, 2002); David D. Mitchell, *Black Theology and Youths at Risk* (New York: Peter Lang, 2001); Frederick L. Ware, *Methodologies of Black Theology* (Cleveland: Pilgrim, 2002); Dwight N. Hopkins, *Introducing Black Theology of Liberation* (Maryknoll, N.Y.: Orbis, 1999); Dwight N. Hopkins, *Heart and Head: Black Theology—Past, Present and Future* (New York: Palgrave Macmillan, 2002); and Thomas, *Living Stones*.

1. Contemporary Models of Theological Anthropology

1. For a fuller engagement with the history, origin, and theological concerns of the Europeans who traveled to the land of Native Americans, see Dwight N. Hopkins, *Down, Up, and Over: Slave Religion and Black Theology* (Minneapolis: Fortress, 1999).

2. See David H. Kelsey's "Human Being," in *Christian Theology: An Introduction to Its Traditions and Tasks*, ed. Peter C. Hodgson and Robert H. King (Philadelphia: Fortress, 1985), 167–93. Quotes here are from p. 167. See also James H. Evans Jr., *We Have Been Believers: An African American Systematic Theology* (Minneapolis: Fortress, 1992), 99. Some of these themes are thrashed out in a recent revival of trinitarian theological anthropology among European American theologians. For instance, see Stanley J. Grenz, *The Social God and the Relational Self: A Trinitarian Theology of the Imago Dei* (Louisville, Ky.: Westminster John Knox, 2001); Amy Plantinga Pauw, *The Supreme Harmony of All: The Trinitarian Theology of Jonathan Edwards* (Grand Rapids: Eerdmans, 2002); and Ian A. McFarland, *Difference and Identity: A Theological Anthropology* (Cleveland: Pilgrim, 2001). The first text argues against juxtaposing God and humanity via rationality; instead, Grenz asserts the connection of relationality or communion found in the paradigm of the Trinity. The second work engages the relation between the first and second persons of the Trinity relative to a social model, and the relation between the third person of the trinity and a psychological model. The third book prefers the concept "person" because of its use in the doctrine of the Trinity; McFarland sees this focus as an authentic portrayal of relationality because it helps to reconfigure the debate from intrinsic human qualities to who makes us human beings.

Perhaps still one of the best European treatments of theological anthropology is Wolfhart Pannenberg's magisterial work *Anthropology in Theological Perspective* (Edinburgh: T & T Clark, 1999). In addition to his discussion of the doctrinal debates in historical and contemporary discourses, Roman Catholic and Protestant, Pannenberg's innovative approach looks first at the human condition with the tools of sociology, cultural anthropology, psychology, and human biology and discerns their importance for theology and religion.

3. David Maldonado Jr. ("Doing Theology and the Anthropological Questions" in *Teologia en Conjunto: A Collaborative Hispanic Protestant Theology*, ed. Jose David Rodriguez and Loida I. Martell-Otero [Louisville, Ky.: Westminster John Knox, 1997], 98–99) defines two aspects of theological anthropology in this manner: "The first question relates to the essence of the human being. Here the question is, What is the essential nature of the human being? The second relates to the human predicament or condition. This question is, What is the human situation? The former relates to human essence, while the second addresses the human condition and experience."

4. For a look at the tradition of European and European American "adjectival" theologies, see Donald W. Musser and Joseph L. Price, eds., *A New Handbook of Christian Theology* (Nashville: Abingdon, 1992); Dorothee Soelle, *Thinking about God: An Introduction to Theology* (Philadelphia: Trinity Press International, 1990); Terrence W. Tilley, *Postmodern Theologies: The Challenge of Religious Diversity* (Maryknoll, N.Y.: Orbis, 1995); David Ford, ed., *The Modern Theologians* (Cambridge, Mass.: Blackwell, 1997); and John Macquarrie, *Twentieth-Century Religious Thought* (Philadelphia: Trinity Press International, 1989).

5. All theological anthropologies have adjectives in front of them. Traditionally, and even today, the dominating theologies, which rely primarily on the experiences of European and European American genealogies, do not self-name themselves as

European or European American or white. They simply imply that their theological anthropologies are neutral or universal or represent all humankind or speak for all humankind. Yet, in reality, they are very specific and confined mainly to one set of experiences. The thinking of the European and European American traditions represents a small part of human history and tradition. These are very small populations in a truly global context of religious knowledge and theological interpretations. Historically and today, European and European American traditions have pictured themselves as the center of God-talk within the United States and globally because they have, and continue to use, missions, the media, money, and the military to propagate their local experiences of the gospel of Jesus Christ.

6. His earlier pro-modernist views are apparent in David Tracy, *Blessed Rage for Order: The New Pluralism in Theology* (New York: Seabury, 1978), while his more recent acknowledgment of the harm caused by European dominance over Third World peoples can be seen in *Dialogue with the Other* (Grand Rapids: Eerdmans, 1990) and *On Naming the Present* (Maryknoll, N.Y.: Orbis, 1994). Tracy later critiqued *Blessed Rage for Order* for its modernist claims; see "Conversation with David Tracy," in *Cross Currents* (Fall 1999): 301.

7. European democracy, the rise of bourgeois revolutions starting in the eighteenth century and the continued expansion of European money, military, and missionaries throughout the world had its underside—intensification of colonization and control of peoples in Africa, Asia, the Caribbean, Latin America, and the Pacific Islands. Similarly, European American democracy (remember that the U.S. constitution was written by and for an elite group of white men with wealth) has a genealogy of maintaining asymmetrical racial, class, and gender relations in the U.S.A. Hence, American democracy might better be described as American democracies. For a more objective account of what American democracy has meant, see Ronald Takaki, *A Different Mirror: A History of Multicultural America* (Boston: Little, Brown, 1993).

8. Lois Malcolm, "An Interview with David Tracy: The Impossible God," *Christian Century* (February 13–20, 2002): 24–25.

9. See Emmanuel Kant's pioneering 1784 essay "What Is Enlightenment?" for the intellectual foundations and emotional moods of the beginning of European thinkers at this period. The Enlightenment emphasized the human being's ability to think as the starting point for dealing with all dimensions of reality. Consequently, one finds a growing accent on human reason as authoritative adjudicator, individual experience as verification, and the human context as the locus for objectivity. See Peter Gay, *The Enlightenment: An Interpretation* (New York: Norton, 1966); Bertrand Russell, *A History of Western Philosophy* (New York: Simon & Schuster, 1972); Antony Flew, *An Introduction to Western Philosophy: Ideas and Argument from Plato to Popper* (New York: Thames & Hudson, 1991); and Simon Critchley and William R. Schroeder, eds., *A Companion to Continental Philosophy* (Cambridge, Mass.: Blackwell, 1999).

10. On the rise of postmodernity as well as its implications for the study of religions, see Terrence W. Tilley, *Postmodern Theologies: The Challenge of Religious Diversity* (Maryknoll, N.Y.: Orbis, 1995); and David Batstone, Eduardo Mendieta, Lois Ann Lorentzen, and Dwight N. Hopkins, eds., *Liberation Theologies, Postmodernity, and the Americas* (New York: Routledge, 1997).

11. Tracy, *Blessed Rage*, 8.

12. Ibid., 10.

13. Ibid., 8.

14. Ibid., 9–10.

15. David Tracy, *The Analogical Imagination: Christian Theology and the Culture of Pluralism* (New York: Crossroad, 1981), 9.

16. Ibid., 36.

17. Ibid., 101.

18. See David Tracy, *Plurality and Ambiguity* (San Francisco: Harper & Row, 1987), 9.

19. Ibid., 26.

20. Ibid., 89.

21. Ibid., 106.

22. Ibid. See also David Tracy, *On Naming the Present: God, Hermeneutics, and Church* (Maryknoll, N.Y.: Orbis, 1994), 10.

23. David Tracy, *Dialogue with the Other: The Inter-Religious Dialogue* (Grand Rapids: Eerdmans, 1990).

24. Ibid., 41, 95.

25. Ibid., 1–2.

26. Ibid., 117.

27. Ibid., 17–18, 20–21.

28. David Tracy, "African American Thought: The Discovery of Fragments," in *Black Faith and Public Talk: Critical Essays on James H. Cones' Black Theology and Black Power*, ed. Dwight N. Hopkins (Maryknoll, N.Y.: Orbis, 1999), 30. Also see Malcolm, "An Interview with David Tracy," 24–27.

29. Hopkins, *Black Faith and Public Talk*, 35.

30. Malcolm, "An Interview with David Tracy," 27.

31. Ibid., 70.

32. Tracy, *Plurality and Ambiguity*, 8.

33. Tracy, *The Analogical Imagination*, 5.

34. For comments on the impact of postmodernity and globalization on social interactions (i.e., wealth, race, gender, etc.), see note 10 and Dwight N. Hopkins, Lois Ann Lorentzen, Eduardo Mendieta, and David Batstone, eds., *Religions/Globalizations: Theories and Cases* (Durham, N.C.: Duke University Press, 2001).

35. In *Plurality and Ambiguity*, Tracy creates an elaborate defense for healthy human community in the U.S.A. by way of conversation, understanding, and interpretation (see pages x and 7–19). Also see his *Dialogue with the Other*, 41; earlier he writes, "For hermeneutics lives or dies by its ability to take history and language seriously, to allow the other (whether person, event, or text) to claim our attention as other, not as a projection of our present fears, hopes and desires" (4).

36. Ibid., 435–36.

37. See "Black Power: Statement by the National Committee of Negro Churchmen," in *Black Theology: A Documentary History*, vol. 1: 1966–79, eds. James H. Cone and Gayraud S. Wilmore (Maryknoll, N.Y.: Orbis, 1993), 19.

38. Tracy, *On Naming the Present*, 11, 21.

39. Tracy, *Plurality and Ambiguity*, 106.

40. George A. Lindbeck, *The Nature of Doctrine: Religion and Theology in a Postliberal Age* (Philadelphia: Westminster, 1984). See also Lindbeck, "*Fides ex auditu* and the Salvation of Non-Christians: Contemporary Catholic and Protestant Positions," in *The Gospel and the Ambiguity of the Church*, ed. Vilmos Vajta (Philadelphia: Fortress, 1974), 119.

41. George Lindbeck, "The Infallibility Debate," in *The Infallibility Debate*, ed. John J. Kirvan (New York: Paulist, 1971), 114–15.

42. Ibid., 110.

43. George A. Lindbeck, "The Church's Mission to a Postmodern Culture," in *Postmodern Theology: Christian Faith in a Pluralist World*, ed. Fredric B. Burnham (San Francisco: HarperSanFrancisco, 1989), 54.

44. Ibid., 47.

45. Ibid., 23.

46. Lindbeck, *Nature of Doctrine*, 17–18.

47. Ibid., 129.

48. Ibid., 118.

49. Ibid., 125–26.

50. Ibid., 83–84. Also see George A. Lindbeck, "Barth and Textuality," *Theology Today* 43/3 (October 1986): 367.

51. Lindbeck, *Nature of Doctrine*, 127; Lindbeck, "Barth and Textuality," 376; and Lindbeck, "Church's Mission," 53.

52. Lindbeck, *Nature of Doctrine*, 127.

53. One of the failures of most educational policy makers is to avoid the existence of different types of English in the U.S.A. Ebonics or black English remains a vibrant means of communication even today. See William Labov, *Language in the Inner City: Studies in the Black English Vernacular* (Philadelphia: University of Pennsylvania Press, 1976); Jim Haskins and Hugh F. Butts, *The Psychology of Black Language* (New York: Barnes & Noble, 1973); Geneva Smitherman, *Talkin and Testifyin: The Language of Black America* (Detroit: Wayne State University Press, 1977); Winifred Kellersberger Vass, *The Bantu-Speaking Heritage of the United States* (Los Angeles: Center for Afro-American Studies, University of California Los Angeles, 1979); Marjorie Harness Goodwin, *He-Said-She-Said: Talk As Social Organization among Black Children* (Bloomington: Indiana University Press, 1990); Edith A. Folb, *Black Vernacular Vocabulary: A Study of Intra/Intercultural Concerns and Usage* (Los Angeles: Center for Afro-American Studies, University of California Los Angeles, 1972); and J. L. Dillard, *Black English: Its History and Usage in the United States* (New York: Random House, 1972). Also see the interwoven importance between language and religion in Dwight N. Hopkins and George C. L. Cummings, eds., *Cut Loose Your Stammering Tongue: Black Theology in the Slave Narratives* (Louisville, Ky.: Westminster John Knox, 2003).

54. See Itumeleng Mosala, *Biblical Hermeneutics and Black Theology in South Africa* (Grand Rapids: Eerdmans, 1989).

55. William Styron, *The Confessions of Nat Turner* (New York: Random House, 1966); Henry Irving Tragle, *The Southhampton Slave Revolt of 1831: A Compilation of Source Material* (Amherst: University of Massachusetts Press, 1971); Herbert Aptheker, *Nat Turner's Slave Rebellion* (New York: Humanities, 1966); and Stephen

B. Oates, *The Fires of Jubilee: Nat Turner's Fierce Rebellion* (New York: Harper & Row, 1975).

56. Rosemary Radford Ruether, *Sexism and God-Talk: Toward a Feminist Theology* (Boston: Beacon, 1993 [1983]), 13.

57. Ibid., 18–19.

58. Ibid., 19.

59. Ibid., 20.

60. Ibid., 32; and Rosemary Radford Ruether, *To Change the World: Christology and Cultural Criticism* (New York: Crossroad, 1981), 54–56.

61. Rosemary Radford Ruether, *New Woman New Earth: Sexist Ideologies and Human Liberation* (New York: Seabury, 1975), 125.

62. Ibid., 111.

63. Ibid., 113–14.

64. Ibid., 4.

65. Rosemary Radford Ruether, *Introducing Redemption in Christian Feminism* (Sheffield: Sheffield Academic, 1998), 75.

66. Ruether, *Sexism and God-Talk*, 113.

67. Ibid., 137.

68. Ibid., 232–33. See also Ruether, *To Change the World*, 11.

69. Ruether, *To Change the World*, 17.

70. For additional writings on James H. Cone, see Hopkins, ed., *Black Faith and Public Talk*; the entirety of *Union Seminary Quarterly Review* 48/1–2 (1994), which focuses on James H. Cone's *Martin & Malcolm & America: A Dream or a Nightmare?* as public theology; Dwight N. Hopkins, "James H. Cone," in *Key Figures in African American Thought*, ed. L. R. Gordon (Oxford: Blackwell, 1997); Dwight N. Hopkins, "Postmodernism, Black Theology of Liberation, and the U.S.A.: Michel Foucault and James H. Cone," *Journal of Hispanic/Latino Theology* 3/4 (May 1996); Rufus Burrow Jr., *James H. Cone and Black Liberation Theology* (Jefferson, N.C.: McFarland, 1994); and Harry H. Singleton III, *Black Theology and Ideology: Deideological Dimensions in the Theology of James H. Cone* (Collegeville, Minn.: Liturgical, 2002).

71. James H. Cone, *God of the Oppressed* (San Francisco: HarperSanFrancisco, 1975), 138.

72. James H. Cone, *A Black Theology of Liberation* (Maryknoll, N.Y.: Orbis, 1986 [1970]), 85.

73. Cone, *God of the Oppressed*, 139.

74. Ibid., 141–45.

75. Ibid., 145–46.

76. James H. Cone, *Black Theology and Black Power* (Maryknoll, N.Y.: Orbis, 1997), 28.

77. Cone, *A Black Theology of Liberation*, 101.

78. Cone, *Black Theology and Black Power*, 52–53.

79. Cone, *God of the Oppressed*, 141–62.

80. Cone, *Black Theology and Black Power*, 47.

81. On the origins, contours, problematic, and theological and ethical program of womanist theology, see Stephanie Y. Michem, *Introducing Womanist Theology* (Maryknoll, N.Y.: Orbis, 2002); Dwight N. Hopkins, chapter 4, "Womanist

Theology," in *Introducing Black Theology of Liberation* (Maryknoll, N.Y.: Orbis, 1999); and Diana L. Hayes, chapter 7, "The Vision of Black Women: Womanist Theology," in *And Still We Rise: An Introduction to Black Liberation Theology* (New York: Paulist, 1996).

82. Jacquelyn Grant, "The Sin of Servanthood: And the Deliverance of Discipleship," in *A Troubling in My Soul: Womanist Perspectives On Evil & Suffering*, ed. Emilie M. Townes (Maryknoll, N.Y.: Orbis, 1993), 200.

83. Ibid., 208.

84. Ibid., 208–14.

85. Jacquelyn Grant, "Servanthood Revisited: Womanist Explorations of Servanthood Theology," in Hopkins, ed., *Black Faith and Public Talk*, 133.

86. Ibid.

87. Emilie M. Townes, *In A Blaze of Glory: Womanist Spirituality as Social Witness* (Nashville: Abingdon, 1995), 11.

88. Ibid., 48–49.

89. Ibid.

90. Ibid., 11.

91. This quote comes from a conversation I had with Karen Baker-Fletcher on February 4, 2005. An elaborated discussion of these seven points can be found in her book *My Sister, My Brother: Womanist and Xodus God-Talk* (Maryknoll, N.Y.: Orbis, 1997), 150–60, coauthored with her husband, Garth Kasimu Baker-Fletcher. Furthermore, these seven are extensions of her original five found in her book *A Singing Something: Womanist Reflections on Ana Julia Cooper* (New York: Crossroad, 1994), 188–204.

92. Linda E. Thomas, "Womanist Theology, Epistemology, and a New Anthropological Paradigm," in *Living Stones in the Household of God: The Legacy and Future of Black Theology*, ed. Linda E. Thomas (Minneapolis: Fortress, 2004), 38.

93. Kelly Delaine Brown Douglas, "Womanist Theology: What Is Its Relationship to Black Theology?" in Cone and Wilmore, *Black Theology*, 2:292–98.

94. Renee L. Hill, "Who Are We For Each Other?: Sexism, Sexuality and Womanist Theology," in ibid., 2:346. For nuanced interpretations of Alice Walker's definition of womanism, see the entire section on womanist theology found in Cone and Wilmore, *Black Theology*, vol. 2.

95. Miguel H. Diaz, *On Being Human: U.S. Hispanic and Rahnerian Perspectives* (Maryknoll, N.Y.: Orbis, 2001), xv, 32, 45.

96. David Maldonado Jr., "Doing Theology and the Anthropological Question," in *Teologia en Conjunto: A Collaborative Hispanic Protestant Theology*, ed. Jose David Rodriguez and Loida I. Martell-Otero (Louisville, Ky.: Westminster John Knox, 1997), 106–7.

97. Ibid., 100, 106–10.

98. Ibid., 107–10.

99. Virgil Elizondo, *Galilean Journey: The Mexican-American Promise*, rev. ed. (Maryknoll, N.Y.: Orbis, 2000), 19, 124.

100. Ibid., xv. These seven intellectuals represent the seven themes sequentially as presented in the text: Virgilio Elizondo, Roberto S. Goizueta, Orlando O. Espin, Ada María Isasi-Díaz, Maria Pilar Aquino, Alejandro Garcia-Rivera, and Sixto J. Garcia.

101. Ada María Isasi-Díaz, *Mujerista Theology* (Maryknoll, N.Y.: Orbis, 1996), 1.

102. Ibid., 128–44.

103. Fumitaka Matsuoka, *Out of Silence: Emerging Themes in Asian American Churches* (Cleveland: United Church Press, 1995), 63 and chapter 2.

104. Ibid., 34–39.

105. Ibid, 73–74.

106. Jung Ha Kim, "The Labour of Compassion: Voices of 'Churched' Korean American Women," *Voices from the Third World* 24/1 (June 2001): 16–18.

107. Ibid., 17.

108. Clara Sue Kidwell, Homer Noley, and George E. Tinker, *A Native American Theology* (Maryknoll, N.Y.: Orbis, 2001), 85–86.

109. Ibid., 15, 12.

110. Ibid., 109.

111. Ibid., 109–10, 126–27.

112. Andrea Smith, "Walking in Balance: The Spirituality-Liberation Praxis of Native Women," in *Native American Religious Identity: Unforgotten Gods*, ed. Jace Weaver (Maryknoll, N.Y.: Orbis, 1998), 190. On page 195, however, Smith does indicate the growing concern of Indian women about increased sexual and domestic violence in their communities.

2. Culture: Labor, Aesthetic, and Spirit

1. Randwedzi Nengwekhulu, "The Dialectical Relationship between Culture and Religion in the Struggle for Resistance and Liberation," in *Culture, Religion, and Liberation*, ed. Simon S. Maimela (Pretoria: Penrose, 1994), 19. Dr. Nengwekhulu is Lecturer at the Institute of Development Management in Gaborone, Botswana.

2. Raymond Williams, *The Long Revolution* (New York: Columbia University Press, 1984 [1961]).

3. Stuart Hall, "Cultural Studies: Two Paradigms," in *Culture/Power/History: A Reader in Contemporary Social Theory*, ed. Nicholas B. Dirks, Geoff Eley, and Sherry B. Ortner (Princeton, N.J.: Princeton University Press, 1994), 522, 524.

4. Ibid., 522.

5. Ibid., 523, 524.

6. W. Emmanuel Abraham, "Crisis in African Cultures," in *Person and Community: Ghanaian Philosophical Studies I*, ed. Kwasi Wiredu and Kwame Gyekye (Washington, D.C.: Council for Research in Values and Philosophy, 1992), 13.

7. Edward P. Wimberly and Anne Streaty Wimberly, *Liberation and Human Wholeness: The Conversion Experiences of Black People in Slavery and Freedom* (Nashville: Abingdon, 1986), explore some of the emotional and psychological realities of black culture. Similarly, see William H. Grier and Price M. Cobbs (two psychiatrists), *Black Rage* (New York: Basic, 1968), and Ellis Cose, *The Rage of a Privileged Class* (New York: HarperCollins, 1993).

8. Abraham, "Crisis in African Cultures," 14.

9. See Melville J. Herskovits, *Myth of the Negro Past* (Boston: Beacon, 1990 [1941]); E. Franklin Frazier, *The Negro Family in the United States* (Chicago: Univer-

sity of Chicago Press, 1966 [1939]); William Bascom, *African Folktales in the New World* (Bloomington: Indiana University Press, 1992); and Richard M. Dorson, "African and Afro-American Folklore: A Reply to Bascom and Other Misguided Critics," *Journal of American Folklore* 88, no. 348 (April–June 1975): 151–64.

10. See Sterling Stuckey, *Slave Culture* (New York: Oxford University Press, 1977); Roger D. Abrahams, ed., *Afro-American Folktales: Stories from Black Traditions in the New World* (New York: Pantheon, 1985); Jacob Drachler, *African Heritage: Stories, Poems, Songs, Folk Tales and Essays from Black Africa Revealing the Rich Cultural Roots of Today's Black Americans* (London: Collier, 1969); William D. Piersen, *Black Legacy: America's Hidden Heritage* (Amherst: University of Massachusetts Press, 1993); and Molefe Kete Asante, *The Afrocentric Idea* (Philadelphia: Temple University Press, 1987).

11. See Angela Y. Walton-Raji, *Black Indian Genealogy Research: African American Ancestors among the Five Civilized Tribes* (Bowie, Md.: Heritage, 1993); William Loren Katz, *Black Indians: A Hidden Heritage* (New York: Alladin, 1997); and Jack D. Forbes, *Africans and Native Americans: The Language of Race and the Evolution of Red-Black Peoples* (Urbana: University of Illinois Press, 1993).

12. In my *Down, Up, and Over: Slave Religion and Black Theology* (Minneapolis: Fortress, 1999), I argue for black culture being constituted by three strands, one of which is a reinterpretation of the negative slavemaster culture and white supremacist Christian doctrines. In retrospect, it would have been helpful to acknowledge the Native American/American Indian influence on the making of African American culture.

13. Abraham, "Crisis in African Cultures," 29.

14. Amilcar Cabral, "National Liberation and Culture," in his *Return to the Source: Selected Speeches of Amilcar Cabral* (New York: Monthly Review, 1973), 41.

15. Ibid., 41–42.

16. Ibid., 43–44, 50.

17. Ibid., 55.

18. Lucius T. Outlaw, "Race and Class in the Theory and Practice of Emancipatory Social Transformation," in *Philosophy Born of Struggle: Anthology of Afro-American Philosophy from 1917*, ed. Leonard Harris (Dubuque, Iowa: Kendall/Hunt, 1983), 122.

19. Ibid., 122–23.

20. Barry Hallen, *The Good, the Bad and the Beautiful: Discourse about Values in Yoruba Culture* (Bloomington: Indiana University Press, 2000).

21. Ibid., 114–15.

22. Ibid., 115.

23. Ibid., 117.

24. Ibid., 118–19.

25. Ibid. 120–21.

26. J. P. Odoch Pido, "Personhood and Art: Social Change and Commentary among the Acoli," in *African Philosophy as Cultural Inquiry*, ed. Ivan Karp and D. A. Masolo (Bloomington: Indiana University Press, 2000), 112.

27. Ibid.

28. Ibid.

29. Innocent C. Onyewuenyi, "Traditional African Aesthetics: A Philosophical Perspective," in *The African Philosophy Reader*, ed. P. H. Coetzee and A. P. J. Roux (New York: Routledge, 1998), 398.

30. Ibid., 399.

31. Kwame Gyekye, *African Cultural Values: An Introduction* (Accra, Ghana: Sankofa, 1998), xiii.

32. Ibid., 4–5.

33. Patrick A. Kalilombe, "Spirituality in the African Perspective," in *Paths of African Theology*, ed. Rosino Gibellini (Maryknoll, N.Y.: Orbis, 1994), 115.

34. Ibid., 118–19.

35. Ibid., 122.

36. Ibid. Kalilombe quotes John Pobee, *Toward an African Theology* (Nashville: Abingdon, 1979), 49.

37. Ibid.

38. For a detailed and interesting look at how the spirituality of the living dead ancestors, the unborn, and reincarnation play into the notion of contemporary culture, see Kofi Asare Opoku, *West African Traditional Religions* (Accra, Ghana: FEP International Private Limited, 1976), 25–39, and Ogbu U. Kalu, "Ancestral Spirituality and Society in Africa," in *African Spirituality: Forms, Meanings, and Expressions*, ed. Jacob K. Olupona (New York: Crossroad, 2000), 54–55. In my present argument, these contributions are not by necessity germane to my claims; hence I omit a full treatment at this time.

39. Kalilombe, "Spirituality in the African Perspective," 132–33.

40. Mercy Amba Oduyoye, "Spirituality of Resistance and Reconstruction," in *Women Resisting Violence*, ed. Mary John Mananzan, Mercy Amba Oduyoye, Elsa Tamez, J. Shannon, Mary C. Grey, and Letty M. Russell (Maryknoll, N.Y.: Orbis, 1996), 163.

41. Ibid., 167. See also her *Daughters of Anowa: African Women and Patriarchy* (Maryknoll, N.Y.: Orbis, 1995), especially chapters 4, 5, and 6.

42. Kwame Gyekye agrees with Oduyoye when he states, "In talking about cultural values, I do not imply by any means that there are no cultural disvalues or negative features of the African [traditional] cultures. There are, of course; and they are legion" (*African Cultural Values*, 171, 174). Likewise, Kalilombe challenges traditional spirituality by stating that the seeds of negative spirituality preexisted foreign contact, particularly the failure to allow for some forms of "individualistic ambition, aggressiveness, and self-interested acquisitiveness" ("Spirituality in the African Perspective," 129).

43. See Anna Mary Mukamwezi Kayonga, "African Women and Morality," in *Moral and Ethical Issues in African Christianity: A Challenge for African Christianity*, ed. J. N. K. Mugambi and A. Nasimiyu-Wasike (Nairobi, Kenya: Acton, 1999), 141–45; Isabel Apawo Phiri, Devakarsham Betty Govinden, and Sarojini Nadar, eds., *Her-Stories: Hidden Histories of Women of Faith in Africa* (Pietermaritzburg, South Africa: Cluster, 2002); Musimbi R. A. Kanyoro and Nyambura J. Njoroge, eds., *Groaning in Faith: African Women in the Household of God* (Nairobi, Kenya: Acton, 1996); and Ama Ata Aidoo, "The African Woman Today," in *Sisterhood, Feminisms and Power: From Africa to Diaspora*, ed. Obioma Nnaemeka (Trenton, N.J.: Africa World, 1998), 39–50.

44. For further appreciation of my normative claim of the poor, see my *Heart and Head: Black Theology Past, Present, and Future* (New York: Palgrave Macmillan, 2002) and *Introducing Black Theology of Liberation* (Maryknoll, N.Y.: Orbis, 1999).

45. bell hooks, *Rock My Soul: Black People and Self-Esteem* (New York: Atria, 2003), 12.

46. Ibid., 11.

47. For additional works on the communal culture of resistance within African American scholarship, see Archie Smith Jr., *Navigating the Deep River: Spirituality in African American Families* (Cleveland: United Church Press, 1997); Flora Wilson Bridges, *Resurrection Song: African-American Spirituality* (Maryknoll, N.Y.: Orbis, 2001); Lee H. Butler, Jr., *A Loving Home: Caring for African American Marriage and Families* (Cleveland: Pilgrim, 2000); Homer U. Ashby Jr., *Our Home Is over Jordan: A Black Pastoral Theology* (St. Louis: Chalice, 2003); and Teresa L. Fry Brown, *God Don't Like Ugly: African American Women Handing on Spiritual Values* (Nashville: Abingdon, 2000).

48. From J. N. K. Mugambi's lecture given at the Pan African Consultation on Religion and Poverty in Nairobi, Kenya, July 20, 2002. Notes in author's possession.

3. Selves and the Self: I Am Because We Are

1. Ifeanyi A. Menkiti, "Person and Community in African Traditional Thought," in *African Philosophy: An Introduction*, 2nd ed., ed. Richard A. Wright (Washington, D.C.: University Press of America, 1979), 157. Similar analysis is found in Kwasi Wiredu, "The African Concept of Personhood," in *African-American Perspectives on Biomedical Ethics*, ed. Harley E. Flack and Edmund D. Pellegrino (Washington, D.C.: Georgetown University Press, 1992), 104–17.

2. For further treatment of the notion of self in relation to the new common wealth, see my *Heart and Head: Black Theology Past, Present and Future* (New York: Palgrave Macmillan, 2002).

3. An extended critical intervention in the conversation about the plurality of God's liberating spirituality among humanity can be found in my *Down, Up, and Over: Slave Religion and Black Theology* (Minneapolis: Fortress, 1999).

4. Kwame Gyekye, *Tradition and Modernity: Philosophical Reflections on the African Experience* (New York: Oxford University Press, 1997), 41–42. Also see his *An Essay on African Philosophical Thought: The Akan Conceptual Scheme* (Philadelphia: Temple University Press, 1995).

5. Kwame Gyekye, *African Cultural Values: An Introduction* (Accra, Ghana: Sankofa, 1998), 35.

6. Ibid., 36.

7. Gyekye, *Tradition and Modernity*, 45–46.

8. Ibid.

9. Benezet Bujo, *Foundations of an African Ethic: Beyond the Universal Claims of Western Morality* (New York: Crossroad, 2001), 87–88.

10. Ibid., 88.

11. Kofi Asare Opoku, "In Pursuit of Community: An African Perspective," in *Healing For God's World: Remedies from Three Continents*, ed. Kofi Asare Opoku, Kim Young-Bock, and Antoinette Clark Wire (New York: Friendship, 1991), 18–19.

12. Hannah W. Kinoti, "African Morality: Past and Present," in *Moral and Ethical Issues in African Christianity*, ed. J. N. K. Mugambi and A. Nasimiyu-Wasike (Nairobi, Kenya: Acton, 1999), 78.

13. See the chapter on nature in Clara Sue Kidwell, Homer Noley, and George E. Tinker, *A Native American Theology* (Maryknoll, N.Y.: Orbis, 2001).

14. Opoku, "In Pursuit of Community," 21–22.

15. Bujo, *Foundations of an African Ethic*, 34–35.

16. N. K. Dzobo, "Values in a Changing Society: Man, Ancestors, and God," in *Person and Community: Ghanaian Philosophical Studies I*, ed. Kwasi Wiredu and Kwame Gyekye (Washington, D.C.: Council for Research in Values and Philosophy, 1992), 226.

17. Bujo, *Foundations of an African Ethic*, 1–2. Also examine Kinoti, "African Morality," 76, and Opoku, "In Pursuit of Community," 18.

18. Kim Yong-Bock, "Covenant with the Poor: Toward a New Concept of Economic Justice," in *Healing for God's World: Remedies from Three Continents*, ed. Kofi Asare Opoku, Kim Yong-Bock, and Antoinette Clark Wire (New York: Friendship, 1991), 80.

19. Ibid., 81–82. Yong-Bock supplies additional biblical passages as data: Mic. 2:2-5; Deut. 10:17-18, 14-15; 16:19; Ps. 82:3; Exod. 23:3; 2 Sam. 22:28; Isa. 1:21-23; 25:4; 61:1; Amos 2:6; 4:1; Leviticus 19 and 23; Hos. 12:8-9; Luke 1:53; 4:18ff.; 5:29-32; 6:5, 20, 21, 24, 25; 14:15-24; 16:19ff.; 18:18ff.; 21:1ff.; and Matt. 26:31-46. Also see Englebert Mveng, "Impoverishment and Liberation: A Theological Approach for Africa and the Third World," in *Paths of African Theology*, ed. Rosino Gibellini (Maryknoll, N.Y.: Orbis, 1994), 163, for further biblical warrants for a communal political economy.

As we employ biblical pointers, we are aware of shortcomings even in the text itself. For instance, one has to be careful how the exodus theme is used. Robert Allen Warrior ("A Native American Perspective: Canaanites, Cowboys, and Indians," in *Voices from the Margins: Interpreting the Bible in the Third World*, ed. R. S. Sugirtharajah [Maryknoll, N.Y.: Orbis, 1991, 287–95]) cautions against such a theme because there existed indigenous people already in Canaan who are violently conquered by the Hebrew people exiting from slavery in Egypt. And Renita Weems (*Battered Love: Marrigae, Sex, and Violence in the Hebrew Prophets*, Overtures to Biblical Theology [Minneapolis: Fortress, 1995]) decries the pornographic domestic violence language that some of the biblical prophets deployed as tropes.

20. Kwasi Wiredu ("The Moral Foundations of an African Culture," in Wiredu and Gyekye, *Person and Community*, 194), Kwame Gyekye (*An Essay on African Philosophical Thought*, 19–20, 154), and N. K. Dzobo ("Values in a Changing Society," 226–27) argue for a form of humanism that I take to imply an obligation to the poor's well-being.

21. Mary N. Getui, "Material Things in Contemporary African Society," in *Moral and Ethical Issues in African Christianity: A Challenge for African Christianity*, ed. J. N. K. Mugambi and A. Nasimiyu-Wasike (Nairobi, Kenya: Acton, 1999), 59.

22. Young-Bock, "Covenant with the Poor," 98.

23. At this point, again, it would be helpful to examine the concept of common wealth found in my *Heart and Head*. The argument here relies to a certain degree on lines of pursuit followed in my previous text.

24. Laurenti Magesa, *African Religion: The Moral Traditions of Abundant Life* (Maryknoll, N.Y.: Orbis, 1997), 277–78.

25. Ambrose Moyo, "Material Things in African Society: Implications for Christian Ethics," in Mugambi and Nasimiyu-Wasike, *Moral and Ethical Issues in African Christianity*, 53. Magesa concurs but stresses communal land as a gift directly from God and public property entrusted to society's members for their own use. See his *African Religion*, 280.

26. Mario O. Castillo Rangel is a professor at the Northern Caribbean University in Mandeville, Jamaica. He gave a speech on political economy to the Pan African Seminar on Religion and Poverty, July 25, 2003, in Jamaica. As a member of that seminar, I have a copy of his text.

27. Gyekye, *An Essay on African Philosophical Thought*, 157–58.

28. Young-Bock, "Covenant with the Poor," 98.

29. Archie Smith Jr., *The Relational Self: Ethics and Therapy from a Black Church Perspective* (Nashville: Abingdon, 1982), 51.

30. Ibid., 14–15.

31. Homer U. Ashby Jr., *Our Home Is over Jordan: A Black Pastoral Theology* (St. Louis: Chalice, 2003), 49–50.

32. Bujo, *Foundations of an African Ethic*, 87.

33. See Kwasi Wiredu, *Cultural Universals and Particulars: An African Perspective*, African Systems of Thought (Bloomington: Indiana University Press, 1996), 71. Wiredu compares the complexity of African indigenous culture and its take on prioritizing selves in order to enhance both the collective and the individual with the complexity of the eighteenth-century European Enlightenment and its nineteenth-century, monopoly capitalist industrial revolutions, which featured an aggressive, unbridled notion of privately accumulating wealth at the expense of others and nature. These revolutions resulted in hierarchical racial, gender, and colonial discrepancies among the selves. The late nineteenth century likewise saw intensification of monopolization among the descendants of Europe in the United States of America.

34. See Bujo, *Foundations of an African Ethic*, 87.

35. J. P. Odoch Pido, "Personhood and Art: Social Change and Commentary among the Acoli," in *African Philosophy as Cultural Inquiry*, ed. Ivan Karp and D. A. Masolo (Bloomington: Indiana University Press, 2000), 106.

36. Bujo, *Foundations of an African Ethic*, 87.

37. See Wiredu, *Cultural Universals and Particulars*, 58, 71–72, 129.

38. Amilcar Cabral, *Return to the Source: Selected Speeches of Amilcar Cabral* (New York: Monthly Review, 1973), 65.

39. Ibid., 66.

40. John S. Mbiti, *African Religions and Philosophy* (New York: Anchor, 1970), 3.

41. Kofi Asare Opoku, *West African Traditional Religion* (Accra, Ghana: FEP International, 1978), 26.

42. Gyekye, *An Essay on African Philosophical Thought*, 19–20. Gyekye plumbs the same point in his *African Cultural Values: An Introduction* (Accra, Ghana:

Sankofa, 1998), 24. And see Wiredu, *Cultural Universals and Particulars*: "Every human being . . . has an intrinsic value, since he is seen as possession in himself a part of God" (130).

43. Kwame Nkrumah, *Consciencism: Philosophy and Ideology for Decolonization* (New York: Monthly Review, 1970), 68–69.

44. See Gyekye, "Person and Community in African Thought," in Wiredu and Gyekye, *Person and Community*, 110.

45. Gyekye, *African Cultural Values*, 25–26.

46. Pido, "Personhood and Art," 106.

47. Opoku, *West African Traditional Religion*, 10.

48. Gyekye, *An Essay on African Philosophical Thought*, 100–101.

49. Opoku, *West African Traditional Religion*, 91.

50. N. K. Dzobo, "Knowledge and Truth: Ewe and Akan Conceptions," in Wiredu and Gyekye, *Person and Community*, 73.

51. Wiredu, *Cultural Universals and Particulars*, 21.

52. See ibid., 21–23, for an extended and fascinating engagement with these notions of reflective perception, abstraction, and inference.

53. Getui, "Material Things in Contemporary African Society," 59.

54. Smith, *The Relational Self*, 80.

55. Ibid., 66–67. And the immediate discussion regarding three options for choice into self freedom comes from 81–89.

56. Ibid., 86–87.

57. See the following regarding the wealthy of the United States: Robert L. Allen, *Black Awakening in Capitalist America: An Analytic History* (Garden City, N.Y.: Doubleday, 1969); Manning Marable, *How Capitalism Underdeveloped Black America* (Boston: South End, 1983); David Rockefeller, *Memoirs* (New York: Random House, 2002); Nelson W. Aldrich Jr., *Old Money* (New York: Vintage, 1989); Michael Parenti, *Democracy for the Few* (New York: St. Martin's, 1977); G. William Domhoff, *Who Rules America Now?* (Englewood Cliffs, N.J.: Prentice-Hall, 1983); Richard C. Edwards, Michael Reich, and Thomas E. Weisskopf, eds., *The Capitalist System* (Englewood Cliffs, N.J.: Prentice-Hall, 1972); David N. Smith, *Who Rules the Universities?* (New York: Monthly Review, 1974); Frances Fox Piven and Richard A. Cloward, *The New Class War* (New York: Pantheon, 1982); and Felix Greene, *The Enemy: What Every American Should Know about Imperialis*m (New York: Vintage, 1971).

58. Gyekye, *An Essay on African Philosophical Thought*, 157–59.

59. See Bujo (*Foundations of an African Ethic*, 6) and Gyekye (*African Cultural Values*, 50) for further attention to these concepts.

60. Refer to Bujo, *Foundations of an African Ethic*, 92–93.

61. One of the most lucid discussions of self-concept as self-esteem is found in bell hooks, *Rock My Soul: Black People and Self-Esteem* (New York: Atria, 2003).

62. I laid the path of these sources and this concern in my 1988 PhD dissertation, *Black Theology U.S.A. and South Africa: Politics, Culture, and Liberation*, published one year later under the same name by Orbis Books in Maryknoll, New York. As I approach the twentieth anniversary of that dissertation, everything I've ever written revolves around and expands from those core sources and focused con-

cerns. As my ancestors would say, "Lord willing and the creek don't rise," I remain on the path.

63. One can find a successful model in the text *The Story of Four Schools: The Findings of the Change from Within Project Initiated at the University of the West Indies (Jamaica)* (Mona Campus, University of the West Indies: Jamaica, circa 1996). Visionary and courageous educators chose Jamaican urban schools with high violence and crime levels. Resulting from the change-from-within methodology, test scores increased, sports teams brought back trophies, musically inclined students emerged, crime and violence decreased, and the students, teachers, and staff added to the national pedagogical and cultural treasure of Jamaica.

64. Teresia M. Hinga, "The Biblical Mandate for Social Transformation: A Feminist Perspective," in *Moral and Ethical Issues in African Christianity: Exploratory Issues in Moral Theology*, ed. J. N. K. Mugambi and A. Nasimiyu-Wasike, African Christianity 3 (Nairobi, Kenya: Acton, 1992), 38–41.

65. I extrapolate and surmise this tripartite outline from Gyekye, *An Essay on African Philosophical Thought*, 158–61.

66. Gyekye, *Tradition and Modernity*, 66. See also his "Person and Community," 115–17; Opoku, *West African Traditional Religion*, 11; and Bujo, *Foundations of an African Ethic*, 163.

67. Anna Mary Mukamwezi Kayonga, "African Women and Morality," in Mugambi and Nasimiyu-Wasike, *Moral and Ethical Issues in African Christianity*, 137.

68. Philomena N. Mwaura, "Gender Mainstreaming in African Theology: An African Woman's Perspective," *Voices from the Third World* 24/1 (2001): 169–70.

69. Nyambura J. Njoroge, *An African Christian Feminist Ethic of Resistance and Transformation* (Legon, Ghana: Legon Theological Studies Series, 2000), 124, 126.

70. See Weems, *Battered Love*.

71. Mercy Amba Oduyoye, "Feminist Theology in an African Perspective," in *Paths of African Theology*, ed. Rosino Gibellini (Maryknoll, N.Y.: Orbis, 1994), 178.

72. W. Emmanuel Abraham gives a convincing ethnographic and philosophical account of the socially derived and maintained categories of parenting. His research concludes the sharing of motherhood and fatherhood and wife and husband roles between women and men. W. Emmanuel Abraham, "Crisis in African Cultures," in Wiredu and Gyekye, *Person and Community*, 19.

73. Jacquelyn Grant, "Servanthood Revisited: Womanist Explorations of Servanthood Theology," in *Black Faith and Public Talk: Critical Essays on James H. Cone's Black Theology and Black Power*, ed. Dwight N. Hopkins (Maryknoll, N.Y.: Orbis, 1999), 133.

4. Race: Nature and Nurture

1. For a comprehensive look at the tradition and theory of the one-drop rule, see F. James Davis, *Who Is Black? One Nation's Definition* (University Park: Pennsylvania State University Press, 2001). Compare Scott L. Malcolmson, *One Drop*

of Blood: The American Misadventure of Race (New York: Farrar, Straus, and Giroux, 2000).

2. Kwame Anthony Appiah, "Racisms," in *Anatomy of Racism*, ed. David Theo Goldberg (Minneapolis: University of Minnesota Press, 1990), 3–17.

3. Joel Kovel, *White Racism: A Psychohistory* (New York: Columbia University Press, 1984 [1970]). Also review Lawrence J. Friedman, *The White Savage: Racial Fantasies in the Postbellum South* (Englewood Cliffs, N.J.: Prentice-Hall, 1970).

4. Charles W. Mills, *The Racial Contract* (Ithaca, N.Y.: Cornell University Press, 1997).

5. Ian F. Haney Lopez, *White by Law: The Legal Construction of Race* (New York: New York University Press, 1996).

6. G. William Domhoff, *Who Rules America Now?* (Englewood Cliffs, N.J.: Prentice-Hall, 1983); Richard C. Edwards, Michael Reich, and Thomas E. Weisskopf, eds., *The Capitalist System: A Radical Analysis of American Society* (Englewood Cliffs, N.J.: Prentice-Hall, 1972); and Nelson W. Aldrich Jr., *Old Money: The Mythology of America's Upper Class* (New York: Vintage, 1989).

7. Dalton Conley, *Being Black and Living in the Red: Race, Wealth, and Social Policy in America* (Berkeley: University of California Press, 1999); Melvin L. Oliver and Thomas M. Shapiro, *Black Wealth, White Wealth: A New Perspective On Racial Inequality* (New York: Routledge, 1997); Oliver Cox, *Caste, Class, and Race* (New York: Modern Reader, 1948); and Manning Marable, *How Capitalism Underdeveloped Black America* (Boston: South End, 1983).

8. Francis Cress Welsing, *The Isis Papers: The Keys to the Colors* (Chicago: Third World, 1991); Molefe Asante, *The Afrocentric Idea* (Philadelphia: Temple University Press, 1987); Cheikh Anta Diop, *The African Origin of Civilization: Myth or Reality* (Westport, Conn.: Lawrence Hill, 1974), 251–52; Anthony T. Browder, *From the Browder File: 22 Essays on the African American Experience* (Institute of Karmic Guidance, 1989); and Lucius T. Outlaw, *On Race and Philosophy* (New York: Routledge, 1996), 97–134.

9. Winthrop D. Jordan, *White Over Black: American Attitudes toward the Negro, 1550–1812* (New York: Norton, 1995 [1968]). Also peruse Langston Hughes's engaging fictional work, *The Ways of White Folks* (New York: Vintage, 1971 [1934]).

10. Spencer Wells, *The Journey of Man: A Genetic Odyssey* (Princeton, N.J. Princeton University Press, 2002).

11. Ibid., 55–66, 75, 83, 100, 110–17, 125, 129, 182.

12. Lin Jin, Lynn B. Jorde, et al., "Worldwide DNA Sequence Variation in a 10-Kilobase Noncoding Region on Human Chromosome 22," *Proceedings of the National Academy of Sciences* 97/21 (October 10, 2000): 11354, 11355, 11358; Lynn B. Jorde, Alan R. Rogers, et al., "Microsatellite Diversity and the Demographic History of Modern Humans," *Proceedings of the National Academy of Sciences* 94 (April 1997): 3100–103. See also Sarah A. Tishkoff and S. M. Williams, "Genetic Analysis of African Populations: Dissecting Human Evolutionary History and Complex Disease," *Nature Reviews Genetics* 3/8 (2002): 611–21; and E. Zietkiewice, Sarah A. Tishkoff, et al., "Nuclear DNA Variability Data Support a Recent Common Origin of *Homo sapiens*," *Gene* 205 (1997): 161–71.

13. Wells, *Journey of Man*, 120. See also Steve Olson, *Mapping Human History: Discovering the Past through Our Genes* (New York: Houghton Mifflin, 2002), 126–27.

14. Albert Churchward, *Origin and Evolution of the Human Race* (Whitefish, Mont.: Kessinger, 1997). In addition, see Wells, *Journey of Man*, 37.

15. Christopher B. Stringer, "The Evolution of Modern Humans: Where Are We Now?" author's copy; Christopher B. Stringer, "Modern Human Origins: Progress and Prospects," *Philosophical Transactions of the Royal Society of London* (2002): 563–69; Christopher B. Stringer and Robin McKie, *African Exodus: The Origins of Modern Humanity* (New York: Henry Holt, 1998).

16. Wells, *Journey of Man*, 36. Raymond A. Dart, *Adventures with the Missing Link* (New York: Harper & Brothers, 1959), 1–10.

17. Wells, *Journey of Man*, 71.

18. See William Mosley, *What Color Was Jesus?* (Chicago: African American Images, 1987), 7. Mosley is quoting from Ben Ammi's *God, the Black Man and Truth* (Chicago: Communicators, 1982), 7. For more on the rivers and location in Eden, see Prince Vuyani Ntintili's "The Presence and Role of Africans in the Bible," in *Holy Bible: The African American Jubilee Edition, Contemporary English Version* (New York: American Bible Society, 1999), 100–101.

19. David T. Adamo, *Africa and the Africans in the Old Testament* (Eugene, Ore.: Wipf and Stock, 1998), 59.

20. Modupe Oduyoye, *The Sons of the Gods and the Daughters of Men* (Ibadan, Nigeria: Sefer, 1998 [1984]), 42.

21. Kenan Malik, *The Meaning of Race: Race, History and Culture in Western Society* (New York: New York University Press, 1996), 4; Wells, *Journey of Man*, 30.

22. Charles W. Mills, *Blackness Visible: Essays on Philosophy and Race* (Ithaca, N.Y.: Cornell University Press, 1998), 50–53.

23. See my *Heart and Head: Black Theology Past, Present, and Future* (New York: Palgrave Macmillan, 2002).

24. Peter J. Paris, *The Spirituality of African Peoples: The Search for a Common Moral Discourse* (Minneapolis: Fortress, 1995), 22.

25. In addition to John Brown, who led armed rebellions against the institution of slavery in North America, other race traitors (i.e., those who saw their humanity defined by black, brown, red, and yellow peoples and not the arrogant and assumed voice of whites) can be found in the following excellent books: Jennifer Harvey, Robin Hawley Gorsline, and Karin A. Case, eds., *Doing Our First Works Over: White Theologians and Ethicists Talk about Race* (Cleveland: Pilgrim, 2004); and Jim Perkinson's *A White Theology of Solidarity: Signified Upon and Sounded Out* (New York: Palgrave Macmillan, 2004).

26. See Malik, *The Meaning of Race*, 15–17.

27. Robert E. Hood, *Begrimed and Black: Christian Traditions on Blacks and Blackness* (Minneapolis: Fortress, 1994), 26.

28. Ibid., 27.

29. Ibid., 33.

30. Ibid., 30.

31. Ibid., 35–37.

32. Plato, "The Republic, Book IV:431," in *Plato: Complete Works*, ed. John M. Cooper (Indianapolis: Hackett, 1997), 1063. See also Marimba Ani, *Yurugu: An African-Centered Critique of European Cultural Thought and Behavior* (Trenton, N.J.: Africa World, 1994), 29–33, esp. 32.

33. Gay L. Byron, *Symbolic Blackness and Ethnic Difference in Early Christian Literature* (New York: Routledge, 2002), 33.

34. Ibid., 35.

35. Hood, *Begrimed and Black*, 38, 39.

36. Byron, *Symbolic Blackness*.

37. Hood, *Begrimed and Black*, 93–94.

38. Ibid., 95–96, 115–17, 125–28.

39. Ibid., 12.

40. Shawn Kelley, *Racializing Jesus: Race, Ideology and the Formation of Modern Biblical Scholarship* (New York: Routledge, 2002), 26, and Hood, *Begrimed and Black*, 96.

41. David Theo Goldberg, *Racist Culture: Philosophy and the Politics of Meaning* (Cambridge, Mass.: Blackwell, 1993), 21, and Hood, *Begrimed and Black*, 100.

42. For works on Africa before the massive violence of European Christian invaders, see Kevin Shillington, *History of Africa,* rev. ed. (New York: St. Martin's, 1995); Roland Oliver, ed., *The Dawn of African History* (New York: Oxford University Press, 1968); K. B. C. Onwubiko, *History of West Africa: AD 1000–1800, Book One* (Onitsha, Nigeria: Africana-FEP, 1985); G. T. Stride and C. Ifeka, *Peoples and Empires of West Africa: West Africa in History 1000–1800* (Nairobi, Kenya: Thomas Nelson, 1982); and Walter Rodney, *How Europe Underdeveloped Africa* (Washington, D.C.: Howard University Press, 1974).

43. Kelley, *Racializing Jesus*, 28; and Martin Bernal, *Black Athena: The Afroasiatic Roots of Classical Civilization, Volume One: The Fabrication of Ancient Greece 1785–1985* (New Brunswick, N.J.: Rutgers University Press, 1987), 201–4. Bernal writes that it "is generally accepted that a more clear-cut racism grew up after 1650 and that this was greatly intensified by the increased colonization of North America, with its twin policies of extermination of the Native Americans and enslavement of Africans" (201–2).

44. Goldberg, *Racist Culture*, 24.

45. Kelley, *Racializing Jesus*, 25.

46. Quoted in Emmanuel Chukwudi Eze, *Race and the Enlightenment: A Reader* (Cambridge, Mass.: Blackwell, 1997), 55.

47. Quoted in ibid., 33.

48. Goldberg, *Racist Culture*, 27–28.

49. Hood, *Begrimed and Black*, 137–39.

50. Goldberg, *Racist Culture*, 33, and Bernal, *Black Athena*, 203. For more on polygenesis versus monogenesis, see Goldberg, *Racist Culture*, 65–66, and Hood, *Begrimed and Black*, 139ff. On Voltaire's pro-polygenesis views, see Thomas F. Gossett, *Race: The History of an Idea in America* (New York: Schocken, 1971), 44–45.

51. Goldberg, *Racist Culture*, 30, and Kelley, *Racializing Jesus*, 33–39. Kelley also writes that the "reconfiguration of antiquity is an essential part of the process of creating an identity for the German people" (44).

52. Bernal, *Black Athena*, 202.

53. Rodney, *How Europe Underdeveloped Africa*. See also Eric Williams, *Capitalism and Slavery* (Chapel Hill: University of North Carolina Press, 1944); W. E. B. DuBois, *The Suppression of the Atlantic Slave-Trade to the United States: 1638–1870* (New York: Social Science, 1954); and Oliver Cox, *Capitalism as a System* (New York: Monthly Review, 1964). Malik (*The Meaning of Race*, 41–42) questions the relation between the reification of Enlightenment concepts and the origin of modern racism. Still, he sees the nexus among the philosophies, racism, and the rise of capitalist political economy.

54. Kelley, *Racializing Jesus*, 48, 47.

55. Ibid., 49–51.

56. Malik, *The Meaning of Race*, 115.

57. Reginald Horsman, *Race and Manifest Destiny: The Origins of American Racial Anglo-Saxonism* (Cambridge: Harvard University Press, 1981), 43–46.

58. Gossett, *Race*, 32–33, and Horsman, *Race and Manifest Destiny*, 46.

59. For detailed discussion on the eighteenth-century monogenesis and polygenesis claims, see Gossett, *Race*, 35–77, and Horsman, *Race and Manifest Destiny*, 46–61.

60. Jordan, *White Over Black*, 483ff.

61. Malik, *The Meaning of Race*, 83–84.

62. Ibid., 87–88.

63. Michael Barkun, *Religion and the Racist Right: The Origins of the Christian Identity Movement* (Chapel Hill: University of North Carolina Press, 1994), 151–58.

64. Gossett, *Race*, 156, and chapter 7, "Race and Social Darwinism." See also Malik, *The Meaning of Race*, 99–100, 113–14.

65. Emevwo Biakolo, "Categories of Cross-cultural Cognition and the African Condition," in *The African Philosophy Reader*, ed. H. Coetzee and A. P. J. Roux (New York: Routledge, 1998), 2.

66. See my *Down, Up and Over: Slave Religion and Black Theology* (Minneapolis: Fortress, 2000); Jordan, *White Over Black*; George M. Fredrickson, *The Black Image in the White Mind: The Debate on Afro-American Character and Destiny, 1817–1914* (New York: Harper Torchbooks, 1971); and Barkun, *Religion and the Racist Right*, 152–58.

67. Quotes found in Lee D. Baker, *From Savage to Negro: Anthropology and the Construction of Race, 1896 to 1954* (Berkeley: University of California Press, 1998), 27, 28.

68. Matthew 28 has Jesus telling disciples to go forth and spread the gospel.

69. Refer to a similar analysis offered by Jean-Marc Ela, *African Cry* (Maryknoll, N.Y.: Orbis, 1986), 22, where he writes: "The arrival of the Christianity of the West in the African savannas and forests, then, was not by virtue of its inner dynamism. The missionary expansion of the churches has sometimes been credited to the breath of the Holy Spirit reaching tornado-pitch. The explanation by supernatural causes is inadequate. The success of the nineteenth-century missions is not really all that miraculous. Mission structures were the effect of colonial power in Africa."

70. Ibid., 11.

71. Tsenay Serequeberhan, *The Hermeneutics of African Philosophy: Horizon and Discourse* (New York: Routledge, 1994), 58–59; V. Y. Mudimbe, *The Invention of Africa: Gnosis, Philosophy, and the Order of Knowledge* (Bloomington: Indiana University Press, 1988), 44–49.

72. Colin A. Palmer, "The First Passage: 1502–1619," in *To Make Our World Anew: A History of African Americans*, ed. Robin D. G. Kelley and Earl Lewis (New York: Oxford University Press, 2000), 9.

73. Gwinya H. Muzorewa, *The Origins and Development of African Theology* (Maryknoll, N.Y.: Orbis, 1985), 24–26. And see Ela, *African Cry*, 21–22.

74. Jesse N. K. Mugambi, *African Christian Theology: An Introduction* (Nairobi, Kenya: Heinemann Kenya, 1989), 32.

75. Quoted in Muzorewa, *Origins and Development*, 29. See also Ela, *African Cry*, 15, 19–20; Mugambi, *African Christian Theology*, 30.

76. Quoted in Ogbu U. Kalu, "Church Presence in Africa: A Historical Analysis of the Evangelization Process," in *African Theology En Route*, ed. Kofi Appiah-Kubi and Sergio Torres (Maryknoll, N.Y.: Orbis, 1979), 18.

77. Quoted in Mercy Amba Oduyoye, *Hearing and Knowing: Theological Reflections on Christianity in Africa* (Maryknoll, N.Y.: Orbis, 1986), 31.

78. Simon S. Maimela, *Proclaim Freedom to My People* (Johannesburg, South Africa: Skotaville, 1987), 7–13; John W. de Gruchy, *The Struggle in South Africa* (Grand Rapids: Eerdmans, 1979), 1–14; Charles Villa-Vicencio, *Trapped in Apartheid* (Cape Town, South Africa: David Philip, 1988), 43–52; and Richard Elphick and Rodney Davenport, eds., *Christianity in South Africa: A Political, Social, and Cultural History* (Berkeley: University of California Press, 1987), 47.

79. José Míguez Bonino, *Doing Theology in a Revolutionary Situation* (Philadelphia: Fortress, 1975), xxv, xxvi. See also Julio De Santa Ana, "Scripture, Community, and Mission in the Framework of Latin American Liberation Theology," in *Scripture, Community, and Mission*, ed. Philip L. Wickeri (Hong Kong: Christian Conference of Asia; London: Council for World Missions, 2002), 323–39.

80. Quoted in Bonino, *Doing Theology*, 4.

81. Lloyd Stennette, "The Situation of Blacks in Brazil," in *The Challenge of Basic Christian Communities*, ed. Sergio Torres and John Eagleson, (Maryknoll, N.Y.: Orbis, 1981), 46–49.

82. Mauro Batista, "Black and Christian in Brazil," in Torres and Eagleson, *The Challenge of Basic Christian Communities*, 52, 53.

83. Silvia Regina De Lima Silva, "Black Latin American Theology: A New Way to Sense, to Feel, and to Speak of God," in *Black Faith and Public Talk: Critical Essays on James H. Cone's Black Theology and Black Power*, ed. Dwight N. Hopkins (Maryknoll, N.Y.: Orbis, 1999), 191–92.

84. The de Enciso reference comes from Patrick "Pops" Hylton, *The Role of Religion in Caribbean History from Amerindian Shamanism to Rastafarianism* (Washington, D.C.: Billpops, 2002), 16–18, also 4–8.

85. Ibid., 37, 38; see also 21–24 regarding Cuba. For an additional overview of Roman Catholic and Protestant missionary work in the Caribbean, see Armando Lampe, *Christianity in the Caribbean: Essays on Church History* (Kingston, Jamaica: University of the West Indies Press, 2001), especially chapters 1–3.

86. Winston Arthur Lawson, *Religion and Race: African and European Roots in Conflict—A Jamaican Testament* (New York: Peter Lang, 1998), 67. Also see

Dianne M. Stewart, *Three Eyes for the Journey: African Dimensions of the Jamaican Religious Experience* (New York: Oxford University Press, 2004).

87. Lampe, *Christianity in the Caribbean*, 235.

88. Guboo Ted Thomas, "The Land Is Sacred: Renewing the Dreaming in Modern Australia," in *The Gospel Is Not Western: Black Theologies from the Southwest Pacific*, ed. G. W. Trompf (Maryknoll, N.Y.: Orbis, 1987), 93. On the historic contact with John Cook, see Anne Pattel-Gray, *The Great White Flood: Racism in Australia* (Atlanta: Scholars, 1998), 15–30, and Anne Pattel-Gray, *Through Aboriginal Eyes: The Cry from the Wilderness* (Geneva: World Council of Churches Publications, 1991).

89. Pattel-Gray, *The Great White Flood*, 19–20, 126, 140, and 171.

90. Ibid., 167.

91. Paul Jacobs and Saul Landau with Eve Pell, *To Serve the Devil, Volume 2: Colonials and Sojourners* (New York: Vintage, 1971), 11–13, 15.

92. Haunani-Kay Trask, *From a Native Daughter: Colonialism and Sovereignty in Hawaii* (Monroe, Maine: Common Courage, 1993), 7; see also Jacobs and Landau, *To Serve the Devil*, 19–24.

93. Suliana Siwatbau, "A Theology for Justice and Peace in the Pacific," in Trompf, *The Gospel Is Not Western*, 192.

94. James Massey, *Roots of Dalit History, Christianity, Theology and Spirituality* (Delhi, India: Indian Society for Promoting Christian Knowledge, 1996), 20–24.

95. V. Davasahayam, "Pollution, Poverty and Powerlessness: A Dalit Perspective," in *A Reader in Dalit Theology*, ed. Arvin. Nirmal (Madras, India: Gurukul Lutheran Theological College & Research Institute, no date), 1–2, 9; M. E. Prabhakar, "The Search for a Dalit Theology," in ibid., 45; Sara K. Catterji, "Why Dalit Theology?" in ibid., 26–27; M. Azariah, "Doing Theology in India Today," in ibid., 85, 89.

96. From conversations with Roger Gaikwad, director of the Senate Centre for Extension and Pastoral Theological Research of Serampore College, Kolkata, India (January 1, 2004).

97. K. Rajaratnam, "Contemporary Challenges: Our Theological Task," in *Dalits and Women: Quest for Humanity*, ed. V. Devasahayam (Madras, India: Gurukul Lutheran Theological College & Research Institute, 1992), 6.

98. S. Manickam, "Missions' Approaches to Caste," in Devasahayam, *Dalits and Women*, 61.

99. Jacob S. Dharmaraj, *Colonialism and Christian Mission: Postcolonial Reflections* (Delhi, India: Indian Society for Promoting Christian Knowledge, 1993), xvi, 18–19, 61–62. Also see Catterji, "Why Dalit Theology?" 26–27; Manickam, "Missions' Approaches," 60–67; Massey, *Roots of Dalit History*, 32, 81; and Monica Jyotsna Melanchthon, "A Dalit Reading of Genesis 10—11:9," in *Scripture, Community, and Mission*, ed. Philip L. Wickeri (Hong Kong: Christian Conference of Asia; London: Council for World Mission, 2003), 166–81.

5. Conclusion as Introduction

1. On this syncretized racialized religio-culture, see my *Down, Up, and Over; Slave Religion and Black Theology* (Minneapolis: Fortress, 2000), chapter 3.

2. Bruce Jackson, ed., *The Negro and His Folklore in Nineteenth-Century Periodicals* (Austin: University of Texas Press, 1967), 148–50. Other versions of the Tar Baby cycle can be found in J. Mason Brewer, ed., *American Negro Folklore* (Chicago: Quadrangle, 1968), 7–9, originally published as "A Familiar Legend" in *The Hillsborough* [N.C.] *Recorder*, August 5, 1874. See also Langston Hughes and Arna Bontemps, eds., *The Book of Negro Folklore* (New York: Dodd, Mead, 1958), 1–2.

3. Jackson, ed., *The Negro and His Folklore*, 150. The story is taken from William Owens, "Folklore of the Southern Negro," *Lippincott's Magazine* 20 (December 1877). However, in the same book (152–53), Rabbit wins a similar race against Wolf when Rabbit adheres to his vocation of tricking the strong. In fact, Buh Rabbit outwits Buh Wolf to such an extent that Rabbit saddles and rides Wolf up to Miss Dinah's house and wins her as his wife.

4. Other notable black folklore, trickster agents are discovered in Zora Neale Hurston, "High John De Conquer," in Hughes and Bontemps, *The Book of Negro Folklore*, 93–102; the John and master tales in Zora Neale Hurston, *Every Tongue Got to Confess: Negro Folk-Tales from the Gulf States* (New York: HarperCollins, 2001), 86–101, (these tales were originally collected in the late 1920s); Steve Sanfield, *The Adventures of High John the Conqueror* (Little Rock: August House, 1996); Julius Lester, *Uncle Remus: The Complete Tales* (New York: Phyllis Fogelman, 1999); Daryl Cumber Dance, ed., *From My People: 400 Years of African American Folklore* (New York: Norton, 2002), chapter 1; and the Signifying Monkey paradigm found in Roger D. Abrahams, *Deep Down in the Jungle: Negro Narrative Folklore from the Streets of Philadelphia*, rev. ed. (New York: Aldine, 1970) (the fieldwork was performed in 1958–59).

5. Leonara Herron and Alice M. Bacon, "Conjuring and Conjure-Doctors," in *Mother Wit from the Laughing Barrel: Readings in the Interpretation of Afro-American Folklore*, ed. Alan Dundes (New York: Garland, 1981), 359–68. Reprinted from *Southern Workman* 24 (1895): 117–18, 193–94, 209–11. The stories in this article were collected in 1878.

6. Hughes and Bontemps, *The Book of Negro Folklore*, 193–98. For another instance of the use of conjure as lawyer, see Newbell Niles Pucket, *Folk Beliefs of the Southern Negro* (Montclair, N.J.: Patterson Smith, 1968 [1926]), 277–78.

7. Pucket, *Folk Beliefs*, 209, 232–33, 234–35.

8. Cornelia Walker Bailey, *God, Dr. Buzzard, and the Bolito Man: A Saltwater Geechee Talks about Life on Sapelo Island* (New York: Doubleday, 2000), 189. Note that conjure remains a vibrant worldview and cultural practice on the islands off the coast of Georgia and South Carolina.

9. Herron and Bacon, "Conjuring and Conjure-Doctors," 361.

10. Charles W. Chesnutt, *The Conjure Woman and Other Conjure Tales* (Durham, N.C.: Duke University Press, 1993), 55–69.

11. Puckett, *Folk Beliefs*, 330.

12. Bailey, *God, Dr. Buzzard*, 146.

13. Shine stories can be found in Abrahams, *Deep Down in the Jungle*, 8, 81, 127; Dance, *From My People*, 488–89; and Dundes, *Mother Wit*, 335, 646–47.

14. Dance, *From My People*, 76ff., 131ff., 490ff.; Hughs and Bontemps, *The Book of Negro Folklore*, 359–61; and Dundes, *Mother Wit*, 335, 646–47.

15. Sarah Bradford, *Harriet Tubman: The Moses of Her People* (Secaucus, N.J.: Citadel, 1961 [1868]), 24–25.

16. Ibid., 84.

17. Ibid., 29.

18. John Oliver Killens, Introduction to *The Trial Record of Denmark Vesey* (Boston: Beacon, 1970), 70, 161.

19. Ibid., 64.

20. Ibid., 13, 42, 43, 62.

21. Ibid., 85.

22. For other examples of Christian witness, see Eric Foner, ed., *Nat Turner* (Englewood Cliffs, N.J.: Prentice-Hall, 1971); Gayraud S. Wilmore, *Black Religion and Black Radicalism: An Interpretation of the Religious History of African Americans* (Maryknoll, N.Y.: Orbis, 1998); Gloria Wade-Gayles, ed., *My Soul Is a Witness: African-American Women's Spirituality* (Boston: Beacon, 1995); and Adam Clayton Powell, *Keep the Faith, Baby!* (New York: Trident, 1967).

Index